READINGS IN CLASSICAL MYTH

Edited by

Graeme Ward

Department of Classics
McMaster University

Copyright © 2013 by Graeme Ward

All rights reserved. This book or any portion thereof may not be reproduced or used in any manner whatsoever without the express written permission of the publisher.

Printed in Canada.

First Printing, 2013

Dept. of Classics
McMaster University
L8S 4M2

Table of Contents

I. Homer's *Iliad*

    Achilles and Agamemnon 2

    The Battle Recommences 10

    Diomedes Fights the Gods 13

    Hector Returns to Troy 15

    Embassy Appeals to Achilles 18

    Hera Outwits Zeus 20

    Achilles Returns to Battle 22

    The Gods Fight Each Other .24

    The Death of Hector 25

    Achilles and Priam 27

        Adapted from Samuel Butler, Homer. The Iliad of Homer (London: Longmans, Green and Co., 1898)

II. Homer's *Odyssey*

    Odysseus, the Man of Many Ways 31

    Menelaus' Sojourn in Egypt .32

    Aphrodite and Ares' Affair 33

    The Cyclops 35

    The Sorceress Circe 41

    Odysseus in the Underworld 44

    Further Adventures 50

    Odysseus' Revenge 52

        Adapted from Samuel Butler, Homer. The Odyssey (London A.C. Fifield, 1900)

III.   Hesiod

    Theogony 59

    Works and Days 67

        Adapted from Hugh G. Evelyn-White, Hesiod. Theogony, and Works and Days (Cambridge, MA: Harvard University Press; London: William Heinemann Ltd., 1914)

IV.   Ovid's *Metamorphoses*

    Creation and the Four Ages of Man 72

    The Flood, Deucalion and Pyrrha 75

    Jupiter and Io 77

    Jupiter and Europa 80

    Actaeon and Diana 80

    Tireisias 81

    Arachne 82

    Niobe 84

    Marsyas 86

    Jason and Medea 86

    Minos and the Minotaur 88

    Pygmalion, Venus, and Adonis 89

    Orpheus and Dionysos 91

    Polyphemus, Galatea, Acis; Scylla and Glaucis 92

        Adapted from Brookes More, Ovid. Metamorphoses (Boston: Cornhill Publishing Co. 1922)

V. Vergil's *Aeneid*

A Roman Hero 97

The Fall of Troy 98

Aeneas and Dido 102

Aeneas in the Underworld 104

Adapted from Theodore C. Williams, Vergil. Aeneid (Boston: Houghton Mifflin Co. 1910)

VI. Vergil's *Georgics*

Orpheus and Eurydice 110

Adapted from J. B. Greenough, Vergil. Georgics (Boston: Ginn & Co., 1900).

VII. The *Homeric Hymns*

Athena 112

Apollo 113

Aphrodite 115

Artemis 116

Dionysus 117

Hermes 118

Demeter 123

Adapted from Hugh G. Evelyn-White, Anonymous. Homeric Hymns (Cambridge, MA: Harvard University Press; London, William Heinemann Ltd., 1914)

VIII. Sappho

Sappho, *Poem 1* 130

Adapted from E. M. Cox, Sappho. The Poems of Sappho (London: Williams and Norgate, 1924).

IX. Aeschylus' *Prometheus Bound*

Aeschylus, Prometheus Bound 131

Adapted from G. M. Cookson, Aeschylus. Four plays (Oxford: Basil Blackwell, 1922).

X. Aeschylus' *Agamemnon*

Aeschylus, Agamemnon 137

Adapted from Herbert Weir Smyth, Aeschylus. Agamemnon (Cambridge, MA: Harvard University Press, 1926)

XI. Aeschylus' *Eumenides*

Aeschylus, Eumenides 149

Adapted from Herbert Weir Smyth, Aeschylus. Eumenides (Cambridge, MA: Harvard University Press, 1926)

XII. Sophocles' *Oedipus the King*

Sophocles, Oedipus the King 157

Adapted from Sir Richard Jebb, Sophocles. The Oedipus Tyrannus of Sophocles (Cambridge: Cambridge University Press, 1887)

XIII. Sophocles' *Oedipus at Colonus*

Sophocles, Oedipus at Colonus 166

Adapted from Sir Richard Jebb, Sophocles. Oedipus at Colonus of Sophocles (Cambridge: Cambridge University Press, 1889)

XIV. Euripides' *Hippolytus*

Euripides, Hippolytus 177

Adapted from E. P. Coleridge, Euripides. The Plays of Euripides (London: G. Bell & Sons, Ltd., 1910).

XV. Euripides' *Bacchae*

Euripides, Bacchae 188

Adapted from T. A. Buckley, Euripides. The Tragedies of Euripides (London. Henry G. Bohn. 1850).

Reading 1:
Homer's *Iliad*

The *Iliad* and the *Odyssey* were both credited by ancient Greeks to a single poet: Homer. We can say very little, however, with certainty about him. Although many regions claimed him, his birthplace is unknown. We have no evidence of the period, moreover, in which he might have written. Scholars have estimated that these works belong to a period between the tenth and seventh centuries BCE, while most place it in the second half of the eighth century. Even if the poems themselves were written during this period, we should understand them to represent the final forms (more or less) of a centuries-old evolution of their respective stories as oral poems, which were passed down over many generations. While presenting stories set in Bronze-Age Greece (c. 1200 BCE) five hundred years earlier, therefore, the poems nevertheless reflect the cultural, political, and social changes that had occurred between that period and that of the written form that we see today. As such, they can be seen as an amalgam of different ages of Ancient Greece.

Iliad tells the tale of only a few weeks near the end of the mythic Trojan War, at which point the Greeks have been fighting the Trojans for ten years. It begins with the conflict between Agamemnon, the chief leader of the Greeks at Troy, and Achilles, the supreme warrior. This conflict produces Achilles' great anger, which drives both the themes and narrative of the poem. Achilles nurses his anger, sulking in his tent, while the Greeks soldiers and their leaders face the Trojans and their great champion, Hector. Despite Agamemnon admitting his mistake, and sending embassies to Achilles offering gifts, Achilles remains aloof. Hector's slaying of Achilles' companion, Patroclus, finally draws Achilles out from his tent, and is the turning point of the poem. Achilles' great fury is now directed against Hector, whom he eventually kills before the city's walls. The climax of the poem is the encounter between Priam, the elderly king of Troy, and Achilles. Priam comes to Achilles' tent to beg for the body of his son, Hector, and Achilles, allowing his anger to relent (if only for awhile), agrees. The actions of the heroes in *Iliad* are also influenced by the Greek gods, who mingle with mortals, and support or harm them according to their individual will. The destructive consequences of inhuman anger, the irresistible power of divine fate, and both the glory and sorrow of war are just several of the many themes this great poem explores.

1a) Achilles and Agamemnon (Homer, Iliad, 1. 1-611, passim)

Sing, goddess, of the anger of Achilles, son of Peleus, which brought so many evils upon the Achaeans. Many brave souls did it send hurrying down to Hades, and many heroes did it give up as food for dogs and vultures – so was the will of Zeus fulfilled. It began on the day on which the son of Atreus, king of men, and glorious Achilles, first argued with one another.

And which of the gods was it that drove them to conflict? It was the son of Zeus and Leto, for he was angry with the king, and sent a plague upon the Greek host to afflict the people, because the son of Atreus had dishonored Chryses, his priest. Now Chryses had come to the ships of the Achaeans to free his daughter, and had brought with him a great ransom: moreover he bore in his hand the sceptre of Apollo, wreathed with a suppliant's wreath, and he pled before the Achaeans, but most of all the two sons of Atreus, who were their chiefs.

"Sons of Atreus, and all other Achaeans, may the gods who dwell in Olympus grant you the power to sack the city of Priam, and to reach your homes in safety; but free my daughter, and accept a ransom for her, in reverence to Apollo, son of Zeus."

On this the rest of the Achaeans with one voice were for respecting the priest and taking the ransom that he offered; but not so Agamemnon, who spoke fiercely to him and sent him roughly away.

"Old man, Do no let me find you loitering around our ships, nor coming ever again. Your sceptre of the god and your wreath shall not help you. I will not free her. She shall grow old in my house at Argos far from her own home, busying herself with her loom and visiting my bed! So go, and do not provoke me or it shall be the worse for you!"

The old man was terrified and obeyed. He did not speak a word, but went by the shore of the sounding sea and prayed to King Apollo, whom lovely Leto had borne.

"Hear me, god of the silver bow, you who protect Chryse and holy Cilla and rule Tenedos with your might. Hear me, Sminthean god, If I have ever decorated your temple with garlands, or burned for you thigh-bones in the fat of bulls or goats, grant my prayer, and let your arrows avenge my tears upon the Danaans."

Thus did he pray, and Apollo heard his prayer. He came down furious from the summits of Olympus, with his bow and his quiver upon his shoulder, and the arrows rattled at his back with a rage that trembled within him. He set himself down away from the ships with a face as dark as night, and his silver bow rang death as he shot his arrow in the midst of the Greeks.

First he struck their mules and their hounds, but then he aimed his shafts at the people themselves, and all day long the pyres of the dead were burning. For nine whole days he shot his arrows among them, but on the tenth day Achilles called them all in assembly, inspired to do this by Hera, who saw the Achaeans dying, and had compassion for them. Then, when they were all together, Achilles rose and spoke among them.

"Son of Atreus, I feel that we should now turn for home if we wish to escape destruction, for we are being cut down by war and plague at the same time. Let us ask some priest or seer, or some reader of dreams (for dreams, too, are from Zeus) who can tell us why Phoebus Apollo is so angry, and say whether it is for some vow that we have broken, or the sacrifice of a hecatomb that we have not performed, and whether he will accept the savour of lambs and goats without blemish, so as to take away the plague from us."

With these words he sat down, and Calchas son of Thestor, wisest of augurs, who knew things of the past, present, and future, rose to speak. It was he who had guided the Achaeans with their fleet to Ilium, through the prophecies with which Phoebus Apollo had inspired him. With all truthfulness and goodwill he addressed them thus:

"The god is angry neither about vow nor sacrifice of one hundred bulls, but for his priest's sake, whom Agamemnon has dishonored, since he would not free his daughter nor take a ransom for her. For this reason he has brought these evils upon us, and will yet bring others. He will not deliver the Danaans from this pestilence until Agamemnon has restored the girl without fee or ransom to her father, and has made a holy sacrfice to Chryse. Thus we may perhaps appease Apollo."

When he had thus spoken he sat down, and among them rose the king, son of Atreus, wide-ruling Agamemnon, in great anger. His black heart was filled with fury, and his eyes were blazing like fire. To Calchas first of all he spoke, with a look that threatened violence:

"Prophet of evil, never yet have you spoken to me a pleasant thing; evil is always dear to your heart to prophesy, but a word of good you have never yet spoken, nor brought to pass. And now among the Danaans you claim in prophecy that for this reason the god who strikes from afar brings woes upon them, that I would not accept the glorious ransom for the girl, the daughter of Chryses, since I much prefer to keep her in my home. For certainly I prefer her to Clytemnestra, my wedded wife, since she is not inferior to her, either in form or in stature, or in mind, or in any handiwork. Yet even so will I give her back, if that is better; I would rather the people be safe than perish. But provide me with a prize of honour immediately, lest I alone of the Argives be without one, since that would not be proper. For you all see this, that my prize goes elsewhere."

In answer to him spoke swift-footed brilliant Achilles:

"Most glorious son of Atreus, greediest of all: how shall the great-hearted Achaeans give you a prize? We have no hoard of wealth in common store. Whatever we took by pillage from the cities has been distributed, and it is not right to gather these things back from the army. No. Give back the girl to the god, and we Achaeans will pay you back three and fourfold, if ever Zeus allows us to sack the well-walled city of Troy."

In answer to him spoke lord Agamemnon:

"Although you are mighty, godlike Achil- les, you should not seek to deceive me like this with your wit; for you will not get by me nor persuade me. Are you willing for me to sit here idly in want, while you order me to give her back, while you yourself may keep your prize? No, the great-hearted Achaeans must give me a prize that I find appropriate, and worth just as much. If they do not, I will come and take your prize, or that of Ajax, or I will seize and carry away that of Odysseus. Whomever I come to will be angry. But these things we will consider later. Let us now drag a black ship to the shining sea, and quickly gather suitable rowers into it, and place on board a hecatomb to sacrifice, and embark on it the fair-cheeked daughter of Chryses herself. Let one prudent man be its commander, either Ajax, or Idomeneus, or brilliant Odysseus, or you, son of Peleus, of all men most extreme, so that on our behalf you may appease the god who strikes from afar by offering sacrifice."

Glaring from beneath his brows swift-footed Achilles spoke to him:

"My word! How clothed in shamelessness you are! You always are thinking of gain! How can any man of the Achaeans obey your words with a ready heart, whether to go on a journey or to fight against men with force? It was not on account of our Trojan enemies that I came here to fight, since they have done no wrong to me. They have never driven off my cattle or my horses, nor ever in deep-soiled Phthia did they lay waste the harvest, for many things lie between us shadowy mountains and sounding sea. But we followed you, shameless one, so that you might rejoice, seeking to win recompense from the Trojans for Menelaus and for yourself, dog-face. This you disregard, and take no heed of. And now you threaten that you will yourself take my prize away from me, for which I toiled so much, which the sons of the Achaeans gave to me. Never have I received a prize as good as yours after the Achaeans have sacked a well-inhabited citadel of the Trojans. But my hands always undertake the brunt of furious battle. If ever an apportionment comes, how- ever, your prize is always greater, while I take to my ships a small but dear reward, even though I have worn myself out in the fighting. Now I will go back to Phthia, since it is far better to return home with my beaked ships. I do not intend to pile up riches and wealth for you while I am being dishonoured."

Then the king of men, Agamemnon, answered him:

"Flee then, if your heart urges you. I will not beg you to remain for my sake. With me are others who will honour me, and above all Zeus, the lord of counsel. Of all the kings whom Zeus nurtures, you are the most hateful to me. For strife is always dear to you, and wars and battles. If you are very strong, it was a god, I think, who gave you this gift. Go home with your ships and your companions and lord it over the Myrmidons there. I do not care for you, nor will I heed your wrath. But this is my threat to you: because Phoebus Apollo takes from me the daughter of Chryses, I will send her back with my ship and my companions, but I will myself come to your tent and take the fair-cheeked Briseis, your prize. In this way you will understand how much mightier I am than you, and so others will shrink from declaring themselves my equal and likening themselves to me to my face."

So he spoke. Anger came upon the son of Peleus, and within his shaggy breast his heart was divided, whether he should draw his sharp sword from beside his thigh and slay the son of Atreus, or stay his anger and curb his spirit. Now again the son of Peleus addressed the son of Atreus with violent words, not at all ceasing from his anger:

"You wine-soaked dog-face, with the heart of a fawn! You never have had enough courage to arm for battle along with your people, or to go forth to an ambush with the chiefs of the Achaeans. Doing that seems to you just like death. Indeed, you think it better to deprive of his prize whoever speaks against you in the wide camp of the Achaeans. You people-devouring king! You rule over no- bodies. This is your final piece of insolence. But I will speak against you, and will swear a mighty oath to this. I swear by this staff, that shall never more put forth leaves or shoots since first it left its stump among the mountains, nor shall it again grow green, for the bronze has stripped it on all sides of leaves and bark, and now the sons of the Achaeans carry it in their hands when they act as judges, those who guard the ordinances that come from Zeus. And this shall be for you a mighty oath. Surely some day the sons of the Achaeans one and all, will long for Achilles. And on that day you will not be able to help them at all, for all your grief, when many shall fall dying before man-slaying Hector. But you will eat your heart out and curse yourself because you dishonoured the best of the Achaeans."

So spoke the son of Peleus, and down to the earth he dashed the staff studded with golden nails, and himself sat down, while over against him the son of Atreus continued to vent his wrath. Then among them arose Nestor, sweet of speech, the clear-voiced orator of the Pylians, from whose tongue flowed speech sweeter than honey. Two generations of mortal men had passed away in the course of his lifetime, who had been born and reared with him in sacred Pylos, and he was now king among the third. He with good intent addressed the gathering and spoke among them:

"Comrades, great grief has come upon the land of Achaea. Truly would Priam and the sons of Priam rejoice, and the rest of the Trojans would be most glad at heart, were they to hear all this of you two quarrelling, you who are chief among the Danaans in counsel and chief in war. Listen to me, for you are both younger than I. In earlier times I moved among men more warlike than you, and never did they despise me. So also should you obey, since to obey is better. Agamemnon, mighty though you are, do not take away the girl, but let her be, as the sons of the Achaeans first gave her to noble Achilles as a prize. Son of Peleus, do not be minded to strive with a king, might against might! For it is no common honour that is the portion of a sceptre-holding king, to whom Zeus gives glory. If you are a stronger fighter, and a goddess mother bore you, nevertheless he is the mightier, since he is king over more. Son of Atreus, check your rage. Indeed, I beg you to let go your anger against Achilles, who is for all the Achaeans a mighty bulwark in evil war."

In answer to him spoke lord Agamemnon:

"All these things, old man, to be sure, you have spoken as is right. But this man wishes to be above all others; over all he wishes to rule and over all to be king, and to all to give orders; in this, I think, there is someone who will not obey. If the gods who exist for ever made him a spearman, do they therefore license him to keep uttering insults?"

Brilliant Achilles broke in upon him and replied:

"Surely I will be called cowardly and of no account, if I should yield to you in every matter that you say. On others lay these commands, but do not give orders to me, for I do not think I shall obey you any longer. And another thing I will tell you, and take it to heart: with my hands I will not fight for the girl's sake either with you nor with any other, since you are taking away what you have given. But everything else that is mine by my swift black ship, none of it will you take or carry away against my will. Come, just try, so that these too may know: immediately will your dark blood flow forth about my spear."

So when the two had made an end of contending with violent words, they rose, and broke up the gathering beside the ships of the Achaeans. The son of Peleus went his way to his huts and his balanced ships together with his friend Patroclus, and with his men. But the son of Atreus launched a swift ship on the sea, and chose for

it twenty rowers, and drove on board 100 cattle as a hecatomb for the god, and brought the fair-cheeked daughter of Chryses and set her in the ship; and Odysseus of many wiles went on board to take command.

So these embarked and sailed over the watery ways, while the son of Atreus bade the people purify themselves. And they purified themselves, and cast the defilement into the sea, and offered to Apollo perfect sacrifices of bulls and goats by the shore of the barren sea; and the savour thereof went up to heaven, eddying amid the smoke. Thus were they busied throughout the camp. Agamemnon, however, did not cease from the strife with which he had first threatened Achilles. He called to Talthybius and Eurybates, who were his heralds and ready squires:

"Go to the hut of Achilles, Peleus' son, and take by the hand the fair-cheeked Briseis, and lead her hither; and if he give her not, I will myself go with a larger company and take her; that will be even the worse for him."

So saying he sent them forth, and laid upon them a stern command. Unwilling went the two along the shore of the barren sea, and came to the tents and the ships of the Myrmidons. They found Achilles sitting beside his tent and his black ship; and he was not glad at sight of them. The two, seized with dread and in awe of the king, stood, but spoke no word to him, nor made question. He understood in his heart, however, and spoke:

"Hail, heralds, messengers of Zeus and men, draw near. It is not you who are guilty in my sight, but Agamemnon, who sent you here to take the girl, Briseis. But come, Patroclus, sprung from Zeus, bring forth the girl, and give her to them to lead away. But let these two themselves be witnesses before the blessed gods and mortal men, and before him, that ruthless king, if hereafter there shall be need of me to ward off shameful ruin from the host. Truly he rages with baneful mind, and knows not at all to look both before and after, that his Achaeans might wage war in safety beside their ships."

So he spoke, and Patroclus obeyed his dear comrade, and led from the hut the fair-cheeked Briseis, and gave her to them to lead away. So the two went back beside the ships of the Achaeans, and with them, all unwilling, went the woman. But Achilles burst into tears, and withdrew apart from his comrades, and sat down on the shore of the grey sea, looking forth over the wine-dark deep. Earnestly he prayed to his dear mother with hands outstretched:

"Mother, surely Olympian Zeus, who thunders on high, ought to have given honour into my hands, since you bore me, though to so brief a span of life. But now he has honoured me not a bit. Truly the son of Atreus, wide-ruling Agamemnon has dishonoured me: for he has taken and keeps my prize through his own arrogant act."

So he spoke, weeping, and his lady mother heard him, as she sat in the depths of the sea beside the old man, her father. And speedily she came forth from the grey sea like a mist, and sat down before him, as he wept, and she stroked him with her hand, and spoke to him, and called him by name:

"My child, why do you weep? What sorrow has come upon your heart? Speak out; hide it not in your mind, that we both may know."

Then with heavy moaning spoke swift-footed Achilles to her:

"You know. Why then should I tell the tale to you who knows all? We went forth to Thebe, the sacred city of Eetion, and laid it waste, and brought here all the spoil. This the sons of the Achaeans divided fairly among themselves, except for the son of Atreus, to whom they gave the fair-cheeked daughter of Chryses. However, Chryses, priest of Apollo, who strikes from afar, came to the swift ships of the bronze-clad Achaeans, to free his daughter, bearing ransom past counting. But Agamemnon, son of Atreus, sent him away harshly. So the old man went back again in anger; and Apollo heard his prayer, for he was very dear to him, and sent against the Argives an evil plague. Then the people began to die thick and fast, and the shafts of the god ranged everywhere throughout the wide camp of the Achaeans. But to us the prophet with sure knowledge declared the oracles of the god who strikes from afar. Now, the quick-glancing Achaeans are taking the maiden in a swift ship to Chryse, and are bearing gifts to the god; while the other woman the heralds have just now taken from my tent and led away, the daughter of Briseus, whom the sons of the Achaeans gave me. But, you, if you are able, guard your own son; go to Olympus and make prayer to Zeus, if ever you have gladdened his heart by word or deed. Sit by his side, and clasp his knees, in hope that he might perhaps wish to succour the Trojans, and for those others, the Achaeans, to pen them in among the sterns of their ships and around the sea as they are slain, so that they may all have profit of their king, and that the son of Atreus, wide-ruling Agamemnon may know his blindness in that he did no honour to the best of the Achaeans."

Then Thetis answered him as she wept:

"Alas, my child, why did I rear you, cursed in my child-bearing? I wish that it had been your lot to remain by your ships without tears and without grief, since your span of life is brief and will not last for a long time; but now you are doomed to a speedy death and are laden with sorrow above all men. It was to an evil fate that I bore you in our halls. Yet in order to tell your word to Zeus who delights in the thunderbolt I will myself go to snowy Olympus, in hope that he may be persuaded. But remain by your swift, seafaring ships, and continue your wrath against the Achaeans, and refrain utterly from battle. ... I will go to the house of Zeus with threshold of bronze, and will clasp his knees in prayer, and I think I shall win him."

So saying, she went her way and left him where he was, angry at heart for the fair-girdled woman's sake, whom they had taken from him by force though he was unwilling. Meanwhile Odysseus came to Chryse bringing the holy hecatomb. When they had arrived within the deep harbour, they furled the sail, and stowed it in the black ship... and them- selves went forth upon the shore of the sea. They brought forth the hecatomb for Apollo, who strikes from afar, and the daughter of Chryses also stepped forth from the sea-faring ship. Odysseus of many wiles then lead her to the altar, and place her in the arms of her dear father, saying to him:

"Chryses, Agamemnon, king of men, sent me forth to bring to you your daughter, and to offer to Phoebus a holy hecatomb on the Danaans' behalf, that therewith we may pro- pitiate the lord, who has now brought upon the Argives woeful lamentation."

So saying he placed her in his arms, and he joyfully took his dear child; but they made haste to set in array for the god the holy hecatomb around the well-built altar. Then Chryses lifted up his hands, and prayed aloud for them:

"Hear me, god of the silver bow, who stands over Chryse and holy Cilla, and rules mightily over Tenedos. As before you heard me when I prayed—to me you did honour, and mightily smote the host of the Achaeans—even so now fulfill me this my desire: ward off now from the Danaans the terrible pestilence."

So he prayed, and Phoebus Apollo heard him. Then, when they had prayed, and had sprinkled the barley grains, they first drew back the victims' heads, and cut their throats, and flayed them, and cut out the thighs and covered them with a double layer of fat, and laid raw flesh thereon. And the old man burned them on stakes of wood, and made libation over them of gleaming wine; and beside him the young men held in their hands the five-pronged forks. But when the thigh-pieces were completely burned, and they had tasted the entrails, they cut up the rest and spitted it, and roasted it carefully, and drew all off the spits. Then, when they had ceased from their labour and had made ready the meal, they feasted, nor did their hearts lack anything of the equal feast.

But Thetis did not forget the request of her son, but rose up from the wave of the sea, and at early morning went up to great heaven and Olympus. There she found the far-seeing son of Cronos sitting apart from the rest upon the topmost peak of many-ridged Olympus. So she sat down before him, and clasped his knees with her left hand, while with her right she touched him beneath the chin, and she spoke in prayer to king Zeus, son of Cronos:

"Father Zeus, if ever amid the immortals I gave you aid by word or deed, grant me this prayer: do honour to my son, who is doomed to a speedy death beyond all other men; yet now Agamemnon, king of men, has dishonoured him, for he has taken and keeps his prize by his own arrogant act. But honour him, Olympian Zeus, lord of counsel; and give might to the Trojans, until the Achaeans do honour to my son, and magnify him with recompense."

So she spoke; but Zeus, the cloud-gatherer, spoke no word to her, but sat a long time in silence. ... Finally, greatly troubled, Zeus, the cloud-gatherer spoke to her:

"Surely this will be sorry work, since you will set me on to engage in strife with Hera, when she shall anger me with taunting words. Even now she always upbraids me among the immortal gods, and declares that I give aid to the Trojans in battle. But for the present, depart again, lest Hera note something; and I will take thought for these things to bring all to pass. Come, I will bow my head to you, so that you may be certain; no word of mine may be recalled, nor is false, nor unfulfilled, to which I bow my head."

The son of Cronos spoke, and bowed his dark brow in assent, and the ambrosial locks waved from the king's immortal head; and he made great Olympus quake.

When the two had taken counsel together in this way, they parted; she leapt straightway into the deep sea from gleaming Olympus, and Zeus went to his own palace. All the gods together rose from their seats before the face of their father; no one dared to await his coming, but they all rose up before him. There, then, he took his seat. But Hera, when she saw him, knew that he and the old merman's daughter, silver-footed Thetis, had been making mischief, so she at once began to scold him.

"Trickster," she cried, "which of the gods have you been taking into your counsels now? You are always settling matters in secret behind my back, and have never yet told me, if you could help it, one word of your plans."

"Hera," replied the lord of gods and men, "you must not expect to be informed of all my plans. You are my wife, but you would find it hard to understand them. When it is proper for you to hear, there is no one, god or man, who will be told sooner, but when I mean to keep a matter to myself, you must not pry or ask questions."

"Dread son of Cronos," answered Hera, "what do you mean? I? Pry and ask questions? Never. I let you have your own way in everything. Still, I have a strong worries that the old merman's daughter, Thetis, has been working you over, for she was with you and held your knees this very morning. I believe, therefore, that you have been promising her to give glory to Achilles, and to kill many people at the ships of the Achaeans."

"Woman," said Zeus, "I can do nothing without you suspecting and tracking me. You will gain nothing by it, for I shall only dislike you more, and it will be worse for you. Even if it were as you say what can you do about it? Sit down and hold your tongue as I order you, for once I begin to lay my hands about you, even if all heaven were on your side it would not help you at all."

And Hera was frightened, so she curbed her stubborn will and sat down in silence. But the heavenly gods were worried throughout the house of Zeus, until the cunning workman Hephaestus began to try to placate his mother, Hera.

"It will be intolerable," said he, "if you two fall to arguing and setting heaven in an uproar about a pack of mortals. If such things continue, we shall have no pleasure at our banquet. Let me advise my mother - and she must herself know that it will be better to make friends with our dear father Zeus, so that he not threaten her again and disturb our feast. If the Olympian Thunderer wants to hurl us all from our seats, he can do so, for he is far the strongest, so give him kind words, and he will then soon be in a good humour with us."

As he spoke, he took a double cup of nectar, and placed it in his mother's hand.

"Cheer up, my dear mother," said he, "and make the best of it. I love you dearly, and should be very sorry to see you get a thrashing; however upset I might be, I could not help – there is no resisting Zeus. Once before when I was trying to help you, he caught me by the foot and flung me from the heavenly mountain. All day long from morn till evening, was I falling, till at sunset I came to ground in the island of Lemnos, and there I lay, with very little life left in me, till the Sintians came and healed me."

Hera smiled at this, and as she smiled she took the cup from her son's hands. Then Hephaestus drew sweet nectar from the mixing-bowl, and served it round among the gods, going from left to right; and the blessed gods laughed out a loud applause as they saw him bustling about the heavenly palace.

And for the whole day long till the setting of the sun they feasted, nor did they lack anything of the feast, nor of the beautiful lyre, that Apollo held, nor yet of the Muses, who sang, replying one to the other with sweet voices. But when the bright light of the sun was set, they went, each to his own house, to take their rest, where for each one a palace had been built with cunning skill by the famed Hephaestus, the limping god; and Zeus, the Olympian, lord of the lightning, went to his bed, where of old he took his rest, whenever sweet sleep came upon him. There he went up and slept, and beside him lay Hera, Queen of the golden throne.

1b) The Battle Recommences (Homer, Iliad, 3. 1-540, passim)

But Priam called Helen to him. "My child," he said, "take your seat in front of me so that you may see your former husband, your kinsmen and your friends. I do not blame you – it is the gods, not you who are to blame. It is they that have brought about this terrible war with the Achaeans. Tell me, then, who is that huge hero so great and excellent? I have seen men taller by a head, but none so handsome and so royal. Surely he must be a king."

"Lord," answered Helen, "father of my husband, dear and reverend in my eyes – if only I had chosen death rather than to have come here with your son, far from my bridal chamber, my friends, my darling daughter, and all the companions of my childhood. But it was not so, and my fate is one of tears and sorrow. As for your question, the hero of whom you ask is Agamemnon, son of Atreus, a good king and a brave soldier, brother-in-law as surely as that he lives, to my abhorred and miserable self."

The old man marvelled at him and said, "Happy son of Atreus, child of good fortune. I see that the Achaeans are subject to you in great multitudes. When I was in Phrygia I saw many horsemen, the people of Otreus and of Mygdon, who were camping upon the banks of the river Sangarius; I was their ally, and with them when the Amazons, peers of men, came up against them, but even they were not so many as the Achaeans."

The old man next looked upon Odysseus. "Tell me," he said, "who is that other, shorter by a head than Agamemnon, but broader across the chest and shoulders? His armour is laid upon the ground, and he stalks in front of the ranks as it were some great woolly ram ordering his ewes."

And Helen answered, "He is Odysseus, a man of great craft, son of Laertes. He was born in rugged Ithaca, and excels in all manner of stratagems and subtle cunning."

Priam then caught sight of Ajax and asked, "Who is that great and goodly warrior whose head and broad shoulders tower above the rest of the Argives?"

"That," answered Helen, "is huge Ajax, bulwark of the Achaeans, and on the other side of him, among the Cretans, stands Idomeneus looking like a god, and with the captains of the Cretans round him. Often did Menelaus receive him as a guest in our house when he came visiting us from Crete. I see, moreover, many other Achaeans whose names I could tell you, but there are two whom I can nowhere find, Castor, breaker of horses, and Pollux the mighty boxer; they are children of my mother, and own brothers to myself. Either they have not left Lacedaemon, or else, though they have brought their ships, they will not show themselves in battle for the shame and disgrace that I have brought upon them."

She knew not that both these heroes were already lying under the earth in their own land of Lacedaemon. Meanwhile the heralds were bringing the holy oath-offerings through the city- two lambs and a goatskin of wine, the gift of earth; and Idaeus brought the mixing bowl and the cups of gold. He went up to Priam and said, "Son of Laomedon, the princes of the Trojans and Achaeans bid you come down on to the plain and swear to a solemn covenant. Paris and Menelaus are to fight for Helen in single combat, that she and all her wealth may go with him who is the victor. We are to swear to a solemn covenant of peace whereby we others shall dwell here in Troy, while the Achaeans return to Argos and the land of the Achaeans."

The old man trembled as he heard, but ordered his followers to yoke the horses, and they hastened to do so. He mounted the chariot, gathered the reins in his hand, and Antenor took his seat beside him; they then drove through the Scaean gates on to the plain. When they reached the ranks of the Trojans and Achaeans they left the chariot, and with measured pace advanced into the space between the hosts.

Agamemnon and Odysseus both rose to meet them. The attendants brought oath-offerings and mixed the wine in the mixing-bowls; they poured water over the hands of the chieftains, and the son of Atreus drew the dagger that hung by his sword, and cut wool from the lambs' heads; this the men-servants gave about among the Trojan and Achaean princes, and the son of Atreus lifted up his hands in prayer.

"Father Zeus," he cried, "who rules in Ida, most glorious in power, and thou Sun, who sees and gives ear to all things, Earth and Rivers, and you who in the realms below punishes the soul of him who has broken his oath, witness these rites and guard them, so that they be not vain. If Paris kills Menelaus, let him keep Helen and all her wealth, while we sail home with our ships; but if Menelaus kills Paris, let the Trojans give back Helen and all that she has; let them moreover pay such fine to the Achaeans as shall be agreed upon, in testimony among those that shall be born hereafter. And if Priam and his sons refuse such fine when Paris has fallen, then will I stay here and fight on till I have got satisfaction."

As he spoke he drew his knife across the throats of the victims, and laid them down gasping and dying upon the ground, for the knife had taken their strength. Then they poured wine from the mixing-bowl into the cups, and prayed to the everlasting gods, saying, Trojans and Achaeans among one another,

"Zeus, most great and glorious, and ye other everlasting gods, grant that the brains of them who shall first sin against their oaths - of them and their children- may be shed upon the ground even as this wine, and let their wives become the slaves of strangers." Thus they prayed, but Zeus would not yet grant them their prayer…

When they had armed, each among his own soldiers, they strode fiercely into the open, and both Trojans and Achaeans were struck with awe as they watched them. They stood near one another on the even ground, clutching their spears, and each furious against the other. Paris aimed first, and struck the round shield of the son of Atreus, but the spear did not pierce it, for the shield turned its point. Menelaus next took aim, praying to Father Zeus as he did so. "Lord Zeus," he said, "grant me revenge against Paris who has wronged me; subdue him under my hand, so that in ages yet to come men may shrink from wronging the house of his host."

He poised his spear as he spoke, and hurled it at the shield of Paris. Through shield and armour it went, and tore the shirt by his side, but Paris swerved aside, and thus saved his life. Then the son of Atreus drew his sword, and drove at the projecting part of his helmet, but the sword fell shivered in three or four pieces from his hand, and he cried, looking towards Heaven, "Father Zeus, of all gods you are the most spiteful; I made sure of my revenge, but the sword has broken in my hand, my spear has been hurled in vain, and I have not killed him."

With this he flew at Paris, caught him by the horsehair plume of his helmet, and began dragging him towards the Achaeans. The strap of the helmet that went under his chin was choking him, and Menelaus would have dragged him off to his own great glory had not Zeus's daughter Aphrodite been quick to find and to break the strap, so that the empty helmet came away in his hand. This he flung to his comrades among the Achaeans, and was again springing upon Paris to run him through with a spear, but Aphrodite snatched him up in a moment (as a god can do), hid him under a cloud of darkness, and conveyed him to his own bedchamber.

Then she went to call Helen, and found her on a high tower with the Trojan women crowding round her. She took the form of an old woman who used to dress wool for her when she was still in Sparta, and of whom she was very fond. Thus disguised she plucked her by perfumed robe and said, "Come here; Paris says you are to go to the house; he is on his bed in his own room, shining with beauty and dressed in gorgeous apparel. No one would think he had just come from fighting, but rather that he was going to a dance, or had done dancing and was sitting down."

With these words she made Helen angry. When she saw the beautiful neck of the goddess, her lovely breasts, and sparkling eyes, she marvelled at her and said, "Goddess, why do you try to deceive me? Are you going to send me away still further to some man whom you have taken up in Phrygia or fair Meonia? Menelaus has just defeated Paris, and should to take my hateful self back with him. You are come here to betray me. Go lie with Paris yourself; then be goddess no longer, and never go back to Olympus! Worry about him and look after him till he marries, or, for that matter, his slave - but me? I will not go; I cannot stand his bed any longer. I will be a scandal among all the women of Troy. Besides, I have my own problems."

Aphrodite was furious, and said, "Impudent bitch! Don't provoke me. If you do, I'll leave you to your fate and hate you as much as I have loved you. I will stir up fierce hatred between Trojans and Achaeans, and you shall come to a bad end." At this Helen was frightened. She wrapped her mantle about her and went in silence, following the goddess and unnoticed by the Trojan women. When they came to the house of Paris the servants set about their work, but Helen went into her own room, and the laughter-loving goddess took a seat and set it for her facing Paris. On this Helen, daughter of aegis-bearing Zeus, sat down, and sceptically began to tear a strip off her husband.

"So you've retreated from the fight," she said. "If only you had fallen by the hand of that brave man who was my husband. You used to brag that you were a better man with hands and spear than Menelaus – go, and challenge him again! But I suggest you not go, for if you are foolish enough to meet him in single combat, you will soon be slain by his spear."

And Paris answered, "Wife, do not insult me with your criticisms. This time, with the help of Athena, Menelaus has vanquished me; another time I may myself be victor, for I too have gods that will stand by me. Come, let us lie down together and make love. Never yet have I been so passionately desired you as at now - not even when I first carried you off from Sparta and sailed away with you - not even when I slept with you on the island of Cranae was I so filled with desire for you as now." On this he led her towards the bed, and his wife went with him.

Thus they laid on the bed together, but the son of Atreus raged among the ranks, looking everywhere for Paris, and no man, neither Trojan nor Greek, could find him. If they had seen him they had no intention to hide him, for all of them hated him as they did death itself. Then Agamemnon, king of men, spoke, saying, "Hear me, Trojans, Dardanians, and allies. The victory has been with Menelaus. Therefore give back Helen with all her wealth, and pay such fine as shall be agreed upon, in testimony among them that shall be born hereafter."

1c) Diomedes Fights the Gods (Homer, Iliad, 5. 1-445, passim)

Then Pallas Athena put courage into the heart of Diomedes, son of Tydeus, so that he might excel all other Argives, and cover himself with glory. She made a stream of fire from his shield and helmet like the star that shines most brilliantly in summer after its bath in the waters of Oceanus – such a fire she kindled on his head and shoulders as she ordered him to hurry into the thickest of the fight.

Furiously did the battle rage between the ranks. As for Diomedes, you could not say whether he was more among the Achaeans or the Trojans. He rushed across the plain like a winter torrent that has burst its barrier in full flood; no dams, no walls of fruitful vineyards can embank it when it is swollen with rain from heaven, but in a moment it comes tearing onward, and lays many a field waste that many a strong man hand has reclaimed - just so were the dense phalanxes of the Trojans routed by the son of Tydeus, and many though they were, they dared not abide his assault.

Now when the son of Lycaon saw him scouring the plain and driving the Trojans headlong before him, he aimed an arrow and hit the front part of his armour near the shoulder: the arrow went right through the metal and pierced the flesh, so that the armour was covered with blood. On this the son of Lycaon shouted in triumph, "Brave Trojans, come on; the bravest of the Achaeans is wounded, and he will not hold out much longer if Lord Apollo was indeed with me when I sped from Lycia here."

Thus he boasted; but his arrow had not killed Diomedes, who withdrew and made for the chariot and horses of Sthenelus, the son of Capaneus. "Dear son of Capaneus," he said, "come down from your chariot, and draw the arrow out of my shoulder."

Sthenelus sprang from his chariot, and drew the arrow from the wound, after which the blood came spouting out through the hole that had been made in his shirt. Then Diomedes prayed, saying,

"Hear me, daughter of untiring, aegis-bearing Zeus, if ever you loved my father well and stood by him in the thick of a fight, do the same now by me; grant me to come within a spear's throw of that man and kill him. He has been too quick for me and has wounded me; and now he is boasting that I shall not see the light of the sun much longer."

Thus he prayed, and Pallas Athena heard him; she made his limbs nimble and quickened his hands and his feet. Then she went up close to him and said, "Fear not, Diomedes, to battle with the Trojans, for I have set in your heart the spirit of your kingly father Tydeus. Moreover, I have withdrawn the veil from your eyes, that you know gods and men apart. If, then, any other god comes here and offers battle, do not fight him; but should Zeus' daughter Aphrodite come, strike her with your spear and wound her."

When Aeneas saw him thus wreaking havoc among the ranks, he went through the fight amid the rain of spears to see if he could find Pandarus. When he had found the brave son of Lycaon he said, "Pandarus, where is now your bow, your winged arrows, and your renown as an archer, in respect of which no man here can rival you nor is there any in Lycia that can beat you?"

And the two of them had now driven close to Diomedes, and the son of Lycaon spoke first. "Great and mighty son," he said, "of noble Tydeus, my arrow failed to lay you low, so I will now try with my spear." He poised his spear as he spoke and hurled it from him. It struck the shield of the son of Tydeus; the bronze point pierced it and passed on till it reached the breastplate. Then the son of Lycaon shouted out and said, "You are hit clean through the belly; you will not stand out for long, and the glory of the fight is mine."

But Diomedes, all not discourage, answered, "You missed, not hit, and before you two see the end of this business one or other of you shall glut tough-shielded Ares with his blood." With this he hurled his spear, and Athena guided it on to Pandarus's nose near the eye. It went crashing in among his white teeth; the bronze point cut through the root of his to tongue, coming out under his chin, and his glistening armour rang rattling round him as he fell heavily to the ground. The horses started aside for fear, and he lost his life and strength.

Aeneas sprang from his chariot armed with shield and spear, fearing that the Achaeans would carry off the body. He bestrode it as a lion in the pride of strength, with shield and on spear before him and a cry of battle on his lips resolute to kill the first that should dare face him. But the son of Tydeus lifted a mighty rock, so huge and great that as men now are it would take two to lift it; nevertheless he bore it with ease, and with this he struck Aeneas on the groin where the hip meets the pelvis. The stone crushed this joint, and broke both the sinews, while its jagged edges tore away all the flesh. The hero fell on his knees, and propped himself with his hand resting on the ground till the darkness of night fell upon his eyes. And now Aeneas, lord of men, would have perished then and there, had not his mother, Zeus' daughter Aphrodite, who had conceived him by Anchises when he was herding cattle, been quick to see it, and thrown her two white arms about the body of her dear son. She protected him by covering him with a fold of her own fair garment, so that no Danaan would drive a spear into his breast and kill him.

Now the son of Tydeus pursued the Cyprian goddess, spear in hand, for he knew her to be feeble and not one of those goddesses that can lord it among men in battle like Athena or Enyo the waster of cities, and when at last after a long chase he caught her up, he flew at her and thrust his spear into the flesh of her delicate hand. The point tore through the ambrosial robe which the Graces had woven for her, and pierced the skin between her wrist and the palm of her hand, so that the immortal blood, or ichor, that flows in the veins of the blessed gods, came pouring from the wound; for the gods do not eat bread nor drink wine, hence they have no blood such as ours, and are immortal. Aphrodite screamed, and let her son fall, but Phoebus Apollo caught him in his arms, and hid him in a cloud of darkness, so that no Danaan would drive a spear into his breast and kill him; and Diomedes shouted out as he left her, "Daughter of Zeus, leave war and battle alone. Can you not be contented with confusing silly women? If you meddle with fighting you will get what will make you shudder at the very name of war."

The goddess went dazed and painfully away, and Iris, fleet as the wind, drew her from the battle, in pain and with her fair skin all besmirched. She found fierce Ares waiting on the left of the battle, with his spear and his two fleet steeds resting on a cloud; whereon she fell on her knees before her brother and implored him to let her have his horses. "Dear brother," she cried, "save me; and give me your horses to take me to Olympus where the gods dwell. I am badly wounded by a mortal, the son of Tydeus, who would now fight even with father Zeus."

But Athena and Hera, who were looking on, began to taunt Zeus with their mocking talk, and Athena was first to speak. "Father Zeus," she said, "do not be angry with me, but I think Aphrodite must have been persuading some one of the Achaean women to go with the Trojans whom she likes so much, and while caressing one or other of them she must have torn her delicate hand with the gold pin of the woman's brooch."

The lord of gods and men smiled, and called golden Aphrodite to his side. "My child, he said, "it is not for you to be a warrior. From now on, look to your own delightful matrimonial duties, and leave all this fighting to Ares and to Athena."

Thus did they spoke. But Diomedes sprang upon Aeneas, though he knew him to be in the very arms of Apollo. Not one bit did he fear the mighty god, so set was he on killing Aeneas and stripping him of his armour. Three times he sprang forward and tried to slay him, and three times Apollo beat back his gleaming shield. When he was coming on for the fourth time, as though he were a god, Apollo shouted to him with an awful voice and said, "Be careful, son of Tydeus, and draw off; do not think pretend to match yourself against gods, for men that walk the earth cannot hold their own with the immortals."

The son of Tydeus then gave way a little, to avoid the anger of the god, while Apollo took Aeneas out of the crowd and set him in sacred Pergamus, where his temple stood. There, within the mighty sanctuary, Latona and Diana healed him and made him glorious to behold, while Apollo of the silver bow fashioned a phantom in the likeness of Aeneas, and armed as he was.

1d) Hector Returns to Troy (Homer, Iliad, 6. 103-502, passim)

Hector sprang from his chariot, and went about everywhere among the host, brandishing his spears, urging the men on to fight, and raising the dread cry of battle. Thereupon they rallied and again faced the Achaeans, who gave ground and ceased their murderous onset, for they thought that some one of the immortals had come down from starry heaven to help the Trojans, so strangely had they rallied. And Hector shouted to the Trojans, "Trojans and allies, be men, my friends, and fight with might and courage, while I go to Tory and tell the old men of our council and our wives to pray to the gods and vow sacrifices in their honour."

With this he went his way, and the black rim of hide that went round his shield beat against his neck and his ankles. Then Glaucus son of Hippolochus, and the son of Tydeus went into the open space between the hosts to fight in single combat. When they were close to one another Diomedes of the loud war-cry was the first to speak. "Who, my good lord," he said, "are you among men? I have never seen you in battle before, but you are daring beyond all others if you endure my assault. Woe to those fathers whose sons face my might. If, however, you are one of the immortals and have come down from heaven, I will not fight you; for even valiant Lycurgus, son of Dryas, did not live long when he took to fighting with the gods. It was he who drove the nursing women who were in charge of frenzied Dionysos through the land of Nysa, and they flung their thyrsi on the ground as murderous Lycurgus beat them with his ox-goad. Dionysos himself plunged terror-stricken into the sea, and Thetis took him to her bosom to comfort him, for he was scared by the fury with which the man reviled him. Thereupon the gods who live at ease were angry with Lycurgus and the son of Cronos struck him blind, nor did he live much longer after he had become hateful to the immortals. Therefore I will not fight with the blessed gods; but if you are of them that eat the fruit of the ground, draw near and meet your doom."

And the son of Hippolochus answered, "Son of Tydeus, why ask me of my lineage? Men come and go as leaves year by year from the trees. Those of autumn the wind sheds upon the ground, but when spring returns the forest buds with fresh vines. Even so is it with the generations of mankind, the new spring up as the old are passing away. If, then, you would learn my descent, it is one that is well known to many. There is a city in the heart of Argos, pasture-land of horses, called Ephyra, where Sisyphus lived, who was the craftiest of all mankind. He was the son of Aeolus, and had a son named Glaucus, who was father to Bellerophon, whom heaven endowed with the most surpassing comeliness and beauty. But Proetus devised his ruin, and being stronger than he, drove him from the land of the Argives, over which Zeus had made him ruler. For Antea, wife of Proetus, lusted after him, and would have had him lie with her in secret; but Bellerophon was an honourable man and would not, so she told lies about him to Proetus. 'Proetus,' said she, 'kill Bellerophon or die, for he would have had converse with me against my will.' The king was angered, but shrank from killing Bellerophon, so he sent him to Lycia with lying letters of introduction, written on a folded tablet, and containing much ill against the bearer. He bade Bellerophon show these letters to his father-in-law, to the end so that he would thus perish; Bellerophon therefore went to Lycia, and the gods convoyed him safely.

"When he reached the river Xanthus, which is in Lycia, the king received him with all good-will, feasted him nine days, and sacrificed nine cattle in his honour, but when rosy-fingered Dawn appeared upon the tenth day, he questioned him and desired to see the letter from his son-in-law Proetus. When he had received the wicked letter he first commanded Bellerophon to kill that savage monster, the Chimaera, who was not a human being, but a goddess, for she had the head of a lion and the tail of a serpent, while her body was that of a goat, and she breathed forth flames of fire; but Bellerophon slew her, for he was guided by signs from heaven. He next fought the far-famed Solymi, and this, he said, was the hardest of all his battles. Thirdly, he killed the Amazons, women who were the equals of men, and as he was returning thence the king devised yet another plan for his destruction; he picked the bravest warriors in all Lycia, and placed them in ambuscade, but not a man ever came back, for Bellerophon killed every one of them. Then the king knew that he must be the valiant offspring of a god, so he kept him in Lycia, gave him his daughter in marriage, and made him of equal honour in the kingdom with himself; and the Lycians gave him a piece of land, the best in all the country, fair with vineyards and tilled fields, to have and to hold.

"The king's daughter bore Bellerophon three children, Isander, Hippolochus, and Laodameia. Zeus, the lord of counsel, lay with Laodameia, and she bore him noble Sarpedon; but when Bellerophon came to be hated by all the gods, he wandered all desolate and dismayed upon the Alean plain, gnawing at his own heart, and shunning the path of man. Mars, insatiate of battle, killed his son Isander while he was fighting the Solymi; his daughter was killed by Artemis of the golden reins, for she was angered with her; but Hippolochus was father to myself, and when he sent me to Troy he urged me again and again to fight ever among the foremost and outdo my peers, so as not to shame the blood of my fathers who were the noblest in Ephyra and in all Lycia. This, then, is the descent I claim."

Thus did he speak, and the heart of Diomedes was glad. He planted his spear in the ground, and spoke to him with friendly words. "In that case," he said, "you are an old friend of my father's house. Great Oeneus once entertained Bellerophon for twenty days, and the two exchanged presents. Oeneus gave a belt rich with purple, and Bellerophon a double cup, which I left at home when I set out for Troy. I do not remember Tydeus, for he was taken from us while I was yet a child, when the army of the Achaeans was cut to pieces before Thebes. From now on, however, I must be your host in Argos, and you mine in Lycia, if I should ever go there; let us avoid one another's spears even during a general engagement; there are many noble Trojans and allies whom I can kill, if I overtake them and heaven delivers them into my hand; so again with yourself, there are many Achaeans whose lives you may take if you can; we two, then, will exchange armour, that all present may know of the old ties that subsist between us."

With these words they sprang from their chariots, grasped one another's hands, and swore friendship. But the son of Cronos made Glaucus take lose his wits, for he exchanged his golden armour for bronze, the worth of a hundred head of cattle for the worth of nine.

Now when Hector reached the Scaean gates and the oak tree, the wives and daughters of the Trojans came running towards him to ask after their sons, brothers, kinsmen, and husbands: he told them to set about praying to the gods, and many were made sorrowful as they heard him.

Hector hurried from the house… and went down the streets by the same way that he had come. When he had gone through the city and had reached the Scaean gates through which he would go out on to the plain, his wife came running towards him, Andromache, daughter of great Eetion who ruled in Thebe under the wooded slopes of Mt. Placus, and was king of the Cilicians. His daughter had married Hector, and now came to meet him with a nurse who carried his little child in her bosom - a mere baby. Hector's darling son, and lovely as a star. Hector had named him Scamandrius, but the people called him Astyanax, for his father stood alone as chief guardian of Tory. Hector smiled as he looked upon the boy, but he did not speak, and Andromache stood by him weeping and taking his hand in her own.

"Dear husband," she said, "your valour will bring you to destruction; think about your infant son, and on my hapless self who before long shall be your widow - for the Achaeans will attack you and kill you. It would be better for me, should I lose you, to lie dead and buried, for I shall have nothing left to comfort me when you are gone, except sorrow. I have neither father nor mother now. Achilles killed my father when he sacked Thebe, the beautiful city of the Cilicians. He slew him, but did not, out of shame, despoil him; when he had burned him in his wondrous armour, he raised a barrow over his ashes and the mountain nymphs, daughters of aegis-bearing Zeus, planted a grove of elms about his tomb. I had seven brothers in my father's house, but on the same day they all went within the house of Hades. Achilles killed them as they were with their sheep and cattle. My mother – she who was queen of all the lands under Mt. Placus - he brought here as spoils, and freed her for a great sum, but the archer-queen Artemis took her in the house of your father. No! Hector, you who are a father, mother, brother, and dear husband to me, have mercy upon me; stay here upon this wall; do not leave your child fatherless, and your wife a widow; as for the army, place them near the fig-tree, where the city can be best scaled, and the wall is weakest. Three times have the bravest of them come there and assaulted it, under the two Ajaxes, Idomeneus, the sons of Atreus, and the brave son of Tydeus, either of their own bidding, or because some soothsayer had told them."

And Hector answered, "Dear wife, I too have thought about all this, but with what face should I look upon the Trojans, men or women, if I shirked battle like a coward? I cannot do it: I know nothing except to fight bravely in the front ranks of the Trojan army and win renown alike for my father and myself. I know well that the day will surely come when mighty Troy shall be destroyed with Priam and Priam's people, but I do not grieve for that- not even for Hecuba, nor King Priam, nor for my brothers, many and brave who may fall in the dust before their foes – not for any of these do I grieve as for you yourself when the day comes on which some Achaean robs you forever of your freedom, and bears you away in tears. It may be that you will have to work the loom in Argos at the bidding of a mistress, or to fetch water from the springs Messeis or Hypereia, treated brutally by some cruel task-master; then will one say who sees you weeping, 'She was the wife of Hector, the bravest warrior among the Trojans during the war before Ilium.' At this your tears will fall again for him who would have blocked your day of captivity. May I lie dead under the earth that is heaped over my body before I hear your cry as they carry you into slavery."

He stretched his arms towards his child, but the boy cried and nestled in his nurse's breast, scared at the sight of his father's armour, and at the horse-hair plume that nodded fiercely from his helmet. His father and mother laughed to see him, but Hector took the helmet from his head and laid it gleaming upon the ground.

Then he took his darling child, kissed him, and dandled him in his arms, praying over him the while to Zeus and to all the gods. "Zeus," he cried, "grant that my child may be like myself, chief among the Trojans; let him be not less excellent in strength, and let him rule Troy with his might. Then may one say of him as he comes from battle, 'The son is far better than the father.' May he bring back the blood-stained spoils of a soldier whom he has laid low, and let his mother's heart be glad.'"

With this he laid the child again in the arms of his wife, who took him to her own soft breast, smiling through her tears. As her husband watched her his heart yearned towards her and he caressed her fondly, saying, "My own wife, do not take these things too bitterly to heart. No one can hurry me down to Hades before my time, but if a man's hour is come, whether he is brave or a coward, there is no escape for him once he has been born. Go, then, within the house, and busy yourself with your daily duties, your loom, your distaff, and the ordering of your servants; for war is man's matter, and mine above all others of them that have been born in Troy."

He took his plumed helmet from the ground, and his wife went back again to her house, weeping bitterly and often looking back towards him. When she reached her home she found her maidens inside, and told them all to join in her lament; so they mourned Hector in his own house though he was yet alive, for they deemed that they should never see him return safe from battle, and from the furious hands of the Achaeans.

1e) Embassy Appeals to Achilles (Homer, Iliad, 9. 315-652, passim)

Achilles spoke, "Odysseus, noble son of Laertes, I answer you plainly and in all honesty that there should be no more of this flattering, from whomever it may come. I hate as the gates of hell him who says one thing while he hides another in his heart; therefore I will say what

I mean. I will be appeased neither by Agamemnon son of Atreus, nor by any other of the Danaans, for I see that I have no thanks for all my fighting. He that fights fares no better than he that does not; coward and hero are held in equal honour, and death deals the same fate to him who works and him who is idle. I have taken nothing from all my hardships - with my life ever in my hands; as a bird when she has found a morsel takes it to her nestlings, and herself still fares hardly, just so a long night have I been wakeful, and many a bloody battle have I waged by day against those who were fighting for their women. With my ships I have taken twelve cities, and eleven round about Troy have I stormed with my men by land; I took great loot from every one of them, but I gave all up to Agamemnon son of Atreus. He stayed where he was by his ships, yet of what came to him he gave little, and kept much himself.

"Nevertheless he distributed some bits of honour among the chieftains and kings, and they have them still; from me alone of the Achaeans he took the woman whom I enjoyed - let him keep her and sleep with her. Why? Why must the Argives fight the Trojans anyway? What made the son of Atreus gather the army and bring them? Was it not for the sake of Helen? Are the sons of Atreus the only men in the world who love their wives? Any man of common feeling loves and cherishes her who is his own, as I this woman, with my whole heart, though she was but a prize of my spear. Agamemnon has taken her from me; he has played me for a fool; I know his intention; let him tempt me no further, for he shall not move me. Let him look to you, Odysseus, and to the other commanders to save his ships from burning. He has done much without me already. He has built a wall; he has dug a trench deep and wide all round it, and he has planted it within with stakes; but even so he does not stay from the murderous might of Hector. So long as I fought the Achaeans, Hector did not engage in battle far from his city walls; he would come to the Scaean gates and to the oak tree, but no further. Once he stayed to meet me and hardly did he escape my assault: now, however, since I am in no mood to fight him, I will offer sacrifice to Zeus and to all the gods; I will draw my ships into the water and then provide them wit supplies as needed. Tomorrow morning, if you care to look, you will see my ships on the Hellespont, and my men rowing out to sea with might and main. If great Poseidon grants me a fair passage, in three days I shall be in Phthia. I have much there that I left behind me when I came here to my sorrow, and I shall bring back still further loot of gold, of red copper, of fair women, and of iron, my share of the spoils that we have taken; but one prize, he who gave has insolently taken away. Tell him all as I now tell you, and tell him in public that the Achaeans may hate him and beware of him should he think that he can dupe others for his shamelessness.

Ajax son of Telamon then said, "Odysseus, noble son of Laertes, let us go, for I see that our mission is vain. We must now take our answer, unwelcome though it be, to the Danaans who are waiting to receive it. Achilles is savage and remorseless; he is cruel, and cares nothing for the love his comrades lavished upon him more than on all the others. He is implacable - and yet if a man's brother or son has been slain he will accept a fine as amends from him who killed him, and the wrong-doer remains in peace among his own people; but as for you, Achilles, the gods have put a wicked, unforgiving spirit in your heart – and this, all about one single girl, whereas we now offer you the seven best we have, and much else in addition! Be more gracious, respect the hospitality of your own roof. We are with you as messengers from the host of the Danaans, and would prefer that be held nearest and dearest to yourself of all the Achaeans."

"Ajax," replied Achilles, "noble son of Telamon, you have spoken much to my liking, but my blood boils when I think it all over, and remember how the son of Atreus treated me insolently as though I were some vile tramp, and even in the presence of the Argives. Go, then, and deliver your message; say that I will have no concern with fighting till Hector, son of noble Priam, reaches the tents of the Myrmidons in his murderous course, and flings fire upon their ships. For all his lust of battle, I take it he will be held in check when he is at my own tent and ship."

1f) Hera Outwits Zeus (Homer, Iliad, 14. 149-359, passim)

Hera of the golden throne looked down as she stood upon a peak of Olympus and her heart was gladdened at the sight of him who was at once her brother and her brother-in-law, hurrying here and there in the fighting. Then she turned her eyes to Zeus as he sat on the topmost crests of many-fountained Ida, and hated him. She set herself to think how she might outwit him, and in the end she thought that it would be best for her to go to Ida and put on rich clothes, in the hope that Zeus might become lustful for her, and wish to have her. When he would be then sweetly and carelessly asleep, she might dull his eyes and senses.

She went, therefore, to the room, which her son Hephaestus had made her, and the doors of which he had cunningly fastened by means of a secret key so that no other god could open them. Here she entered and closed the doors behind her. She cleansed all the dirt from her fair body with ambrosia, then she anointed herself with olive oil,, very soft, and scented specially for herself - if it were so much as shaken in the bronze-floored house of Zeus, the scent pervaded the universe of heaven and earth. With this she anointed her delicate skin, and then she plaited the fair ambrosial locks that flowed in a stream of golden tresses from her immortal head. She put on the wondrous robe which Athena had made for her with consummate art, and had embroidered with various means; she fastened it about her breast with golden clasps, and she girded herself with a girdle that had a hundred tassels: then she fastened her earrings, three brilliant pendants that glistened most beautifully, through the pierced lobes of her ears, and threw a lovely new veil over her head. She bound her sandals on to her feet, and when she had arrayed herself perfectly to her satisfaction, she left her room and called Venus to come aside and speak to her. "My dear child," she said, "will you do what I am going to ask of you, or will refuse me because you are angry at my being on the Danaan side, while you are on the Trojan?"

Zeus' daughter Aphrodite answered, "Hera, revered queen of goddesses, daughter of mighty Cronos, say what you want, and I will do it for at once, if I can, and if it can be done at all."

Then Hera told her a lying tale and said, "I want you to give me some of those fascinating charms, the spells of which bring all things mortal and immortal to your feet. I am going to the world's end to visit Oceanus (from whom all we gods proceed) and mother Tethys: they received me in their house, took care of me, and brought me up, having taken me over from Rhea when Zeus imprisoned great Cronos in the depths that are under earth and sea. I must go and see them that I may make peace between them; they have been quarrelling, and are so angry that they have not slept with one another this long while; if I can bring them round and restore them to one another's embraces, they will be grateful to me and love me for ever afterwards."

At this, laughter-loving Aphrodite said, "I cannot and must not refuse, for you sleep in the arms of Zeus who is our lord."

As she spoke she loosed from her bosom the curiously embroidered girdle into which all her charms had been wrought- love, desire, and that sweet flattery which steals the judgement even of the most prudent. She gave the girdle to Hera and said, "Take this girdle wherein all my charms reside and lay it in your breast. If you will wear it I promise you that your mission, be it what it may, will not be unsuccessful…"

Hera then went to Gargarus, the topmost peak of Ida, and Zeus, gatherer of the clouds, set eyes upon her. As soon as he did so he became inflamed with the same passionate desire for her that he had felt when they had first enjoyed each other's love, and slept with one another without their dear parents knowing anything about it. He went up to her and said, "What do you want that you have come here from Olympus - and with neither chariot nor horses to convey you?"

Then Hera told him a lying tale and said, "I am going to the world's end, to visit Oceanus, from whom all we gods proceed, and mother Tethys; they received me into their house, took care of me, and brought me up. I must go and see them that I may make peace between them: they have been quarrelling, and are so angry that they have not slept with one another this long time. The horses that will take me over land and sea are stationed on the lowermost spurs of many-fountained Ida, and I have come here from Olympus on purpose to consult you. I was afraid you might be angry with me later on, if I went to the house of Oceanus without letting you know."

And Zeus said, "Hera, you can choose some other time for paying your visit to Oceanus – right now, let us lose ourselves in love and in the enjoyment of one another. Never before have I been so overpowered by passion, neither for goddess nor mortal woman, as I am at this moment for yourself - no, not even when I was in love with the wife of Ixion who bore me Pirithous, peer of gods in counsel, nor yet with Danae the slender-ankled daughter of Acrisius, who bore me the famed hero Perseus. Then there was the daughter of Phoenix, who bore me Minos and Rhadamanthus: there was Semele, and Alcmena in Thebes by whom I begot my lion-hearted son Hercules, while Semele became mother to Bacchus the comforter of mankind. There was queen Ceres again, and lovely Leto, and yourself- but with none of these was I ever so much in love with as I now am with you."

Hera again answered him with a sly tale. "Most dread son of Cronos," she exclaimed, "what are you talking about? Would you have us enjoy one another here on the top of Mount Ida, where everything can be seen? What if one of the deathless gods should see us sleeping together, and tell the others? It would be such a scandal that when I had risen from your embraces I could never show myself inside your house again; but if you are so fixated, there is a room which your son Hepaestus has made me, and he has given it good strong doors; if you would so have it, let us go there and lie down."

And Zeus answered, "Hera, you need not be afraid that either god or man will see you, for I will cover both of us in such a dense golden cloud, that the very sun for all his bright piercing beams shall not see through it."

With this the son of Cronos held his wife in his embrace; from which the earth sprouted them a cushion of young grass, with dew-covered lotus, crocus, and hyacinth, so soft and thick that it raised them well above the ground. Here they laid themselves down and overhead they were covered by a fair cloud of gold, from which there fell glittering dew-drops. Thus, then, did the lord of all things rest peacefully on the crest of Ida, overcome at once by sleep and love, and he held his spouse in his arms.

1g) Achilles Returns to Battle (Homer, Iliad, 18. 13-242, passim)

As Achilles was thinking, Antilochus, the son of Nestor came up to him and told his sad tale, weeping bitterly. "Alas," he cried, "son of noble Peleus, I bring you bad news – if only they were not true! Patroclus has fallen, and a fight is raging about his naked body - for Hector holds his armour."

A dark cloud of grief fell upon Achilles as he listened. He filled both hands with dust from off the ground, and poured it over his head, disfiguring his handsome face, and letting the dirt settle over his shirt so fair and new. He flung himself down at full length, and tore his hair with his hands. The slave-women whom Achilles and Patroclus had taken captive screamed aloud for grief, beating their breasts, and with their limbs failing them for sorrow. Antilochus bent over him the while, weeping and holding both his hands as he lay groaning for he feared that he might plunge a knife into his own throat. Then Achilles gave a loud cry and his mother heard him as she was sitting in the depths of the sea by the old man her father, whereon she screamed, and all the goddess daughters of Nereus that dwelt at the bottom of the sea, came gathering round her…

His mother went up to him as he lay groaning; she laid her hand upon his head and spoke piteously, saying, "My son, why are you thus weeping? What sorrow has now fallen on you? Tell me; do not hide it from me. Surely Zeus has granted you the prayer you made him, when you lifted up your hands and prayed to him that the Achaeans might all of them be pent up at their ships, and rue it bitterly in that you were no longer with them."

Achilles groaned and answered, "Mother, Olympian Zeus has indeed granted me the fulfilment of my prayer, but what good is it to me, seeing that my dear comrade Patroclus has fallen - he whom I valued more than all others, and loved as dearly as my own life? I have lost him; oh, and Hector, when he killed him, stripped him of my wondrous armour, so glorious to behold, which the gods gave to Peleus when they laid you in the couch of a mortal man. If only you were still dwelling among the immortal sea-nymphs, and that Peleus had taken to himself some mortal bride. For now you shall have unending grief because of the death of that son whom you can never welcome home - no, I will not live nor walk about among men unless Hector fall by my spear, and thus pay me for having slain Patroclus son of Menoetius."

Thetis wept and answered, "Then, my son, your end is near - for your own death awaits you full soon after that of Hector."

Then said Achilles in his great grief, "I would die here and now, since I could not save my companion. He has fallen far from home, and in his hour of need my hand was not there to help him. What is there for me? I will not return to my own land, and I have neither saved Patroclus nor my other comrades of whom so many have been slain by mighty Hector; I have stayed here by my ships, a worthless burden upon the earth, I, who in battle have no equal among the Achaeans, though in council there are better than me. Therefore, may strife die both from among gods and men, and anger, in which even a righteous man hardens his heart - which rises up in the soul of a man like smoke, and the taste of which is sweeter than drops of honey. Even so has Agamemnon angered me. And yet - so be it, for it is over; I will force my soul into subjection as I must; I will go; I will pursue Hector who has slain him whom I loved so dearly, and will then obey my doom when it may please Zeus and the other gods to send it. Even Heracles, the best beloved of Zeus - even he could not escape the hand of death, but fate and Hera's fierce anger laid him low, as I too shall lie when I am dead if a like doom awaits me. Till then I will win fame, and will bid Trojan and Dardanian women squeeze tears from their tender cheeks with both their hands in the grievousness of their great sorrow; thus shall they know that he who has held aloof so long will hold aloof no longer. Do not hold me back in the love you bear me, for you shall not move me."

Then silver-footed Thetis answered, "My son, what you have said is true. It is good to save your comrades from destruction, but your armour is in the hands of the Trojans; Hector bears it in triumph upon his own shoulders. I know well that his boasting shall not last, for his end is close at hand; do not go, however, into the heat of battle until you see me return here; tomorrow at the break of day I shall be here, and will bring you goodly armour from King Hephaestus."

At this she left her brave son, and as she turned away she said to the sea-nymphs her sisters, "Dive into the bosom of the sea and go to the house of the old sea-god my father. Tell him everything; as for me, I will go to the cunning workman Hephaestus on high Olympus, and ask him to provide my son with a suit of splendid armour..."

And Achilles dear to Zeus arose, and Athena flung her tasselled aegis round his strong shoulders; she crowned his head with a halo of golden cloud from which she kindled a glow of gleaming fire. As the smoke that goes up into heaven from some city that is being besieged on an island far out at sea - all day men sally from the city and fight their hardest, and at the setting of the sun the line of beacon-fires blazes forth, flaring high for those that dwell near them to see, so that they may come with their ships and assist them - just so did the light flare from the head of Achilles, as he stood by the trench, going beyond the wall- but he aid not join the Achaeans for he heeded the charge which his mother laid upon him.

There did he stand and shout aloud. Athena also raised her voice from afar, and spread unspeakable terror among the Trojans. Ringing as the note of a trumpet that sounds alarm then the foe is at the gates of a city, just so aggressive was the voice of the son of Aeacus, and when the Trojans heard its clarion tones they were fearful; the horses turned back with their chariots for they boded mischief, and their drivers were awe-struck by the steady flame which the grey-eyed goddess had kindled above the head of the great son of Peleus.

Three times did Achilles raise his loud cry as he stood by the trench, and three times the Trojans and their brave allies were thrown into confusion; after which twelve of their noblest champions fell beneath the wheels of their chariots and perished by their own spears. The Achaeans to their great joy then drew Patroclus out of reach of the weapons, and laid him on a litter: his comrades stood mourning round him, and among them fleet Achilles who wept bitterly as he saw his true comrade lying dead upon his bier. He had sent him out with horses and chariots into battle, but his return he was not to welcome.

1h) The Gods Fight Each Other (Homer, Iliad, 21. 382-497, passim)

A furious quarrel broke out among the other gods, for they were on different sides. They fell on one another with a mighty uproar – the earth groaned, and the sky rang out as with a blare of trumpets. Zeus heard as he was sitting on Olympus, and laughed for joy when he saw the gods coming to blows among themselves. They were not long in starting, and Ares piercer of shields opened the battle. Sword in hand he sprang at once upon Athena and reviled her. "Why, you vulture," he said, "have you again set the gods by the ears in the pride and haughtiness of your heart? Have you forgotten how you set Diomedes, son of Tydeus, to wound me, and yourself took visible spear and drove it into me to the hurt of my fair body? You shall now suffer for what you then did to me."

As he spoke he struck her on the terrible tasselled aegis - so terrible that not even can Zeus' lightning pierce it. Here did murderous Ares strike her with his great spear. She drew back and with her strong hand seized a stone that was lying on the plain - great and rugged and black - which men of old had set for the boundary of a field. With this she struck Ares on the neck, and brought him down. Nine roods did he cover in his fall, and his hair was all soiled in the dust, while his armour rang rattling round him. But Athena laughed and vaunted over him saying, "Idiot, have you not learned how far stronger I am than you, but you must still match yourself against me? Thus do your mother's curses now roost upon you, for she is angry and would do you mischief because you have deserted the Achaeans and are helping the Trojans."

She then turned her two piercing eyes elsewhere, whereon Zeus' daughter Aphrodite took Ares by the hand and led him away groaning all the time, for it was only with great difficulty that he had come to himself again. When Queen Hera saw her, she said to Athena, "Look, daughter of aegis-bearing untiring Zeus, that bitch Aphrodite is again taking Ares through the crowd out of the battle; go after her at once."

Thus she spoke. Athena sped after Aphrodite with a will, and assaulted t her, striking her on the breast with her strong hand so that she fell fainting to the ground, and there they both lay stretched at full length. Then Athena vaunted over her saying, "May all who help the Trojans against the Argives prove just as redoubtable and stalwart as Aphrodite did when she came across me while she was helping Ares. Had this been so, we should long since have ended the war by sacking the strong city of Troy."

Hera smiled as she listened. Meanwhile Lord Poseidon turned to Apollo saying, "Phoebus, why should we keep each other at arm's length? Unfittingt, since the others have begun fighting; it will be disgraceful to us if we return to Zeus' bronze-floored mansion on Olympus without having fought each other; so bring it on, you are the younger of the two, and I ought not to attack you, for I am older and have had more experience. Idiot, you have no sense, and forget how we two alone of all the gods fared hardly round about Troy when we came from Zeus' house and worked for Laomedon a whole year at a stated wage and he gave us his orders. I built the Trojans the wall about their city, so wide and fair that it might be impregnable, while you, Phoebus, herded cattle for him in the dales of many valleyed Ida. When, however, the glad hours brought round the time of payment, mighty Laomedon robbed us of all our hire and sent us off with nothing but abuse. He threatened to bind us hand and foot and sell us over into some distant island. He tried, moreover, to cut off the ears of both of us, so we went away in a rage, furious about the payment he had promised us, and yet withheld; in spite of all this, you are now showing favour to his people, and will not join us in bringing the utter ruin of the proud Trojans with their wives and children."

And Lord Apollo answered, "Lord of the earthquake, you would have no respect for me if I were to fight you about a pack of wretched mortals, who come out like leaves in summer and eat the fruit of the field, and presently fall lifeless to the ground. Let us stay this fighting at once and let them settle it among themselves."

He turned away as he spoke, for he would lay no hand on the brother of his own father. But his sister the huntress Artemis, patroness of wild beasts, was very angry with him and said, "So you would fly, Arrow-shooter, and hand victory over to Poseidon with a cheap boast to boot. Wimp, why keep your bow idle in this way? Never let me again hear you bragging in my father's house, as you have often done in the presence of the immortals, that you would stand up and fight with Poseidon."

Apollo gave her no answer, but Zeus' august queen was angry and scolded her bitterly. "You bitch," she cried, "how dare you cross me like this? For all your bow you will find it hard to hold your own against me. Zeus made you as a lion among women, and lets you kill them whenever you choose – better to chase wild beasts and deer upon the mountains than to fight those who are stronger than you are. If you would try war, do so, and find out by pitting yourself against me, how far stronger I am than you are."

She caught both Artemis' wrists with her left hand as she spoke, and with her right she took the bow from her shoulders, and laughed as she beat her with it about the ears while Artemis wriggled and writhed under her blows. Her swift arrows were shed upon the ground, and she fled weeping from under Juno's hand as a dove that flies before a falcon to the cleft of some hollow rock, when it is her good fortune to escape. Even so did she fly weeping away, leaving her bow and arrows behind her.

1i) The Death of Hector (Homer, Iliad, 22. 197-370, passim)

Achilles was still in full pursuit of Hector, as a hound chasing a fawn which he has started from its covert on the mountains, and hunts through glade and thicket. The fawn may try to elude him by crouching under cover of a bush, but he will scent her out and follow her up until he gets her - even so there was no escape for Hector from the fleet son of Peleus…And Athena went after Hector in the form and with the voice of [his brother], Deiphobus. She came close to him and said, "Dear brother, I see you are hard pressed by Achilles who is chasing you at full speed round the city of Priam, let us await his onset and stand on our defence."

Thus did Minerva deceive him with her cunning, and when the two were now close to one another great Hector was first to speak. "I will no longer flee you, son of Peleus," he said, "as I have been doing to this point. Three times have I fled round the mighty city of Priam, without daring to withstand you, but now, let me either slay or be slain, for I am in the mind to face you. Let us, then, give pledges to one another by our gods, who are the fittest witnesses and guardians of all pacts; let it be agreed between us that if Zeus grants me the longer stay and I take your life, I am not to treat your dead body in any unseemly fashion, but when I have stripped you of your armour, I am to give up your body to the Achaeans. And do you likewise."

Achilles glared at him and answered, "Fool, do not talk to me about pacts. There can be no pacts between men and lions – wolves and lambs can never be of one mind, but hate each other through and through. Therefore there can be no understanding between you and me, nor may there be any pacts between us, till one or other shall fall and glut grim Ares with his life's blood. Put forth all your strength; you have need now to prove yourself indeed a bold soldier and man of war. You have no more chance, and Pallas Athena will now vanquish you by my spear: you shall now pay me in full for the grief you have caused me on account of my comrades whom you have killed in battle."

He poised his spear as he spoke and hurled it. Hector saw it coming and avoided it; he watched it and crouched down so that it flew over his head and stuck in the ground beyond; Athena then snatched it and gave it back to Achilles without Hector seeing her; Hector then said to the son of Peleus, "You have missed, Achilles, peer of the gods, and Zeus has not yet revealed to you the hour of my doom, though you made sure that he had done so. You were a false-tongued liar when you deemed that I should forget my valour and quail before you. You shall not drive spear into the back of a runaway - drive it, should heaven so grant you power, drive it into me as I make straight towards you; and now for your own part avoid my spear if you can – if only you might receive the whole of it into your body; if you were once dead the Trojans would find the war an easier matter, for it is you who have harmed them most."

He poised his spear as he spoke and hurled it. His aim was true, for he hit the middle of Achilles' shield, but the spear rebounded from it, and did not pierce it. Hector was angry when he saw that the weapon had sped from his hand in vain, and stood there in dismay for he had no second spear. With a loud cry he called Deiphobus and called to him, but there was no one there; then he saw the truth and said to himself, "Alas! the gods have lured me on to my destruction. I deemed that the hero Deiphobus was by my side, but he is within the wall, and Athena has deceived me; death is now indeed near at hand and there is no way out of it - for so Zeus and his son Apollo the far-shooter have willed it, though to this point they have been ever ready to protect me. My doom has come upon me; let me not then die ingloriously and without a struggle, but let me first do some great thing that shall be told among men hereafter."

As he spoke he drew the keen blade that hung so great and strong by his side, and gathering himself together be sprang on Achilles like a soaring eagle which swoops down from the clouds on to some lamb or timid hare - just so did Hector brandish his sword and spring upon Achilles. Achilles mad with rage darted towards him, with his wondrous shield before his breast, and his gleaming helmet, made with four layers of metal, nodding fiercely forward. The thick tresses of gold with which Vulcan had crested the helmet floated round it, and as the evening star that shines brighter than all others through the stillness of night, just so was the gleam of the spear which Achilles poised in his right hand, fraught with the death of noble Hector. He eyed his fair flesh over and over to see where he could best wound it, but all was protected by the beautiful armour of which Hector had spoiled Patroclus after he had slain him, save only the throat where the collar-bone divides the neck from the shoulders, and this is a most deadly place: here then Achilles struck him as he was coming on towards him, and the point of his spear went right through the fleshy part of the neck, but it did not sever his windpipe so that he could still speak. Hector fell headlong, and Achilles vaunted over him saying, "Hector, you thought that you should come off unharmed when you were spoiling Patroclus, and did not remember me who was not with him. Fool that you were: for I, his companion, mightier far than he, was still left behind him at the ships, and now I have laid you low. The Achaeans shall give him all due funeral rites, while dogs and vultures shall enjoy your corpse."

Then Hector said, as the life ebbed out of him, "I pray you by your life and knees, and by your parents, no not let dogs devour me at the ships of the Achaeans, but accept the rich treasure of gold and bronze which my father and mother will offer you, and send my body home, so that the Trojans and their wives may give me my funeral rites when I am dead."

Achilles glared at him and answered, "Dog! Do not talk to me of knees nor parents; if only I could be as sure of being able to cut your flesh into pieces and eat it raw, for the ill have you done me, as I am that nothing shall save you from the dogs - it shall not be, even if they should bring ten or twenty times that ransom and weigh it out for me on the spot, with promise of yet more afterwards. Though Priam son of Dardanus should bid them offer me your weight in gold, even so your mother shall never lay you out and lament over the son she bore, but dogs and vultures shall utterly devour you."

Hector with his dying breath then said, "I know you what you are, and was sure that I could not move you, for your heart is hard as iron; look to it that I bring not heaven's anger upon you on the day when Paris and Phoebus Apollo, valiant though you be, shall slay you at the Scaean gates."

When he had thus spoken the shrouds of death enfolded him, after which his soul left him and flew down to the house of Hades, lamenting its sad fate that it should enjoy youth and strength no longer. But Achilles said, speaking to the dead body, "Die, die! As for me, I will accept my fate whenever Zeus and the other gods see fit to send it."

As he spoke he drew his spear from the body and set it on one side; then he stripped the blood-stained armour from Hector's shoulders while the other Achaeans came running up to view his corpse's wondrous strength and beauty; and no one came near him without giving him a fresh wound. Then they would turn to their neighbours and say, "It is easier to handle Hector now than when he was flinging fire on to our ships" and as they spoke they would thrust their spears into him again and again.

1j) Achilles and Priam (Homer, Iliad, 24. 320-804, passim)

The old man hurried to mount his chariot, and drove out through the inner gateway and under the echoing gatehouse of the outer court. Before him went the mules drawing the four-wheeled wagon, and driven by wise Idaeus; behind these were the horses, which the old man lashed with his whip and drove swiftly through the city, while his friends followed after, wailing and lamenting for him as though he were on his road to death. As soon as they had come down from the city and had reached the plain, his sons and sons-in-law who had followed him went back to Troy.

But Priam and Idaeus as they showed out upon the plain did not escape the ken of all-seeing Zeus, who looked down upon the old man and pitied him; then he spoke to his son Hermes and said, "Hermes, for it is you who are the most disposed to escort men on their way, and to hear those whom you will hear, go, and escort Priam to the ships of the Achaeans that no other of the Danaans shall see him nor take note of him until he reach the son of Peleus."

Thus he spoke and Hermes, guide and guardian, slayer of Argus, did as he was told. Forthwith he bound on his glittering golden sandals with which he could fly like the wind over land and sea; he took the wand with which he seals men's eyes in sleep, or wakes them just as he pleases, and flew holding it in his hand till he came to Troy and to the Hellespont. To look at, he was like a young man of noble birth in the hey-day of his youth and beauty with the down just coming upon his face.

Hermes opened the gate for the old man, and brought in the treasure that he was taking with him for the son of Peleus. Then he sprang from the chariot on to the ground and said, "Sir, it is I, immortal Hermes, that have come with you, for my father sent me to escort you. I will now leave you, and will not enter into the presence of Achilles, for it might anger him that a god should befriend mortal men thus openly. Go you within, and embrace the knees of the son of Peleus: beg him by his father, his lovely mother, and his son; thus you may move him."

With these words Hermes went back to high Olympus. Priam sprang from his chariot to the ground, leaving Idaeus where he was, in charge of the mules and horses. The old man went straight into the house where Achilles, beloved by the gods, was sitting. There he found him with his men seated at a distance from him: only two, the hero Automedon, and Alcimus of the race of Ares, were busy in attendance about his person, for he had but just done eating and drinking, and the table was still there. King Priam entered without their seeing him, and going right up to Achilles he clasped his knees and kissed the dread murderous hands that had slain so many of his sons.

As when some cruel spite has befallen a man that he should have killed some one in his own country, and must fly to a great man's protection in a land of strangers, and all marvel who see him, just so did Achilles marvel as he beheld Priam. The others looked one to another and marvelled also, but Priam begged Achilles saying, "Think of your father, Achilles, a man like the gods, who is similar to me, at the sad threshold of old age. It may be that those who dwell near him harass him, and there is none to keep war and ruin from him. Yet when he hears of you being still alive, he is glad, and his days are full of hope that he shall see his dear son come home to him from Troy; but I, wretched man that I am, had the bravest in all Troy for my sons, and there is not one of them left. I had fifty sons when the Achaeans came here; nineteen of them were from a single womb, and the others were borne to me by the women of my household. The greater part of them fierce Ares has laid low, and Hector, him who alone was left, him who was the guardian of the city and ourselves, him you have just slain; therefore I have now come to the ships of the Achaeans to ransom his body from you with a great ransom. Fear, Achilles, the wrath of the gods! Think on your own father and have compassion for me, who am the more pitiable, for I have done what no man yet has ever done – I have kissed the hands of the man who slew my son."

Thus spoke Priam, and the heart of Achilles yearned as he thought of his own father. He took the old man's hand and moved him gently away. The two wept bitterly - Priam, as he lay at Achilles' feet, weeping for Hector, and Achilles now for his father and now for Patroclus, till the house was filled with their weeping. But when Achilles had now had enough of grief and had unburdened himself of his sorrow, he left his seat and raised the old man by the hand, in pity for his white hair and beard; then he said,

"Unhappy man, you have indeed been greatly bold; how could you venture to come alone to the ships of the Achaeans, and enter the presence of him who has slain so many of your brave sons? You must have iron courage: sit now upon this seat, and for all our grief we will hide our sorrows in our hearts, for weeping will not avail us. The immortals know no care, yet the lot they spin for mortals is full of sorrow; on the floor of Zeus' palace stand two jars: one filled with evils, and the other with joys. He for whom Zeus, the lord of thunder, mixes the gifts he sends, will meet sometimes with good and sometimes with evil; but he to whom Zeus sends nothing but evils will be pointed at by the finger of scorn, the hand of famine will pursue him to the ends of the world, and he will go up and down the face of the earth, respected neither by gods nor men. Even so did it befall Peleus; the gods endowed him with all good things from his birth upwards, for he reigned over the Myrmidons, excelling all men in prosperity and wealth, and mortal though he was they gave him a goddess for his bride. But even on him too did heaven send misfortune, for there is no race of royal children born to him in his house, save one son who is doomed to die young; nor may I take care of him now that he is growing old, for I must stay here at Troy to be the bane of you and your children. And you too, O Priam, I have heard that you were once happy. They say that in wealth and offspring you surpassed all that is in Lesbos, the realm of Makar to the northward, Phrygia that is more inland, and those that dwell upon the great Hellespont; but from the day when those who dwell in heaven sent this evil upon you, war and slaughter have been about your city continually. Bear up against it, and let there be some intervals in your sorrow. Mourn as you may for your brave son, you will take nothing by it. You cannot raise him from the dead, ere you do so yet another sorrow shall befall you."

And Priam answered, "O lord, do not tell me to be seated, while Hector is still lying uncared for in your tents, but accept the great ransom which I have brought you, and give him to me at once that I may look upon him. May you prosper with the ransom and reach your own land in safety, seeing that you have suffered me to live and to look upon the light of the sun."

Achilles looked at him sternly and said, "Do not anger me! I am of the mind to give up the body of Hector. My mother, daughter of the old man of the sea, came to me from Zeus to tell me deliver it to you. Moreover I know well, O Priam, and you cannot hide it, that some god has brought you to the ships of the Achaeans, otherwise no man however strong and in his prime would dare to come to our host; he could neither pass our guard unseen, nor draw the bolt of my gates thus easily; therefore, provoke me no further, so that I do not sin against the word of Zeus, and fail to endure your presence, suppliant though you are, within my tents…"

As he spoke he laid his hand on the old man's right wrist, in token that he should have no fear; thus then did Priam and his attendant sleep there in the forecourt, full of thought, while Achilles lay in an inner room of the house, with fair Briseis by his side. And now both gods and mortals were fast asleep through the livelong night, but upon Hermes alone, the bringer of good luck, sleep could take no hold for he was thinking all the time how to get King Priam away from the ships without his being seen by the guards. He hovered therefore over Priam's head and said,

"Sir, now that Achilles has spared your life, you seem to have no fear about sleeping in the thick of your foes. You have paid a great ransom, and have received the body of your son; were you still alive and a prisoner, the sons whom you have left at home would have to give three times as much to free you; and so it would be if

Agamemnon and the other Achaeans were to know of your being here."

When he heard this, the old man was afraid and roused his servant. Hermes then yoked their horses and mules, and drove them quickly through the host so that no man perceived them. When they came to the ford of eddying Xanthus, begotten of immortal Zeus, Hermes went back to high Olympus, and Dawn, in robe of saffron, began to break over all the land. Priam and Idaeus then drove on toward the city lamenting and making moan, and the mules drew the body of Hector. No one, neither man nor woman, saw them, till Cassandra, fair as golden Aphrodite standing on Pergamum, caught sight of her dear father in his chariot, and his servant that was the city's herald with him. Then she saw him that was lying upon the bier, drawn by the mules, and with a loud cry she went about the city saying, "Come, Trojan men and women, and look on Hector; if ever you rejoiced to see him coming from battle when he was alive, look now on him that was the glory of our city and all our people."

At this there was not man nor woman left in the city, so great a sorrow had seized them. Hard by the gates they met Priam as he was bringing in the body. Hector's wife and his mother were the first to mourn him: they flew towards the wagon and laid their hands upon his head, while the crowd stood weeping round them. They would have stayed before the gates, weeping and lamenting the livelong day to the going down of the sun, had not Priam spoken to them from the chariot and said, "Make way for the mules to pass you. Afterwards when I have taken the body home you shall have your fill of weeping."

And so they yoked their oxen and mules and gathered together before the city. Nine days long did they bring in great heaps wood, and on the morning of the tenth day with many tears they took Hector out, laid his dead body upon the summit of the pile, and set fire to it. Then when the child of morning rosy-fingered Dawn appeared on the eleventh day, the people again assembled, round the pyre of mighty Hector. When they were got together, they first quenched the fire with wine wherever it was burning, and then his brothers and comrades with many a bitter tear gathered his white bones, wrapped them in soft robes of purple, and laid them in a golden urn, which they placed in a grave and covered over with large stones set close together. Then they built a barrow hurriedly over it keeping guard on every side lest the Achaeans should attack them before they had finished. When they had heaped up the barrow they went back again into the city, and being well assembled they held high feast in the house of Priam their king. Thus, then, did they celebrate the funeral of Hector tamer of horses.

Adapted from Samuel Butler, Homer. The Iliad of Homer (London: Longmans, Green and Co., 1898)

READING 2:
HOMER'S ODYSSEY

The *Odyssey* describes the long, arduous return of Odysseus from Troy to his home, on the Greek island of Ithaca. The Greek champions who fought at Troy were punished by the gods for their treatment of the defeated city, and Odysseus must overcome monsters, hostile inhabitants, jealous nymphs, and the Land of the Dead itself before he can return home. Meanwhile, his dutiful wife, Penelope, and young son, Telemachus, are being eaten out of house and home by a host of suitors who, believing Odysseus now to be dead, seek to marry Penelope and acquire her husband's wealth. The story is primarily known as an adventure, a hero's quest to return to his homeland, overcome dreaded monsters, and rescue his wife from scoundrels. Homer's version of the tale, however, also addresses Greek views of civilization versus barbarism, the nature of divine will, and an individual man's quest to assert his identity and place in the world.

2a) Odysseus, the Man of Many Ways (Homer, *Odyssey*, 1. 1-21)

Tell me, O muse, of that man of many ways, who traveled far and wide after he had sacked the famous town of Troy. He visited many cities, and became acquainted with the manners and customs of many nations. He suffered much by sea while trying to save his own life and bring his men safely home; but do what he might, he could not save his men, for they perished through their own sheer folly in eating the cattle of the Sun-god Hyperion; so the god prevented them from ever reaching home. Tell me, too, about all these things, O daughter of Zeus, from whatever source you may know them.

So now all who escaped death in battle or by shipwreck had got safely home except Odysseus, and he, though he was longing to return to his wife and country, was detained by the goddess Calypso, who had got him into a large cave and wanted to marry him. But as years went by, there came a time when the gods settled that he should go back to Ithaca; even then, however, when he was among his own people, his troubles were not yet over; nevertheless all the gods had now begun to pity him except Poseidon, who still persecuted him without ceasing and would not let him get home.

2b) Menelaus' Sojourn in Egypt (Odyssey, 4. 351-483, passim)

I was trying to come back here, but the gods detained me in Egypt, for my sacrifices had not given them full satisfaction, and the gods are very strict about having their due. Now off Egypt, about as far as a ship can sail in a day with a good stiff breeze behind her, there is an island called Pharos - it has a good harbour from which vessels can get out into open sea when they have taken in water- and the gods becalmed me twenty days without so much as a breath of fair wind to help me forward. We should have run clean out of provisions and my men would have starved, if a goddess had not taken pity upon me and saved me in the person of Idothea, daughter to Proteus, the old man of the sea, for she had taken a great fancy to me.

"Let me tell you," I said, "whichever of the goddesses you may happen to be, that I am not staying here of my own accord, but must have offended the gods that live in heaven. Tell me, therefore, for the gods know everything. Which of the immortals it is that is hindering me in this way, and tell me also how I may sail the sea so as to reach my home."

"Stranger," she replied, "I will make it all quite clear to you. There is an old immortal who lives under the sea hereabouts and whose name is Proteus. He is an Egyptian, and people say he is my father; he is Poseidon's head man and knows every inch of ground all over the bottom of the sea. If you can snare him and hold him tight, he will tell you about your voyage, what courses you are to take, and how you are to sail the sea so as to reach your home. He will also tell you, if you so will, all that has been going on at your house both good and bad, while you have been away on your long and dangerous journey."

"Can you show me," I said, "some tactic by means of which I may catch this old god without his suspecting it and finding me out? For a god is not easily caught - not by a mortal man."

"Stranger," she said, "I will make it all quite clear to you. About the time when the sun shall have reached mid heaven, the old man of the sea comes up from under the waves, heralded by the West wind that furs the water over his head. As soon as he has come up he lies down, and goes to sleep in a great sea cave, where the seals - Halosydne's chickens as they call them - come up also from the grey sea, and go to sleep in shoals all round him; and a very strong and fish-like smell do they bring with them. Early tomorrow morning I will take you to this place and will lay you in ambush. Pick out, therefore, the three best men you have in your fleet, and I will tell you all the tricks that the old man will play you."

"First he will look over all his seals, and count them; then, when he has seen them and tallied them on his five fingers, he will go to sleep among them, as a shepherd among his sheep. The moment you see that he is asleep seize him; put forth all your strength and hold him fast, for he will do his very utmost to get away from you. He will turn himself into every kind of creature that goes upon the earth, and will become also both fire and water; but you must hold him fast and grip him tighter and tighter, till he begins to talk to you and comes back to what he was when you saw him go to sleep; then you may slacken your hold and let him go; and you can ask him which of the gods it is that is angry with you, and what you must do to reach your home over the seas."

Having so said she dived under the waves, whereon I turned back to the place where my ships were ranged upon the shore; and my heart was clouded with care as I went along. When I reached my ship we got supper ready, for night was falling, and camped down upon the beach.

When the child of morning, rosy-fingered Dawn, appeared, I took the three men on whose prowess of all kinds I could most rely, and went along by the sea-side, praying heartily to heaven. Meanwhile the goddess fetched me up four seal-skins from the bottom of the sea, all of them just skinned, for she meant playing a trick upon her father. Then she dug four pits for us to lie in, and sat down to wait till we should come up. When we were close to her, she made us lie down in the pits one after the other, and threw a seal skin over each of us. Our ambuscade would have been intolerable, for the stench of the fishy seals was most distressing- who would go to bed with a sea monster if he could help it? But here, too, the goddess helped us, and thought of something that gave us great relief, for she put some ambrosia under each man's nostrils, which was so fragrant that it killed the smell of the seals.

We waited the whole morning and made the best of it, watching the seals come up in hundreds to bask on the sea shore, until at noon the old man of the sea came up too, and when he had found his fat seals he went over them and counted them. We were among the first he counted, and he never suspected any guile, but laid himself down to sleep as soon as he had done counting. Then we rushed at him with a shout and seized him. He immediately began with his old tricks, and changed himself first into a lion with a great mane; then all of a sudden he became a dragon, a leopard, a wild boar; the next moment he was running water, and then again directly he was a tree, but we stuck to him and never lost hold, till at last the cunning old creature became distressed, and said, "Which of the gods was it, Son of Atreus, that hatched this plot with you for snaring me and seizing me against my will? What do you want?"

"You know that yourself, old man," I answered, "you will gain nothing by trying to put me off. It is because I have been kept so long in this island, and see no sign of my being able to get away. I am losing all heart; tell me, then, for you gods know everything, which of the immortals it is that is hindering me, and tell me also how I may sail the sea so as to reach my home?"

"Then," he said, "if you would finish your voyage and get home quickly, you must offer sacrifices to Zeus and to the rest of the gods before embarking; for it is decreed that you shall not get back to your friends, and to your own house, till you have returned to the heaven fed stream of Egypt, and offered holy hecatombs to the immortal gods that reign in heaven. When you have done this they will let you finish your voyage."

2c) Aphrodite and Ares' Affair (Homer, Odyssey, 8. 266-363, passim)

Meanwhile the bard began to sing the love between Ares and Aphrodite, and how they first began their affair in the house of Hephaestus. Ares gave Aphrodite many presents, and defiled Hesphaestus' marriage bed, so that the Sun, who saw what they were doing, told Hephaestus. Hephaestus was very angry when he heard such dreadful news, so he went to his smithy, forming a plot, got his great anvil into its place, and began to forge some chains which none could either unloose or break, so that they might stay there in that place. When he had finished his snare he went into his bedroom and fastened the bed-posts all over with chains like cobwebs; he also let many hang down from the great beam of the ceiling. Not even a god could see them, so fine and subtle were they. As soon as he had spread the chains all over the bed, he made as though he were setting out for the fair state of Lemnos, which of all places in the world was the one he was most fond of. But Ares kept no blind look out, and as soon as he saw him start, hurried off to his house, burning with love for Aphrodite.

Now Aphrodite had just come in from a visit to her father Zeus, and was sitting down when Mars came inside the house, and said as he took her hand in his own, "Let us go to the bed of Hephaestus: he is not at home, but is gone off to Lemnos among the Sintians, whose speech is barbarous."

She was hardly reluctant, so they went to bed with one another, after which they were caught in the net which cunning Hephaestus had spread for them, and neither could get up nor move hand or foot, but found too late that they were in a trap. Then Hephaestus came up to them, for he had turned back before reaching Lemnos, when his scout the sun told him what was going on. He was in a furious passion, and stood in the vestibule making a dreadful noise as he shouted to all the gods.

"Father Zeus," he cried, "and all you other blessed gods who live forever, come here and see the ridiculous and disgraceful sight that I will show you. Zeus' daughter Aphrodite is always dishonouring me because I am lame. She is in love with Ares, who is handsome and cleanly built, whereas I am a cripple - but my parents are to blame for that, not I; they ought never to have begotten me. Come and see the pair together asleep on my bed. It makes me furious to look at them. They are very fond of one another, but I do not think they will lie there longer than they can help, nor do I think that they will sleep much; there, however, they shall stay till her father has repaid me the sum I gave him for his baggage of a daughter, who is beautiful but not honest."

On this the gods gathered to the house of Hephaestus. Earth-encircling Poseidon came, and Hermes the bringer of luck, and Apollo, but the goddesses all stayed at home because of the shame of the act. Then the givers of all good things stood in the doorway, and the blessed gods roared with inextinguishable laughter, as they saw how cunning Hephaestus had been, after which one would turn towards his neighbour, saying:

"Ill deeds do not prosper, and the weak defeat the strong. See how limping Hephaestus, lame as he is, has caught Ares, who is the quickest god in heaven; and now Ares will be struck with heavy damages."

Thus did they speak to one another, but Apollo said to Hermes, "Messenger Hermes, giver of good things, you would not care how strong the chains were, would you, if you could lie beside Aphrodite?"

"Apollo," answered Hermes, "I only wish I might get the chance, though there were three times as many chains - and you might look on, all of you, gods and goddesses, but would sleep with her just as I would."

The immortal gods burst out laughing as they heard him, but Poseidon took it all seriously, and kept imploring Hephaestus to set Ares free again. "Let him go," he said, "and I will undertake, as you require, that he shall pay you all the damages that are held reasonable among the immortal gods."

"Do not," replied Hephaestus, "ask me to do this; a bad man's bond is bad security; what remedy could I enforce against you if Mars should go away and leave his debts behind him along with his chains?"

"Hephaestus," said Poseidon, "if Ares goes away without paying his damages, I will pay you myself." And Hephaestus answered, "In that case I cannot and must not refuse you."

And then he loosed the bonds that bound them, and as soon as they were free they scampered off, Ares to Thrace and laughter-loving Aphrodite to Cyprus and to Paphos, where her grove is, and her altar, fragrant with burnt offerings. Here the Graces bathed her, and anointed her with oil of ambrosia such as the immortal gods use, and they clothed her in raiment of the most enchanting beauty.

2d) The Cyclops (Homer, Odyssey, 9. 29-567, passim)

The goddess Calypso kept me with her in her cave, and wanted me to marry her, as did also the cunning Aeaean goddess, Circe; but neither of them could persuade me, for there is nothing dearer to a man than his own country and his parents, and however splendid a home he may have in a foreign country, if it is far from father or mother, he does not care about it. Now, however, I will tell you of the many hazardous adventures, which by Zeus' will I met with on my return from Troy…

We sailed onward, always in great distress, until we came to the land of the lawless and inhuman Cyclopes. Now the Cyclopes neither plant nor plough, but trust in fortune, and live on whatever wheat, barley, and grapes as grow wild without any kind of agriculture, and their wild grapes yield them wine as the sun and the rain may grow them. They have neither laws nor assemblies of the people, but live in caves on the tops of high mountains; each is lord and master in his family, and they take no account of their neighbours.

Now near their harbour there lies a wooded and fertile island not quite close to the land of the Cyclopes, but still not far. It is overrun with wild goats, that breed there in great numbers and are never disturbed by men's footsteps… for the Cyclopes have no ships, nor yet shipwrights who could make ships for them; they cannot therefore go from city to city, or sail over the sea to one another's country as people who have ships can do; if they had had these they would have colonized the island, for it is a very good one, and would yield everything in due season. There are meadows that in some places come right down to the sea shore, well watered and full of luscious grass; grapes would grow there excellently; there is level land for ploughing, and it would always yield heavily at harvest time, for the soil is deep. There is a good harbour where no cables are needed, nor yet anchors, nor need a ship be moored, but all one has to do is to beach one's vessel and stay there till the wind becomes fair for putting out to sea again. At the head of the harbour there is a spring of clear water coming out of a cave, and there are poplars growing all round it.

Here we entered, but so dark was the night that some god must have brought us in, for there was nothing whatever to be seen. A thick mist hung all round our ships; the moon was hidden behind a mass of clouds so that no one could have seen the island if he had looked for it, nor were there any breakers to tell us we were close in shore before we found ourselves upon the land itself; when, however, we had beached the ships, we took down the sails, went ashore and camped upon the beach till daybreak.

While we were feasting we kept turning our eyes towards the land of the Cyclopes, which was hard by, and saw the smoke of their stubble fires. We could almost fancy we heard their voices and the bleating of their sheep and goats, but when the sun went down and it came on dark, we camped down upon the beach, and next morning I called a council: "Stay here, my brave companions," I said, "all the rest of you, while I go with my ship and exploit these people myself: I want to see if they are uncivilized savages, or a hospitable and humane race."

I took a goatskin of sweet black wine, which had been given me by Maron, Apollo son of Euanthes, who was priest of Apollo the patron god of Ismarus, and lived within the wooded precincts of the temple. When we were sacking the city we respected him, and spared his life, as also his wife and child; so he made me some presents of great value- seven talents of fine gold, and a bowl of silver, with twelve jars of sweet wine, unblended, and of the most exquisite flavour. Not a man nor woman in the house knew about it, but only himself, his wife, and one housekeeper: when he drank it he mixed twenty parts of water to one of wine, and yet the fragrance from the mixing-bowl was so exquisite that it was impossible to refrain from drinking. I filled a large skin with this wine, and took a purse full of provisions with me, for my mind told me that I might have to deal with some savage who would be of great strength, and would respect neither justice nor custom.

We soon reached his cave, but he was out shepherding, so we went inside and took stock of all that we could see. His cheese-racks were loaded with cheeses, and he had more lambs and kids than his pens could hold. They were kept in separate flocks; first there were the hogs, then the oldest of the younger lambs and lastly the very young ones all kept apart from one another; as for his dairy, all the vessels, bowls, and milk pails into which he milked, were filled with whey. When they saw all this, my men begged me to let them first steal some cheeses, and make off with them to the ship; they would then return, drive down the lambs and kids, put them on board and sail away with them. It would have been indeed better if we had done so but I would not listen to them, for I wanted to see the owner himself, in the hope that he might give me a present. When, however, we saw him my poor men found him ill to deal with.

We lit a fire, offered some of the cheeses in sacrifice, ate others of them, and then sat waiting till the Cyclops should come in with his sheep. When he came, he brought in with him a huge load of dry firewood to light the fire for his supper, and this he flung with such a noise on to the floor of his cave that we hid ourselves for fear at the far end of the cavern. Meanwhile he drove all the ewes inside, as well as the she-goats that he was going to milk, leaving the males, both rams and he-goats, outside in the yards. Then he rolled a huge stone to the mouth of the cave - so huge that twenty-two strong four-wheeled wagons would not be enough to draw it from its place against the doorway. When he had so done he sat down and milked his ewes and goats, all in due course, and then let each of them have her own young. He curdled half the milk and set it aside in wicker strainers, but the other half he poured into bowls that he might drink it for his supper. When he had got through with all his work, he lit the fire, and then caught sight of us, and said:

"Strangers, who are you? Where do come from? Are you traders, or do you sail the sea as pirates, with your hands against every man, and every man's hand against you?"

We were frightened out of our wits by his loud voice and monstrous form, but I managed to say, "We are Achaeans on our way home from Troy, but by the will of Zeus, and stress of weather, we have been driven far out of our course. We are the people of Agamemnon, son of Atreus, who has won infinite renown throughout the whole world, by sacking so great a city and killing so many people. We therefore humbly ask you to show us some hospitality, and otherwise make us such presents as visitors may reasonably expect. May your excellency fear the wrath of the gods, for we are your suppliants, and Zeus takes all respectable travellers under his protection, for he is the avenger of all suppliants and foreigners in distress."

To this he gave me but a pitiless answer, "Stranger," he said, "you are a fool, or else you know nothing of this country. Talk to me, indeed, about fearing the gods or shunning their anger? We Cyclopes do not care about Zeus or any of your blessed gods, for we are ever so much stronger than they. I shall not spare either yourself or your companions out of any regard for Zeus, unless I am in the humour for doing so. And now tell me where you made your ship fast when you came to shore. Was it round the point, or is she lying straight off the land?"

He said this to draw me out, but I was too cunning to be caught in that way, so I answered with a lie; "Poseidon," I said, "sent my ship on to the rocks at the far end of your country, and wrecked it. We were driven on to them from the open sea, but I and those who are with me escaped the jaws of death."

The cruel wretch granted me not one word of answer, but with a sudden lunge he seized two of my men at once and dashed them down upon the ground as though they had been puppies. Their brains splattered upon the ground, and the earth was wet with their blood. Then he tore them limb from limb and supped upon them. He gobbled them up like a lion in the wilderness, flesh, bones, marrow, and entrails, without leaving anything uneaten. As for us, we wept and lifted up our hands to heaven on seeing such a horrid sight, for we did not know what else to do; but when the Cyclops had filled his huge belly, and had washed down his meal of human flesh with a drink of neat milk, he stretched himself full length upon the ground among his sheep, and went to sleep. I was at first inclined to seize my sword, draw it, and drive it into his vitals, but I reflected that if I did we should all certainly be lost, for we should never be able to shift the stone which the monster had put in front of the door. So we stayed sobbing and sighing where we were until morning came.

When the child of morning, rosy-fingered Dawn, appeared, he again lit his fire, milked his goats and ewes, all quite rightly, and then let each have her own young one; as soon as he had got through with all his work, he grabbed two more of my men, and began eating them for his morning's meal. Then, with the utmost ease, he rolled the stone away from the door and drove out his sheep, but he at once put it back again - as easily as though he were merely clapping the lid on to a quiver full of arrows. As soon as he had done so he shouted, and cried "Shoo, shoo," after his sheep to drive them on to the mountain; so I was left to scheme some way of taking my revenge and covering myself with glory.

In the end I thought it would be the best plan to do as follows. The Cyclops had a great club which was lying near one of the sheep pens; it was of green olive wood, and he had cut it intending to use it for a staff as soon as it should be dry. It was so huge that we could only compare it to the mast of a twenty-oared merchant vessel, and able to venture out into open sea. I went up to this club and cut off about six feet of it; I then gave this piece to the men and told them to sharpen it evenly at one end, which they proceeded to do, and lastly I brought it to a point myself, charring the end in the fire to make it harder. When I had done this I hid it under dung, which was lying about all over the cave, and told the men to cast lots which of them should venture along with myself to lift it, and carried it into the monster's eye while he was asleep. The lot fell upon the very four whom I should have chosen, and I myself made five. In the evening the wretch came back from shepherding, and drove his flocks into the cave - this time driving them all inside, and not leaving any in the yards; I suppose some fancy must have taken him, or a god must have prompted him to do so. As soon as he had put the stone back to its place against the door, he sat down, milked his ewes and his goats, and then let each have her own young one; when he had got through with all this work, he grabbed up two more of my men, and made his supper from them. So I went up to him with an ivy-wood bowl of black wine in my hands:

"Look here, Cyclops," I said, "you have been eating a great deal of man's flesh, so take this and drink some wine, so that you may see what kind of drink we had on board my ship. I was bringing it to you as a drink-offering, in the hope that you would take compassion upon me and further me on my way home, whereas all you do is to go on ramping and raving most intolerably. You ought to be ashamed yourself; how can you expect people to come see you any more if you treat them in this way?"

He then took the cup and drank. He was so delighted with the taste of the wine that he begged me for another bowl full. "Be so kind," he said, "as to give me some more, and tell me your name at once. I want to make you a present that you will be glad to have. We have wine even in this country, for our soil grows grapes and the sun ripens them, but this drinks like nectar and ambrosia all in one."

I then gave him some more; three times did I fill the bowl for him, and three times did he drain it without thought or heed; then, when I saw that the wine had got into his head, I said to him as plausibly as I could: "Cyclops, you ask my name and I will tell it you; give me, therefore, the present you promised me; my name is 'Nobody' – this is what my father and mother and my friends have always called me."

But the cruel wretch said, "Then I will eat all Nobody's comrades before Nobody himself, and will keep Nobody for the last. This is the present that I will make him."

As he spoke he reeled, and fell sprawling face upwards on the ground. His great neck hung heavily backwards and a deep sleep took hold upon him. Presently he turned sick, and threw up both wine and the gobbets of human flesh on which he had been gorging, for he was very drunk. Then I thrust the beam of wood far into the embers to heat it, and encouraged my men, so that none of them should become faint-hearted. When the wood, green though it was, was about to blaze, I drew it out of the fire, glowing with heat, and my men gathered round me, for heaven had filled their hearts with courage. We drove the sharp end of the beam into the monster's eye, and bearing upon it with all my weight I kept turning it round and round as though I were boring a hole in a ship's plank with an drill, which two men with a wheel and strap can keep on turning as long as they choose. Just so did we drive the red hot beam into his eye, till the boiling blood bubbled all over it as we worked it round and round, so that the steam from the burning eyeball scalded his eyelids and eyebrows, and the roots of the eye sputtered in the fire. As a blacksmith plunges an axe or hatchet into cold water to temper it - for it is this that gives strength to the iron - and it makes a great hiss as he does so, just so did the Cyclops' eye hiss round the beam of olive wood, and his hideous screams made the cave ring again. We ran away in a fright, but he plucked the beam all besmirched with gore from his eye, and hurled it from him in a frenzy of rage and pain, shouting as he did so to the other Cyclopes who lived on the bleak headlands near him; so they gathered from all quarters round his cave when they heard him crying, and asked what was the matter with him.

"What bothers you, Polyphemus," they said, "that you make such a noise, breaking the stillness of the night, and preventing us from being able to sleep? Surely no man is carrying off your sheep? Surely no man is trying to kill you either by fraud or by force?"

But Polyphemus shouted to them from inside the cave, "Nobody is killing me by deception! Nobody is destroying me by violence!"

"Then," they said, "if nobody is attacking you, you must be ill; when Zeus makes people ill, there is no help for it, and you had better pray to your father Poseidon."

"Then they went away, and I laughed inwardly at the success of my clever trick, but the Cyclops, groaning and in an agony of pain, felt about with his hands till he found the stone and took it from the door; then he sat in the doorway and stretched his hands in front of it to catch anyone going out with the sheep, for he thought I might be foolish enough to attempt this.

As for myself I kept thinking how I could best save my own life and those of my companions; I schemed and schemed, as one who knows that his life depends upon it, for the danger was very great. In the end I thought that this plan would be the best: the male sheep were well grown, and carried a heavy black fleece, so I bound them noiselessly in threes together, with some of the willows on which the wicked monster used to sleep. There was to be a man under the middle sheep, and the two on either side were to cover him, so that there were three sheep to each man. As for myself there was a ram finer than any of the others, so I caught hold of him by the back, hidden myself in the thick wool under his belly, and flung on patiently to his fleece, face upwards, keeping a firm hold on it all the time.

Thus, then, did we wait in great fear of mind till morning came, but when the child of morning, rosy-fingered Dawn, appeared, the male sheep hurried out to feed, while the ewes remained bleating about the pens waiting to be milked, for their udders were full to bursting; but their master in spite of all his pain felt the backs of all the sheep as they stood upright, without being sharp enough to find out that the men were underneath their bellies. As the ram was going out, last of all, heavy with its fleece and with the weight of my crafty self; Polyphemus laid hold of it and said:

"My good ram, what is it that makes you the last to leave my cave this morning? You do not usually let the ewes go before you, but lead the mob with a run whether to flowery mead or bubbling fountain, and are the first to come home again at night; but now you lag last of all. Is it because you know your master has lost his eye, and are sorry because that wicked Nobody and his horrid crew have got him down in his drink and blinded him? But I will have his life yet. If you could understand and talk, you would tell me where the wretch is hiding, and I would dash his brains upon the ground till they flew all over the cave. I should thus have some satisfaction for the harm a this no-good Nobody has done me."

As he spoke he drove the ram outside, but when we were a little way out from the cave and yards, I first got from under the ram's belly, and then freed my comrades; as for the sheep, which were very fat, by constantly heading them in the right direction we managed to drive them down to the ship. The crew rejoiced greatly at seeing those of us who had escaped death, but wept for the others whom the Cyclops had killed. However, I made signs to them by nodding and frowning that they were to hush their crying, and told them to get all the sheep on board at once and put out to sea; so they went aboard, took their places, and smote the grey sea with their oars. Then, when I had got as far out as my voice would reach, I began to jeer at the Cyclops.

"Cyclops," I said, "you should have taken better measure of your man before eating up his comrades in your cave. You wretch, eat up your visitors in your own house? You might have known that your sin would find you out, and now Zeus and the other gods have punished you."

"He got more and more furious as he heard me, so he tore the top from off a high mountain, and flung it just in front of my ship so that it was within a little of hitting the end of the rudder. The sea quaked as the rock fell into it, and the wash of the wave it raised carried us back towards the mainland, and forced us towards the shore. But I grabbed a long pole and kept the ship off, making signs to my men by nodding my head, that they must row for their lives. When we had got twice as far as we were before, I was jeering at the Cyclops again, but the men begged me to hold my tongue.

"Do not," they yelled, "be mad enough to provoke this savage creature further; he has thrown one rock at us already which drove us back again to the mainland, and we made sure it had been the death of us; if he had then heard any further sound of voices he would have pounded our heads and our ship's timbers into a jelly with the rugged rocks he would have heaved at us, for he can throw them a long way."

But I would not listen to them, and shouted out to him in my rage, "Cyclops, if anyone asks you who it was that put your eye out and spoiled your beauty, say it was the valiant warrior Odysseus, son of Laertes, who lives in Ithaca."

On this he groaned, and cried out, "Alas, alas, then the old prophecy about me is coming true. There was a prophet here, at one time, a man both brave and of great stature, Telemus son of Eurymus, who was an excellent seer, and did all the prophesying for the Cyclopes till he grew old; he told me that all this would happen to me some day, and said I should lose my sight by the hand of Odysseus. I have been all along expecting some one of imposing presence and superhuman strength, whereas he turns out to be a little insignificant weakling, who has managed to blind my eye by taking advantage of me in my drunkenness; come here, then, Odysseus, that I may make you presents to show my hospitality, and urge Poseidon to help you forward on your journey - for Poseidon and I are father and son. He, if he so will, shall heal me, which no one else neither god nor man can do."

Then I said, "I wish I could be as sure of killing you outright and sending you down to the house of Hades, as I am that it will take more than Poseidon to cure that eye of yours."

On this he lifted up his hands to the firmament of heaven and prayed, saying, "Hear me, great Poseidon; if I am indeed your own true-begotten son, grant that Odysseus may never reach his home alive; or if he must get back to his friends at last, let him do so late and in a sorry state after losing all his men."

Thus did he pray, and Poseidon heard his prayer. Then he picked up a rock much larger than the first, swung it and hurled it with prodigious force. It fell just short of the ship, but was within a little of hitting the end of the rudder. The sea quaked as the rock fell into it, and the wash of the wave it raised drove us onwards on our way towards the shore of the island.

When at last we got to the island where we had left the rest of our ships, we found our companions lamenting us, and anxiously awaiting our return. We ran our vessel upon the sands and got out of her on to the sea shore; we also boarded the Cyclops' sheep, and divided them equitably amongst us so that none might have reason to complain. As for the ram, my companions agreed that I should have it as an extra share; so I sacrificed it on the sea shore, and burned its thigh bones to Zeus, who is the lord of all. But he heeded not my sacrifice, and only thought how he might destroy my ships and my comrades.

Thus through the livelong day to the going down of the sun we feasted our fill on meat and drink, but when the sun went down and it came on dark, we camped upon the beach. When the child of morning, rosy-fingered Dawn, appeared, I bade my men on board and loose the hawsers. Then they took their places and struck the grey sea with their oars; so we sailed on with sorrow in our hearts, but glad to have escaped death though we had lost our comrades.

2e) The Sorceress Circe (Homer, Odyssey, 10. 1-495, passim)

From there we went on to the island of Aeoli. There lives Aeolus, son of Hippotas, dear to the immortal gods. Aeolus entertained me for a whole month, asking me questions all the time about Troy, the Argive fleet, and the return of the Achaeans. I told him exactly how everything had happened, and when I said I must go, and asked him to further me on my way, he gave me no difficulty, but set about doing so at once. Moreover, he formed for me ox-hide to hold the roaring winds, which he shut up in the hide as in a sack - for Zeus had made him lord over the winds, and he could raise or dispel each of them according to his own pleasure. He put the sack in the ship and bound the mouth so tightly with a silver thread that not even a breath of a side-wind could blow from any quarter. The West wind, which was fair for us did he alone let blow as it chose; but it all came to nothing, for we were lost through our own folly.

Nine days and nights we sailed, and on the tenth day we saw our native land on the horizon. We got so close in that we could see the stubble fires burning, and I, being then dead beat, fell into a light sleep, for I had never let the rudder out of my own hands, that we might get home the faster. On this the men fell to talking among themselves, and said I was bringing back gold and silver in the sack that Aeolus had given me. "Bless me," one would say to his neighbour, saying, "how this man gets honoured and makes friends to whatever city or country he may go. See what fine prizes he is taking home from Troy, while we, who have travelled just as far as he has, come back with hands as empty as we set out with - and now Aeolus has given him ever so much more. Quick - let us see what it all is, and how much gold and silver there is in the sack he gave him."

Thus they talked and evil prevailed. They loosed the sack, after which the wind flew out howling and raised a storm that carried us out to sea and away from our own country. Then I awoke, and knew not whether to throw myself into the sea or to live on and make the best of it; but I bore it, covered myself up, and lay down in the ship, while the men lamented bitterly as the fierce winds bore our fleet back to the Aeolian island.

When we reached it we went ashore to take in water, and dined hard by the ships. Immediately after dinner I took a herald and one of my men and went straight to the house of Aeolus, where

I found him feasting with his wife and family; so we sat down as suppliants on the threshold. They were astounded when they saw us and said, "Odysseus, what brings you here? What god has been ill-treating you? We took great pains to further you on your way home to Ithaca, or wherever it was that you wanted to go to."

"Thus did they speak, but I answered sorrowfully, "My men have undone me; they, and cruel sleep, have ruined me. My friends, mend me this mischief, for you can if you will."

I spoke as convincingly as I could, but they said nothing, till their father answered, "Vilest of mankind, leave at once our island; him whom heaven hates I will not in wisdom help. Be off, for you come here as one hated of heaven." And with these words he sent me sorrowing from his door.

From there we sailed sadly on, glad to have escaped death, though we had lost our comrades, and came to the Aeaean island, where Circe, a great and cunning sorceress, who is sister to the magician Aeetes - for they are both children of the sun by Perse, who is daughter to Oceanus. We brought our ship into a safe harbour without a word, for some god guided us there, and having landed we stayed there for two days and two nights, worn out in body and mind. On the morning of the third day, I took my spear and my sword, and went away from the ship to reconnoitre, and see if I could discover signs of human structures, or hear the sound of voices. Climbing to the top of a high look-out I spotted the smoke of Circe's house rising upwards amid a dense forest of trees, and when I saw this I doubted whether, having seen the smoke, I would not go on at once and find out more, but in the end I thought it best to go back to the ship, give the men their dinners, and send some of them instead of going myself.

So I divided them into two companies and set a captain over each; I gave one company to Eurylochus, while I took command of the other myself. Then we cast lots in a helmet, and the lot fell upon Eurylochus; so he set out with his twenty-two men, and they wept, as also did we who were left behind.

When they reached Circe's house they found it built of cut stones, on a site that could be seen from far, in the middle of the forest. There were wild mountain wolves and lions prowling all round it – poor, bewitched creatures whom she had tamed by her enchantments and drugged into subjection. They did not attack my men, but wagged their great tails, fawned upon them, and rubbed their noses lovingly against them. Presently they reached the gates of the goddess's house, and as they stood there they could hear Circe within, singing most beautifully as she worked at her loom, making a web so fine, so soft, and of such dazzling colours as no one but a goddess could weave. On this Polites, whom I valued and trusted more than any other of my men, said, "There is someone inside working at a loom and singing most beautifully; the whole place echoes with it, let us call her and see whether she is woman or goddess."

They called her and she came down, unfastened the door, and told them to enter. They, thinking no evil, followed her, all except Eurylochus, who suspected mischief and stayed outside. When she had got them into her house, she set them on benches and mixed them a meal with cheese, honey, cake, but she drugged it with evil poisons to make them forget their homes, and when they had drunk, she turned them into pigs by a stroke of her wand, and shut them up in her pigsties. They were like pigs-head, hair, and all, and they grunted just as pigs do; but their senses were the same as before, and they remembered everything.

Thus then were they shut up squealing, and Circe threw them some acorns and beech masts such as pigs eat, but Eurylochus hurried back to tell me about the sad fate of our comrades. He was so overcome with dismay that though he tried to speak he could find no words to do so; his eyes filled with tears and he could only sob and sigh, till at last we forced his story out of him, and he told us what had happened to the others.

"Then I took my sword of bronze and slung it over my shoulders; I also took my bow, and told Eurylochus to come back with me and show me the way. But he laid hold of me with both his hands and spoke piteously, saying, "Sir, do not force me to go with you, but let me stay here, for I know you will not bring one of them back with you, nor even return alive yourself; let us rather see if we cannot escape somehow with the few that are left us, for we may still save our lives."

"Stay where you are, then," I responded, "eating and drinking at the ship, but I must go, for I am bound to do so."

With this I left the ship and went up inland. When I got through the charmed grove, and was near the great house of the enchantress Circe, I met Hermes with his golden wand, disguised as a young man in the hey-day of his youth and beauty with the down just coming upon his face. He came up to me and took my hand within his own, saying, "My poor, wretched man, where are you going over this mountain top, alone and without knowing the way? Your men are shut up in Circe's pigsties, like so many wild boars in their lairs. You surely do not think that you can set them free? I can tell you that you will never get back and will have to stay there with the rest of them. But never mind, I will protect you and get you out of your difficulty. Take this herb, which is one of great virtue, and keep it about you when you go to Circe's house, it will be a talisman to you against every kind of mischief."

Then Hermes went back to high Olympus passing over the wooded island; but I walked onward to the house of Circe, and my heart was clouded with worry as I walked along. When I got to the gates I stood there and called the sorceress, and as soon as she heard me she came down, opened the door, and asked me to come in; so I followed her - very troubled in my mind. She set me on a richly decorated seat, inlaid with silver, there was a footstool also under my feet, and she mixed a mess in a golden goblet for me to drink; but she drugged it. When she had given it me, and I had drunk it without its affecting me, she struck me with her wand. "There now," she cried, "be off to the pigsty, and make your lair with the rest of them."

But I rushed at her with my sword drawn as though I would kill her, at which she fell with a loud scream, clasped my knees, and spoke piteously, saying, "Who are you and where do you come from? How can it be that my drugs have no power to charm you? Never yet was any man able to stand so much as a taste of the herb I gave you; you must be spell-proof; surely you can be none other than the bold hero Odysseus, who Hermes always said would come here some day with his ship while on his way home from Troy; so be it then; sheathe your sword and let us go to bed, that we may make friends and learn to trust each other."

And I answered, "Circe, how can you expect me to be friendly with you when you have just been turning all my men into pigs? And now that you have got me here myself, you plot mischief for me when you ask me to go to bed with you, and will unman me and make me fit for nothing. I shall certainly not consent to go to bed with you unless you will first take your solemn oath to plot no further harm against me." So she swore at once as I had told her, and when she had completed her oath then I went to bed with her.

When Circe saw me sitting there without eating, and in great grief, she came to me and said, "Odysseus, why do you sit like that as though you were dumb, gnawing at your own heart, and refusing both meat and drink? Is it that you are still suspicious? You ought not to be, for I have already sworn solemnly that I will not hurt you." And I said, "Circe, no man with any sense of what is right can think of either eating or drinking in your house until you have set his friends free and let him see them. If you want me to eat and drink, you must free my men and bring them to me that I may see them with my own eyes."

When I had said this she went straight through the court with her wand in her hand and opened the pigsty doors. My men came out like so many prime hogs and stood looking at her, but she went among them and anointed each with a second drug, whereon the bristles that the bad drug had given them fell off, and they became men again, younger than they were before, and much taller and better looking. They recognized me at once, seized me by the hand, and wept for joy till the whole house was filled with the sound of their weeping, and Circe herself was so sorry for them that she came up to me and said, "Odysseus, noble son of Laertes, go back at once to the sea where you have left your ship, and first draw it on to the land. Then, hide all your ship's gear and property in some cave, and come back here with your men."

Meanwhile Circe had been seeing that the men who had been left behind were washed and anointed with olive oil; she had also given them wool cloaks and shirts, and when we came we found them all comfortably at dinner in her house. As soon as the men saw each other face to face and knew one another, they wept for joy and cried aloud till the whole palace rang again. Afterwards, Circe came up to me and said, "Odysseus, noble son of Laertes, tell your men to leave off crying; I know how much you have all of you suffered at sea, and how ill you have fared among cruel savages on the mainland, but that is over now, so stay here, and eat and drink till you are once more as strong and hearty as you were when you left Ithaca; for at present you are weakened both in body and mind; you keep all the time thinking of the hardships - you have suffered during your travels, so that you have no more cheerfulness left in you."

"Odysseus, noble son of Laertes, none of you shall stay here any longer if you do not want to, but there is another journey which you have got to take before you can sail homewards. You must go to the house of Hades and of dread Persephone to consult the ghost of the blind Theban prophet Teiresias, whose reason is still unshaken. To him alone has Persephone left his understanding even in death, but the other ghosts flit about aimlessly."

2f) Odysseus in the Underworld (Homer, Odyssey, 10. 1-640, passim)

Then, when we had got down to the sea shore we drew our ship into the water and got her mast and sails into her; we also put the sheep on board and took our places, weeping and in great distress of mind. Circe, that great and cunning goddess, sent us a fair wind that blew dead aft and stayed steadily with us keeping our sails all the time well filled; so we did whatever needed to be done to the ship's gear and let her go as the wind and helmsman headed her. All day long her sails were full as she held her course over the sea, but when the sun went down and darkness was over all the earth, we got into the deep waters of the river Oceanus, where lie the land and city of the Cimmerians who live enshrouded in mist and darkness which the rays of the sun never pierce neither at his rising nor as he goes down again out of the heavens, but the poor wretches live in one long melancholy night. When we got there we beached the ship, took the sheep out of her, and went along by the waters of Oceanus till we came to the place of which Circe had told us.

Here Perimedes and Eurylochus held the victims, while I drew my sword and dug the trench a cubit each way. I made a drink-offering to all the dead, first with honey and milk, then with wine, and thirdly with water, and I sprinkled white barley over the whole, praying earnestly to the poor feckless ghosts, and promising them that when I got back to Ithaca I would sacrifice a barren heifer for them, the best I had, and would load the pyre with good things. I also particularly promised that Teiresias should have a black sheep to himself, the best in all my flocks. When I had prayed sufficiently to the dead, I cut the throats of the two sheep and let the blood run into the trench, whereon the ghosts came trooping up from Erebus - brides, young bachelors, old men worn out with labour, maids who had been crossed in love, and brave men who had been killed in battle, with their armour still stained with blood; they came from every quarter and flitted round the trench with a strange kind of screaming sound that made me turn pale with fear. When I saw them coming I told the men to be quick and flay the carcasses of the two dead sheep and make burnt offerings of them, and at the same time to repeat prayers to Hades and to Persephone; but I sat where I was with my sword drawn and would not let the poor feckless ghosts come near the blood till Teiresias should have answered my questions.

The first ghost that came was that of my comrade, Elpenor, for he had not yet been laid beneath the earth. We had left his body unburied in Circe's house, for we had had too much else to do. I was very sorry for him, and cried when I saw him: "Elpenor, how did you come down here into this gloom and darkness? You have here on foot quicker than I have with my ship."

"Lord," he answered with a groan, "it was all bad luck, and my own unspeakable drunkenness. I was lying asleep on the top of Circe's house, and never thought of coming down again by the great staircase but fell right off the roof and broke my neck, so my soul down to the house of Hades. And now I beseech you by all those whom you have left behind you, though they are not here, by your wife, by the father who brought you up when you were a child, and by Telemachus who is the one hope of your house, do what I shall now ask you. I know that when you leave this limbo you will again hold your ship for the Aeaean island. Do not go there leaving me unburied behind you, or I may bring heaven's anger upon you; but burn me with whatever armour I have, build a barrow for me on the sea shore, that may tell people in days to come what a poor unlucky fellow I was, and plant over my grave the oar I used to row with when I was yet alive and with my messmates." And I said, "My poor fellow, I will do all that you have asked of me."

Thus, then, did we sit and talked sadly with one another, I on the one side of the trench with my sword held over the blood, and the ghost of my comrade saying all this to me from the other side. Then came the ghost of my dead mother Anticlea, daughter to Autolycus. I had left her alive when I set out for Troy and was moved to tears when I saw her, but even so, for all my sorrow I would not let her come near the blood till I had asked my questions of Teiresias.

Then came also the ghost of Theban Teiresias, with his golden sceptre in his hand. He knew me and said, "Odysseus, noble son of Laertes, why, poor man, have you left the light of day and come down to visit the dead in this sad place? Stand back from the trench and withdraw your sword that I may drink of the blood and answer your questions truly."

"So I drew back, and sheathed my sword, after which when he had drank of the blood he began with his prophecy.

"You want to know," he said, "about your return, but heaven will make this hard for you. I do not think that you will escape the eye of Poseidon, who still nurses his bitter grudge against you for having blinded his son. Still, after much suffering you may get home if you can restrain yourself and your companions when your ship reaches the Thrinacian island, where you will find the sheep and cattle belonging to the sun, who sees and gives ear to everything. If you leave these flocks unharmed and think of nothing but of getting home, you may yet after much labour reach Ithaca; but if you harm them, then I warn you of the destruction both of your ship and of your men. Even though you may yourself escape, you will return in bad plight after losing all your men, [in another man's ship, and you will find trouble in your house, which will be overrun by arrogant people, who are devouring your property under the pretext of paying court and making presents to your wife.

"This," I answered, "must be as it pleases heaven, but tell me truthfully, I see my poor mother's ghost close by us; she is sitting by the blood without saying a word, and though I am her own son she does not remember me and speak to me; tell me, Sir, how I can make her know me."

"Any ghost," he said, "that you let taste of the blood will talk with you like a reasonable being, but if you do not let them have any blood they will go away again."

After this the ghost of Teiresias went back to the house of Hades, for his prophesies had now been spoken, but I sat still where I was until my mother came up and tasted the blood. Then she recognized me at once and spoke fondly to me, saying, "My son, how did you come down to this abode of darkness while you are still alive? It is a hard thing for the living to see these places, for between us and them there are great and terrible waters, and there is Oceanus, which no man can cross on foot, but he must have a good ship to take him. Are you all this time trying to find your way home from Troy, and have you never yet got back to Ithaca nor seen your wife in your own house?"

"Mother," I said, "I was forced to come here to consult the ghost of the Theban prophet Teiresias. I have never yet been near the Achaean land nor set foot on my native country, and I have had nothing but one long series of misfortunes from the very first day that I set out with Agamemnon for Troy, the land of noble horses, to fight the Trojans. But tell me, and tell me true, in what way did you die? Did you have a long illness, or did heaven grant you a gentle, easy passage to eternity? Tell me also about my father, and the son whom I left behind me; is my property still in their hands, or has someone else got hold of it, who thinks that I shall not return to claim it? Tell me again what my wife intends doing, and in what mind she is; does she live with my son and guard my estate securely, or has she made the best match she could and married again?"

"My mother answered, "Your wife still remains in your house, but she is in great distress and spends her whole time in tears both night and day. No one as yet has got possession of your fine property, and Telemachus still holds your lands undisturbed. He has to entertain largely, as of course he must, considering his position as a magistrate, and how everyone invites him; your father remains at his old place in the country and never goes near the town. He has no comfortable bed nor bedding; in the winter he sleeps on the floor in front of the fire with the men and goes about all in rags, but in summer, when the warm weather comes on again, he lies out in the vineyard on a bed of vine leaves thrown anyhow upon the ground. He grieves continually about your never having come home, and suffers more and more as he grows older. As for my own end it was so: heaven did not take me swiftly and painlessly in my own house, nor was I attacked by any illness such as those that generally wear people out and kill them, but my longing to know what you were doing and the force of my affection for you- this it was that was the death of me."

"Then I tried to find some way of embracing my mother's ghost. Three times I sprang towards her and tried to clasp her in my arms, but each time she flitted from my embrace as it were a dream or phantom, and being touched to the quick I said to her, "Mother, why do you not stay still when I wish to embrace you? If we could throw our arms around one another we might find sad comfort in the sharing of our sorrows even in the house of Hades; does Persephone want to lay a still further load of grief upon me by mocking me with a phantom only?"

"My son," she answered, "most ill-fated of all mankind, it is not Persephone that is tricking you, but all people are like this when they are dead. The sinews no longer hold the flesh and bones together; these perish in the fierceness of consuming fire as soon as life has left the body, and the soul flits away as though it were a dream. Now, however, go back to the light of day as soon as you can, and note all these things that you may tell them to your wife hereafter."

"Just so did we speak together, and soon Persephone sent up the ghosts of the wives and daughters of all the most famous men. They gathered in crowds about the blood, and I considered how I might question each of them. In the end I judged that it would be best to draw the sharp blade that hung by my sturdy thigh, and keep them from all drinking the blood at once. So they came up one after the other, and each one as I questioned her told me her race and lineage.

"When Proserpine had dismissed the female ghosts in all directions, the ghost of Agamemnon son of Atreus came sadly up to me, surrounded by those who had perished with him in the house of Aegisthus. As soon as he had tasted the blood he recognized me, and weeping bitterly stretched out his arms towards me to embrace me; but he had no strength nor substance any more, and I too wept and pitied him as I beheld him. "How did you come by your death," I said, "King Agamemnon? Did Poseidon raise his winds and waves against you when you were at sea, or did your enemies put an end to you on the mainland when you were cattle-lifting or sheep-stealing, or while they were fighting in defence of their wives and city?"

"Odysseus," he answered, "noble son of Laertes, I was not lost at sea in any storm of Poseidon's raising, nor did my foes dispatch me on the mainland, but Aegisthus and my wicked wife were the death of me. He asked me to his house, feasted me, and then butchered me most miserably as though I were a fat beast in a slaughter house, while all around me my comrades were slain like sheep or pigs for the wedding breakfast, or picnic, or gorgeous banquet of some great nobleman. You must have seen numbers of men killed either in a general engagement, or in single combat, but you never saw anything so truly pitiable as the way in which we fell in that cloister, with the mixing-bowl and the loaded tables lying all about, and the ground reeking with our-blood. I heard Priam's daughter Cassandra scream as Clytemnestra killed her close beside me. I lay dying upon the earth with the sword in my body, and raised my hands to kill the slut of a murderess, but she slipped away from me; she would not even close my lips nor my eyes when I was dying, for there is nothing in this world so cruel and so shameless as a woman when she has fallen into such guilt as hers was. Fancy murdering her own husband! I thought I was going to be welcomed home by my children and my servants, but her abominable crime has brought disgrace on herself and all women who shall come after - even on the good ones."

And I said, "Truthfully, Zeus has hated the house of Atreus from first to last in the matter of their women's counsels. See how many of us fell for Helen's sake, and now it seems that Clytemnestra hatched mischief against too during your absence."

"Be sure, therefore," continued Agamemnon, "and not be too friendly even with your own wife. Do not tell her all that you know perfectly well yourself. Tell her a part only, and keep your own counsel about the rest. Not that your wife, Odysseus, is likely to murder you, for Penelope is a very admirable woman, and has an excellent spirit. We left her a young bride with an infant at her breast when we set out for Troy. This child no doubt is now grown up happily to man's estate, and he and his father will have a joyful meeting and embrace one another as it is right they should do, whereas my wicked wife did not even allow me the happiness of looking upon my son, but killed me ere I could do so. Furthermore I say - and remember in your heart my advice - do not tell people when you are bringing your ship to Ithaca, but come upon them with stealth, for after all this there is no trusting women! But now tell me, and tell me true, can you give me any news of my son Orestes? Is he in Orchomenus, or at Pylos, or is he at Sparta with Menelaus - for I presume that he is still living."

And I said, "Agamemnon, why do you ask me? I do not know whether your son is alive or dead, and it is not right to talk when one does not know."

"As we sat weeping and talking sadly with one another the ghost of Achilles came up to us with Patroclus, Antilochus, and Ajax who was the finest and goodliest man of all the Danaans after the son of Peleus. The fleet descendant of Aeacus knew me and spoke piteously, saying, "Odysseus, noble son of Laertes, what deed of daring will you undertake next, that you venture down to the house of Hades among us silly dead, who are but the ghosts of them that can labour no more?"

And I said, "Achilles, son of Peleus, foremost champion of the Achaeans, I came to consult Teiresias, and see if he could advise me about my return home to Ithaca, for I have never yet been able to get near the Achaean land, nor to set foot in my own country, but have been in trouble all the time. As for you, Achilles, no one was ever yet so fortunate as you have been, nor ever will be, for you were adored by all us Argives as long as you were alive, and now that you are here you are a great prince among the dead. Do not, therefore, take it so much to heart even if you are dead."

"Say not a word," he answered, "in death's favour; I would rather be a paid servant in a poor man's house and be above ground than king of kings among the dead. But give me news about my son; is he gone to the wars and will he be a great soldier, or is this not so? Tell me also if you have heard anything about my father Peleus - does he still rule among the Myrmidons, or do they show him no respect throughout Hellas and Phthia now that he is old and his limbs fail him? I wish I could just stand by his side, in the light of day, with the same strength that I had when I killed the bravest of our foes upon the plain of Troy – that I could be as I then was and go even for a short time to my father's house, any one who tried to do him violence or supersede him would soon me it."

The ghosts of other dead men stood near me and told me each his own sad tale; but that of Ajax, son of Telamon, alone stayed away – still angry with me for having won the contest in our dispute about the armour of Achilles. Thetis had offered it as a prize, but the Trojan prisoners and Athena were the judges. If only I had never gained the victory in such a contest, for it cost the life of Ajax, who was foremost of all the Danaans after the son of Peleus, alike in stature and prowess.

When I saw him I tried to pacify him and said, "Ajax, will you not forget and forgive even in death, but must the judgment about that hateful armour still bother you? It cost us Argives dear enough to lose such a tower of strength as you were to us. We mourned you as much as we mourned Achilles son of Peleus himself, nor can the blame be laid on anything but on the spite which Zeus bore against the Danaans, for it was this that made him counsel your destruction - come here, therefore, bring your proud spirit into submission, and hear what I can tell you."

He would not answer, but turned away to Erebus and to the other ghosts; nevertheless, I should have made him talk to me in spite of his being so angry, or I should have gone talking to him, only that there were still others among the dead whom I desired to see.

Then I saw Minos, son of Zeus, with his golden sceptre in his hand sitting in judgment on the dead, and the ghosts were gathered sitting and standing round him in the spacious house of Hades, to learn his sentences upon them. After him I saw huge Orion in a meadow full of asphodel driving the ghosts of the wild beasts that he had killed upon the mountains, and he had a great bronze club in his hand, unbreakable for ever and ever. And I saw Tityus son of Gaia stretched upon the plain and covering some nine acres of ground. Two vultures on either side of him were digging their beaks into his liver, and he kept on trying to beat them off with his hands, but could not; for he had violated Zeus' mistress Leto as she was going through Panopeus on her way to Pytho.

I saw also the dreadful fate of Tantalus, who stood in a lake that reached his chin; he was dying to quench his thirst, but could never reach the water, for whenever the poor creature stooped to drink, it dried up and vanished, so that there was nothing but dry ground- parched by the spite of heaven. There were tall trees, moreover, that shed their fruit over his head - pears, pomegranates, apples, sweet figs and juicy olives, but whenever the poor creature stretched out his hand to take some, the wind tossed the branches back again to the clouds.

And I saw Sisyphus at his endless task raising his gigantic stone with both his hands. With hands and feet he tried to roll it up to the top of the hill, but always, just before he could roll it over on to the other side, its weight would be too much for him, and the pitiless stone would come thundering down again on to the plain. Then he would begin trying to push it up hill again, and the sweat ran off him and the steam rose after him.

I stayed where I was in case some other of the mighty dead should come to me. And I would have seen still more of them, whom I wished to see - Theseus and Pirithous, glorious children of the gods - but so many thousands of ghosts came round me and uttered such appalling cries, that I fell into a panic, fearful that Persephone would send up from the house of Hades the head of that awful monster Gorgon. On this I rushed back to my ship and ordered my men to go on board at once and loose the ropes; so they embarked and took their places, whereon the ship went down the stream of the river Oceanus. We had to row at first, but soon a fair wind sprang up.

2g) Further Adventures (Homer, Odyssey, 12. 166-453, passim)

I had hardly finished telling everything to the men before we reached the island of the Sirens, for the wind had been very favourable. Then all of a sudden it fell dead calm; there was not a breath of wind nor a ripple upon the water, so the men furled the sails and stowed them; then taking to their oars they churned the water with the foam they raised in rowing. Meanwhile I look a large wheel of wax and cut it up small with my sword. Then I kneaded the wax in my strong hands till it became soft, which it soon did between the kneading and the rays of the sun-god son of Hyperion. Then I stopped the ears of all my men, and they bound me hands and feet to the mast as I stood upright on the crosspiece; but they went on rowing themselves. When we had got within earshot of the land, and the ship was going at a good rate, the Sirens saw that we were getting in shore and began with their singing.

"Come here," they sang, "renowned Odysseus, honour to the Achaean name, and listen to our voices. No one ever sailed past us without staying to hear the enchanting sweetness of our song - and he who listens will go on his way not only charmed, but wiser, for we know all the ills that the gods laid upon the Argives and Trojans before Troy, and can tell you everything that is going to happen over the whole world."

They sang these words most musically, and as I longed to hear them further I made by frowning to my men that they should set me free; but they quickened their stroke, and Eurylochus and Perimedes bound me with still stronger bonds till we had got out of hearing of the Sirens' voices. Then my men took the wax from their ears and unbound me.

Immediately after we had got past the island I saw a great wave from which spray was rising, and I heard a loud roaring sound. The men were so frightened that they let go of their oars, for the whole sea resounded with the rushing of the waters, but the ship stayed where it was, for the men had left off rowing. I went round, therefore, and encouraged them man by man not to lose heart.

"My friends," I said, "this is not the first time that we have been in danger, and we are in nothing like so bad a case as when the Cyclops shut us up in his cave; nevertheless, my courage and wise counsel saved us then, and we shall live to look back on all this as well. Now, therefore, let us all do as I say, trust in Zeus and row on with might and main. As for you, helmsman, these are your orders; attend to them, for the ship is in your hands; turn her head away from these steaming rapids and hug the rock, or she will give you the slip and be over yonder before you know where you are, and you will be the death of us."

So they did as I told them; but I said nothing about the awful monster Scylla, for I knew the men would not on rowing if I did, but would huddle together in the hold. In one thing only did I disobey Circe's strict instructions - I put on my armour. Then, seizing two strong spears, I took my stand on the ship's bow, for it was there that I expected first to see the monster of the rock, who was to do my men so much harm; but I could not make her out anywhere, though I strained my eyes with looking the gloomy rock all over and over.

Then we entered the straits in great fear of mind, for on the one hand was Scylla, and on the other feared Charybdis kept sucking up the salt water. As she vomited it up, it was like the water in a cauldron when it is boiling over upon a great fire, and the spray reached the top of the rocks on either side. When she began to suck again, we could see the water all inside whirling round and round, and it made a deafening sound as it broke against the rocks. We could see the bottom of the whirlpool all black with sand and mud, and the men were at their wit's ends for fear. While we were taken up with this, and were expecting each moment to be our last, Scylla pounced down suddenly upon us and snatched up my six best men. I was looking at once after both ship and men, and in a moment I saw their hands and feet ever so high above me, struggling in the air as Scylla was carrying them off, and I heard them call out my name in one last despairing cry. As a fisherman, seated, spear in hand, upon some jutting rock throws bait into the water to deceive the poor little fishes, and spears them with the ox's horn with which his spear is shod, throwing them gasping on to the land as he catches them one by one- even so did Scylla land these panting creatures on her rock and munch them up at the mouth of her den, while they screamed and stretched out their hands to me in their mortal agony. This was the most sickening sight that I saw throughout all my voyages.

"When we had passed the Wandering rocks, with Scylla and terrible Charybdis, we reached the noble island of the sun-god, where were the fair cattle and sheep belonging to the sun Hyperion. While still at sea in my ship I could bear the cattle lowing as they came home to the yards, and the sheep bleating. Then I remembered what the blind Theban prophet Teiresias had told me, and how carefully Circe had warned me to shun the island of the blessed sun-god. So being much troubled I said to the men, "My men, I know you are hard-pressed, but listen while I tell you the prophecy that Teiresias made me, and how carefully Circe warned me to shun the island of the blessed sun-god, for it was here, she said, that our worst danger would lie. Head the ship, therefore, away from the island."

"Meanwhile Eurylochus had been giving evil counsel to the men, "Listen to me," he said, "my poor comrades. All deaths are bad enough but there is none so bad as starvation. Why should not we drive in the best of these cows and offer them in sacrifice to the immortal gods? If we ever get back to Ithaca, we can build a fine temple to the sun-god and enrich it with every kind of ornament; if, however, he is determined to sink our ship out of revenge for these homed cattle, and the other gods are of the same mind, I for one would rather drink salt water once for all and have done with it, than be starved to death by inches in such a desert island as this is."

Thus spoke Eurylochus, and the men approved his words. Now the cattle, so fair and sizable, were feeding not far from the ship; the men, therefore drove in the best of them, and they all stood round them saying their prayers, and using young oak-shoots instead of barley, for there was no barley left. When they had done praying they killed the cows and dressed their carcasses; they cut out the thigh bones, wrapped them round in two layers of fat, and set some pieces of raw meat on top of them. They had no wine with which to make drink-offerings over the sacrifice while it was cooking, so they kept pouring on a little water from time to time while the inward meats were being grilled; then, when the thigh bones were burned and they had tasted the inward meats, they cut the rest up small and put the pieces upon the spits.

By this time I woke from my deep sleep and turned back to the ship and to the sea shore. As I drew near I began to smell hot roast meat, so I groaned out a prayer to the immortal gods. "Father Zeus," I exclaimed, "and all you other gods who live in everlasting bliss, you have done me cruel harm by the sleep into which you have sent me; see what fine work these men of mine have been making in my bsence."

For six days my men kept driving in the best cows and feasting upon them, but when Zeus the son of Cronos had added a seventh day, the fury of the gale abated; we therefore went on board, raised our masts, spread sail, and put out to sea. As soon as we were well away from the island, and could see nothing but sky and sea, the son of Cronos raised a black cloud over our ship, and the sea grew dark beneath it. We not get on much further, for in another moment we were caught by a terrific squall from the West that snapped the forestays of the mast so that it fell, while all the ship's gear tumbled about at the bottom of the vessel. The mast fell upon the head of the helmsman in the ship's stern, so that the bones of his head were crushed to pieces, and he fell overboard as though he were diving, with no more life left in him.

Then Zeus let loose his thunderbolts, and the ship went round and round, and was filled with fire and brimstone as the lightning struck it. The men all fell into the sea; they were carried about in the water round the ship, looking like so many seagulls, but the god presently deprived them of all chance of getting home again. I stuck to the ship till the sea knocked her sides from her keel (which drifted about by itself) and struck the mast out of her in the direction of the keel.

Hence I was carried along for nine days till on the tenth night the gods stranded me on the Ogygian island, where dwells the great and powerful goddess Calypso. She took me in and was kind to me, but I need say no more about this, for I told you and your noble wife all about it yesterday, and I hate saying the same thing over and over again."

2h) Odysseus' Revenge (Homer, Odyssey, 21. 1-434; 22. 1-21, passim)

Athena placed the idea in Penelope's mind to make the suitors test their skill with the bow and with the iron axes, in contest among themselves, as a means of bringing about their destruction. She went upstairs and got the store room key, which was made of bronze and had a handle of ivory; she then went with her maidens into the store room at the end of the house, where her husband's treasures of gold, bronze, and wrought iron were kept, and where was also his bow, and the quiver full of deadly arrows that had been given him by a friend whom he had met in Sparta - Iphitus the son of Eurytus. She sat down with it on her knees, weeping bitterly as she took the bow out of its case, and when her tears had relieved her, she went to the court where the suitors were, carrying the bow and the quiver, with the many deadly arrows that were inside it. Along with her came her maidens, bearing a chest that contained iron and bronze which her husband had won as prizes. When she reached the suitors, she stood by one of the bearing-posts supporting the roof of the cloister, holding a veil before her face, and with a maid on either side of her. Then she said:

"Listen to me you suitors, who persist in abusing the hospitality of this house because its owner has been long absent, and without other pretext than that you want to marry me; this, then, being the prize that you are contending for, I will bring out the mighty bow of Odysseus, and whoever of you shall string it and send his arrow through each one of twelve axes, him will I follow and quit this house of my lawful husband, so powerful, and so abounding in wealth. But even so I don't doubt that I shall remember it in my dreams."

As she spoke, she told the swineherd, Eumaeus, to set the bow and the pieces of iron before the suitors, and Eumaeus wept as he took them to do as she had bidden him. Hard by, the stockman wept also when he saw his master's bow, but Antinous scolded them. "You rustic fools," he said, "stupid simpletons; why should you add to the sorrows of your mistress by crying in this way? She has enough to grieve her in the loss of her husband; sit still, therefore, and eat your dinner in silence, or go outside if you want to cry, and leave the bow behind you. We suitors shall have to contend for it with might and main, for we shall find it no light matter to string such a bow as this is. There is not a man of us all who is such another as Odysseus; for I have seen him and remember him, though I was then only a child."

This was what he said, but all the time he was expecting to be able to string the bow and shoot through the iron, whereas in fact he was to be the first that should taste of the arrows from the hands of Odysseus, whom he was dishonouring in his own house – egging the others on to do so also.

Then Telemachus spoke. "Great heavens!" he exclaimed, "Zeus must have robbed me of my senses. Here is my dear and excellent mother saying she will quit this house and marry again, yet I am laughing and enjoying myself as though there were nothing happening. But, suitors, as the contest has been agreed upon, let it go forward. It is for a woman whose peer is not to be found in Pylos, Argos, or Mycene, nor yet in Ithaca nor on the mainland. You know this as well as I do; what need have I to speak in praise of my mother? Come on, then, make no excuses for delay, but let us see whether you can string the bow or no. I too will make trial of it, for if I can string it and shoot through the iron, I shall not suffer my mother to quit this house with a stranger, not if I can win the prizes which my father won before me."

As he spoke he sprang from his seat, threw his crimson cloak from him, and took his sword from his shoulder. First he set the axes in a row, in a long groove that he had dug for them, and had made straight by a line. Then he stamped the earth tight round them, and everyone was surprised when they saw him set up so orderly, though he had never seen anything of the kind before. This done, he went on to the pavement to make trial of the bow; three times did he tug at it, trying with all his might to draw the string, and thrice he had to leave off, though he had hoped to string the bow and shoot through the iron. He was trying for the fourth time, and would have strung it had not Odysseus made a sign to check him in spite of all his eagerness. So he said:

"Damn! I shall either be always feeble and of no prowess, or I am too young, and have not yet reached my full strength so as to be able to hold my own if any one attacks me. You others, therefore, who are stronger than I, make trial of the bow and get this contest settled."

On this he put the bow down, leaning against the door [that led into the house] with the arrow standing against the top of the bow. Then he sat down on the seat from which he had risen, and Antinous said:

"Come on each of you, one at a time, going towards the right from the place at which the cupbearer begins when he is handing round the wine."

The rest agreed, and Leiodes son of Oenops was the first to rise. He was sacrificial priest to the suitors, and sat in the corner near the mixing-bowl. He was the only man who hated their evil deeds and was indignant with the others. He was now the first to take the bow and arrow, so he went on to the pavement to perform his trial, but he could not string the bow, for his hands were weak and unused to hard work, they therefore soon grew tired, and he said to the suitors, "My friends, I cannot string it; let another have it; this bow shall take the life and soul out of many a chief among us, for it is better to die than to live after having missed the prize that we have so long striven for, and which has brought us so long together. Someone of us is even now hoping and praying that he may marry Penelope, but when he has seen this bow and tried it, let him woo and make bridal offerings to some other woman, and let Penelope marry whoever makes her the best offer and whose lot it is to win her."

At this he put the bow down, letting it lean against the door, with the arrow standing against the tip of the bow. Then he took his seat again on the seat from which he had risen; and Antinous rebuked him saying, "Leiodes, what are you talking about? Your words are monstrous and intolerable; it makes me angry to listen to you. Shall, then, this bow take the life of many a chief among us, merely because you cannot bend it yourself? True, you were not born to be an archer, but there are others who will soon string it."

Then the swineherd and the stockman left the cloisters together, and Odysseus followed them. When they had got outside the gates and the outer yard, Odysseus said to them quietly:

"Stockman, and you, swineherd - I have something in my mind which I am in doubt whether to say or no; but I think I will say it. What manner of men would you be to stand by Odysseus, if some god should bring him back here all of a sudden? Say which you are disposed to do - to side with the suitors, or with Odysseus?"

"Father Zeus," answered the stockman, "I wish that this could be so! If some god were to bring Odysseus back, you should see with what might and main I would fight for him."

In similar words Eumaeus prayed to all the gods that Odysseus might return; when, therefore, he saw for certain what intentions they had, Odysseus said, "It is I, Odysseus, who am here. I have suffered much, but at last, in the twentieth year, I have come back to my own country. I find that you two alone of all my servants are glad that I should do so, for I have not heard any of the others praying for my return. To you two, therefore, will I unveil the truth as it shall be. If heaven shall deliver the suitors into my hands, I will find wives for both of you, will give you house and holding close to my own, and you shall be to me as though you were brothers and friends of Telemachus. I will now give you convincing evidence, so that you may recognize me and be assured. See - here is the scar from the boar's tooth that ripped me when I was out hunting on Mount Parnassus with the sons of Autolycus."

As he spoke he drew his rags aside from the great scar, and when they had examined it thoroughly, they both of them wept about Odysseus, threw their arms round him and kissed his head and shoulders, while Odysseus kissed their hands and faces in return. The sun would have gone down upon their mourning if Odysseus had not checked them and said:

"Stop your crying, in case someone comes outside and sees us, and tells those who are inside. When you go in, do so separately; I will go first, and you follow afterwards. Here will be our plan: the suitors will all try to prevent me from getting hold of the bow and quiver. Eumaeus: you place it in my hands when you are carrying it about, and tell the women to close the doors of their apartment. If they hear any groaning or uproar as of men fighting about the house, they must not come out; they must keep quiet, and stay where they are at their work. And I command you, Philoetius, to secure the doors of the outer court, and to bind them securely at once."

When he had finished speaking, he went back to the house and took the seat that he had left. His two servants then followed him inside. Then, when the suitors had made their offerings and had drunk each as much as he desired, Odysseus craftily said:

"Suitors of the illustrious queen…I appeal especially to Eurymachus, and to Antinous who has just spoken with so much reason. Cease shooting for the present and leave the matter to the gods, but in the morning let heaven give victory to whom it will. For the moment, however, give me the bow, so that I may prove the power of my hands among you all, and see whether I still have as much strength as I used to have, or whether travel and neglect have made an end of it."

This made them all very angry, for they feared he might string the bow; Antinous therefore insulted him fiercely saying, "Wretched creature, you have not so much as a grain of sense in your whole body; you ought to think yourself lucky in being allowed to dine unharmed among your superiors, without having any smaller portion served to you than we others have had, and in being allowed to hear our conversation. No other beggar or stranger has been allowed to hear what we say among ourselves; the wine must have been doing you harm, as it does with all those drink immoderately. I can tell you that it will go hardly for you if you string the bow: you will find no mercy from any one here, for we shall at once ship you off to king Echetus, who kills every one that comes near him: you will never get away alive, so drink and keep quiet without getting into a quarrel with men younger than yourself."

Penelope then said to him. "Antinous, it is not right that you should ill-treat any guest of Telemachus who comes to this house. If the stranger should prove strong enough to string the mighty bow of Odysseus, can you suppose that he would take me home with him and make me his wife? Even the man himself can have no such idea in his mind: none of you need let that disturb his feasting; it would be out of all reason."

"Queen Penelope," answered Eurymachus, "we do not suppose that this man will take you away with him; it is impossible; but we are afraid that some of the lowlife, man or woman among the Achaeans, should go gossiping around and say, 'These suitors are feeble men; they are paying court to the wife of a brave man whose bow not one of them was able to string, and yet a beggarly tramp who came to the house strung it at once and sent an arrow through the iron.' This is what will be said, and it will be a scandal for us."

Eurymachus," Penelope answered, "people who persist in eating up the estate of a great chieftain and dishonouring his house must not expect others to think well of them. Why then should you mind if men talk as you think they will? This stranger is strong and well-built, he says moreover that he is of noble birth. Give him the bow, and let us see whether he can string it or no. I say - and it shall surely be - that if Apollo grants him the glory of stringing it, I will give him a cloak and shirt of good wear, with a javelin to keep off dogs and robbers, and a sharp sword. I will also give him sandals, and will see him sent safely wherever he wants to go."

Then Telemachus said, "Mother, I am the only man either in Ithaca or in the islands that are over against Elis who has the right to let anyone have the bow or to refuse it. No one shall force me one way or the other, not even though I choose to make the stranger a present of the bow right away, and let him take it away with him. Go, then, within the house and busy yourself with your daily duties, your loom, your distaff, and the ordering of your servants. This bow is a man's matter, and mine above all others, for it is I who am master here."

She went wondering back into the house, and laid her son's saying in her heart. Then going upstairs with her handmaids into her room, she mourned her dear husband till Athena sent sweet sleep over her eyelids.

The swineherd now picked up the bow and was for taking it to Odysseus, but the suitors clamoured around him from all parts of the cloisters, and one of them said, "You idiot, where are you taking the bow to? Are you out of your wits? If Apollo and the other gods will grant our prayer, your own boarhounds shall get you into some quiet little place, and worry you to death."

Eumaeus was frightened at the outcry they all raised, so he put the bow down then and there, but Telemachus shouted out at him from the other side of the court, and threatened him saying, "Eumaeus, bring the bow on in spite of them, or young as I am I will pelt you with stones back to the country, for I am the better man of the two. I wish I was as much stronger than all the other suitors in the house as I am than you, I would soon send some of them off sick and sorry, for they plan trouble."

Thus did he speak, and all of them laughed heartily, which put them in a better humour with Telemachus; so Eumaeus brought the bow on and placed it in the hands of Odysseus. When he had done this, he called Euryclea apart and said to her, "Euryclea, Telemachus says you are to close the doors of the women's apartments. If they hear any groaning or uproar as of men fighting about the house, they are not to come out, but are to keep quiet and stay where they are at their work." Euryclea did as she was told and closed the doors of the women's apartments.

Meanwhile, Philoetius slipped quietly out and secured the gates of the outer court. There was a ship's cable of fiber lying in the gatehouse, so he secured the gates with it and then came in again, resuming the seat that he had left, and keeping an eye on Odysseus, who had now got the bow in his hands, and was turning it every way about, and proving it all over to see whether the worms had been eating into its two horns during his absence. Then would one turn towards his neighbour saying, "This is some tricky old bowman; either he has got one like it at home, or he wants to make one, in such workmanlike style does the old vagabond handle it." Another said, "I hope he may be no more successful in other things than he is likely to be in stringing this bow."

But Odysseus, when he had taken it up and examined it all over, strung it as easily as a skilled bard strings a new peg of his lyre and makes the twisted gut fast at both ends. Then he took it in his right hand to test the string, and it sang sweetly under his touch like the twittering of a swallow. The suitors were dismayed, and turned pale as they heard it; at that moment, moreover, Zeus thundered loudly as a sign, and the heart of Odysseus rejoiced as he heard the omen that the son of scheming Cronos had sent him.

He took an arrow that was lying upon the table - for those which the suitors were so shortly about to taste were all inside the quiver - he laid it on the centerpiece of the bow, and drew the notch of the arrow and the string toward him, still seated on his seat. When he had taken aim he let fly, and his arrow pierced every one of the handle-holes of the axes from the first onwards till it had gone right through them, and into the outer courtyard. Then he said to Telemachus:

"Your guest has not disgraced you, Telemachus. I did not miss what I aimed at, and I was not long in stringing my bow. I am still strong, and not as the suitors insult me with being. Now, however, it is time for them to prepare supper while there is still daylight, and then otherwise to flaunt themselves with song and dance which are the crowning ornaments of a banquet."

As he spoke he made a sign with his eyebrows, and Telemachus girded on his sword, grasped his spear, and stood armed beside his father's seat. Then Odysseus tore off his rags, and sprang on to the broad pavement with his bow and his quiver full of arrows. He shed the arrows on to the ground at his feet and said, "The mighty contest is at an end. I will now see whether Apollo will grant it to me to hit another mark which no man has yet hit!" At this he aimed a deadly arrow at Antinous, who was about to take up a gold cup to drink his wine and already had it in his hands. He had no thought of death - who among all the revelers would think that one man, however brave, would stand alone among so many and kill him? The arrow struck Antinous in the throat, and the point went clean through his neck, so that he fell over and the cup dropped from his hand, while a thick stream of blood gushed from his nostrils. He kicked the table from him and upset the things on it, so that the bread and roasted meats were all soiled as they fell over on to the ground.

Adapted from Samuel Butler, Homer. The Odyssey (London A.C. Fifield, 1900)

READING 3:

HESIOD

Unlike Homer, we feel more confident in our information about Hesiod, the author of *Theogony* and *Works and Days*. Ancient Greeks considered him a contemporary of Homer, and if that is accurate, it should place him sometime during the eighth to seventh centuries BCE. Hesiod was a native of Boeotia, a relatively rich region for agriculture in ancient Greece, often dominated by the great city of Thebes. Like Homer, Hesiod addresses the goddesses of poetry and music, the Muses, to help him pronounce his works. *Theogony* offers a "genealogy of the gods." It tells the tale of the creation of the universe, the gods and their descendants, their wars with the Titans and, finally, the creation of humans. There were many versions of this Greek form of Genesis, and although Hesiod's is but one, it remains the most celebrated, and today is considered the standard version. It offers us not only a vivid account of the trials and conflict that created the world of gods and humans, but also about the nature of the gods themselves, their attributes, and their power.

Works and Days has a very different scope. Much of it is told from the perspective of Hesiod himself, advising and criticizing his wayward brother, Perses, regarding the proper life of both a farmer and citizen of the community. While some of the poem comprises very specific agricultural tips (somewhat like a Greek "Farmer's Almanac"), it also offers explanations for the generations of humankind, and the power of Zeus as a guarantor for Justice (Dike). It thus describes the nature of the relationship between humanity and the divine, and how to live a just life.

3a) Theogony (Hesiod, Theogony, 1-917, passim)

Let us begin to sing of the Muses of Helicon, who hold the great and holy shrine there, and dance on soft feet around the deep-violet spring and the altar of the almighty son of Cronos, and, when they have washed their tender bodies in Permessus or in the Horse's Spring or Olmeius, make their fair, lovely dances upon highest part of Helicon and move with vigorous feet. Thence they arise and go forth by night, enveloped in thick mist, and sing their song with lovely voice, praising Zeus the holder of the aegis and queenly Hera of Argos, who walks on golden sandals, and the daughter of Zeus the aegis-holder, bright-eyed Athena, and Phoebus Apollo, and Artemis who delights in arrows, and Poseidon who both holds and shakes the earth, and reverend Themis and quick-glancing Aphrodite, and Hebe, with the crown of gold, and fair Dione, Leto, Iapetus, and Cronos the crafty counsellor, Eos and great Helius, and bright Selene, Earth too, and great Oceanus, and dark Night, and the sacred race of all the other immortals who endure forever. Such goddesses taught Hesiod glorious songs one day while he was shepherding his lambs under holy Helicon, and these were the first words the goddesses said to me, the Muses of Olympus, daughters of Zeus who holds the aegis:

"Shepherds of the wilderness, wretched things of shame, mere bellies, we know how to speak many false things as though they were true; but we know, when we will, to utter true things."

So spoke the articulate daughters of great Zeus, and they plucked and gave me a rod, a shoot of sturdy laurel, a marvellous thing, and breathed into me a divine voice to celebrate things that shall be and things there were before; and they told me to sing of the race of the blessed gods who live eternally, but always to sing of themselves both first and last.

Mnemosyne (Memory), who reigns over the hills of Eleuther, bore the Muses in Pieria by union with the father, the son of Cronos, as a respite of ills and a rest from sorrow. For nine nights did wise Zeus lie with her, entering her holy bed remote from the immortals. And when a year was passed and the seasons came round as the months waned, and many days passed, she bore nine daughters, all of one mind, whose hearts are set upon song and their spirit free from care, a little way from the highest peak of snowy Olympus.

There are their bright dancing-places and beautiful homes, and beside them the Graces and Desire live in delight. And they, uttering through their lips a lovely voice, sing the laws of all and the nobility of the immortals, pronouncing their lovely voice. Then they went to Olympus, delighting in their sweet voice with heavenly song, and the dark earth echoed around them as they chanted, and a lovely sound rose up beneath their feet as they went to their father. And he was reigning in heaven, himself holding the lightning and glowing thunderbolt, when he had overcome by his might his own father Cronos; and he distributed justly to the immortals their portions and declared their privileges…

Hail, children of Zeus! Grant us a lovely song and celebrate the holy race of the immortal gods who endure forever, those that were born of Earth and starry Heaven and gloomy Night and them that briny Sea did rear. Tell how at the first gods and earth came to be, and rivers, and the boundless sea with its raging swell, and the gleaming stars, and the wide heaven above, and the gods who were born of them, givers of good things, and how they divided their wealth, and how they shared their honours among them, and also how at first they took wrinkled

Olympus. These things declare to me from the beginning, you Muses who dwell in the house of Olympus, and tell me which of them first came to be.

Truly, first Chaos came into being, but then wide-bosomed Earth, the enduring seat of all the immortals who hold the peaks of snowy Olympus, and murky Tartarus in the depth of the widely-walked Earth, and Eros (Love), fairest among the immortals, who unnerves the limbs and overcomes the mind and wise counsels of all gods and all men within them. From Chaos came forth Erebus and black Night; but of Night were born Aether and Day, whom she conceived and bore from union in love with Erebus.

And Earth first bore starry Heaven, equal to herself, to cover her on every side, and to be an ever-sure abode for the blessed gods. And she brought forth long Hills, graceful haunts of the goddess-Nymphs who dwell amongst the glens of the hills. She bore also the fruitless deep with his raging swell, Pontus, without sweet union of love. But afterwards she lay with Heaven and bare deep-swirling Oceanus, Coeus and Crius and Hyperion and Iapetus, Theia and Rhea, Themis and Mnemosyne and gold-crowned Phoebe and lovely Tethys. After them was born wily Cronos, youngest and most terrible of her children, and he hated his lusty father.

She bore the Cyclopes, overbearing in spirit, Brontes, and Steropes and stubborn-hearted Arges, who gave Zeus the thunder and made the thunderbolt: in all else they were like the gods, but one eye only was set in the middle of their foreheads. And they were surnamed Cyclopes because one orbed eye was set in their foreheads. They were skilled in strength and might and craft. Three other sons were born of Earth and Heaven, great and hardy beyond telling, Cottus and Briareos and Gyes, arrogant children.

From their shoulders sprang a hundred arms, not to be overcome, and each had fifty heads upon his shoulders on their strong bodies, and irresistible was the stubborn strength that was in their great forms. For of all the children that were born of Earth and Heaven, these were the most terrible, and they were hated by their own father from the first. And he used to hide them all away in a secret place of Earth as soon as each was born, and would not allow them to come up into the light: and Heaven rejoiced in his evil acts. But vast Earth groaned within, being distressed, and she made the element of grey flint and shaped a great sickle, and told her plan to her dear sons. And she spoke, cheering them, while she was vexed in her dear heart:

"My children, born from a sinful father, if you will obey me, we should punish the vile outrage of your father; for he first thought of doing shameful things." So she said, but fear seized them all, and none of them uttered a word. But great, wily Cronos took courage and answered his dear mother: "Mother, I will attempt to accomplish this deed, for I do not revere our father of evil name, for he first thought of doing such shameful things." So he answered: and vast Earth rejoiced greatly in spirit, and hid him in an ambush, and put in his hands a jagged sickle, and revealed to him the whole plot.

And Heaven came, bringing on night and longing for love, and he lay about Earth spreading himself full upon her. Then the son from his ambush stretched forth his left hand and in his right took the great long sickle with jagged teeth, and swiftly lopped off his own father's genitals and cast them away to fall behind him. And not in vain did they fall from his hand; for all the bloody drops that gushed forth Earth received, and as the seasons moved round she bore the strong Erinyes and the great Giants with gleaming armour, holding long spears in their hands, and the Nymphs whom they call Meliae all over the boundless earth.

And so soon as he had cut off the genitals with flint and cast them from the land into the surging sea, they were swept away for a long time: and a white foam spread around them from the immortal flesh, and in it there grew a maiden. First she drew near holy Cythera, and from there, afterwards, she came to Cyprus, surrounded by sea, and came forth an awful and lovely goddess, and grass grew up about her beneath her shapely feet. She gods and men call Aphrodite, and the foam-born goddess and rich-crowned Cytherea, because she grew amid the foam, and Cytherea because she reached Cythera, and Cyprogenes because she was born in billowy Cyprus, and Philommedes because sprang from the genitals. And with her went Eros, and pleasant Desire followed her at her birth from the start and as she went into the assembly of the gods. This honour she has from the beginning, and this is the portion allotted to her among men and undying gods, the whisperings of maidens and smiles and tricks with sweet delight and love and graciousness.

But these sons whom be begot himself great Heaven used to call "Titans" in warning, for he said that they strained and arrogantly performed a fearful deed, and that vengeance for it would come afterwards. And Night bore hateful Doom and black Fate and Death, and she bore Sleep and the legions of nightmares. And again, the goddess murky Night, although she lay with none, bore Blame and painful Suffering, and the Hesperides who guard the rich, golden apples and the trees bearing fruit beyond glorious Ocean.

Also she bore the ruthless, avenging Furies and the Fates, Clotho and Lachesis and Atropos who give men at their birth both evil and good to have. As for the Furies, they pursue the transgressions of men and of gods: and these goddesses never cease from their dread anger until they punish the sinner with a sore penalty. Also deadly Night bore Nemesis to afflict mortal men, and after her, Deceit and Affection and hateful Old-Age and hard-hearted Eris (Strife).

But horrible Strife bore painful Toil and Forgetfulness and Hunger and tearful Pain, Battles also, and Murder, Manslaughter, Quarrel, Falsehood, Dispute, Lawlessness and Ruin, all of one nature, and Oath who most troubles men upon earth when anyone wilfully swears a false oath.

And Sea bore Nereus, the eldest of his children, who is true and does not lie: and men call him the Old Man of the Sea because he is trusty and gentle and does not forget the laws of righteousness, but thinks just and generous thoughts. And yet again he begot great Thaumas and proud Phorcys, having mated with Earth, and fair-cheeked Ceto and Eurybia who has a heart of stone within her. And Thaumas wedded Electra the daughter of deep-flowing Ocean, and she bore him swift Iris and the long-haired Harpies, Aello (Storm-swift) and Ocypetes (Swift-flier) who on their swift wings keep pace with the blasts of the winds and the birds; for quick as time they dart along.

Ceto bore to Phorys the fair-cheeked Graiae, sisters grey from their birth: and both deathless gods and men who walk on earth call them Graiae, Pemphredo well-clad, and saffron-robed Enyo, and the Gorgons who dwell beyond glorious Ocean in the frontiers toward Night where the clear-voiced Hesperidesare—Sthenno, and Euryale, and Medusa—dwell, and who suffered a woeful fate: Medusa was mortal, but the other two were undying and did not grow. With her lay Dark-haired Poseidon in a soft meadow amid spring flowers.

And when Perseus cut off her head, there sprang forth great Chrysaor and the horse Pegasus who is called this because he was born near the springs (pegae) of Ocean; and Crysaor, because he held a golden blade (aor) in his hands. Now Pegasus flew away and left the earth, the mother of flocks, and came to the deathless gods: and he dwells in the house of Zeus and bears to wise Zeus the thunder and lightning. But Chrysaor was joined in love to Callirrhoe, the daughter of glorious Ocean, and begot three-headed Geryones. Him mighty Heracles killed in Erythea by his shuffling oxen on that day when he drove the wide-browed oxen to holy Tiryns, and had crossed the ford of Ocean and killed Orthus and Eurytion the herdsman in the dim stead out beyond glorious Ocean…

But Rhea submitted in love to Cronos and bore splendid children: Hestia, Demeter, and golden-sandled Hera and strong Hades, pitiless in heart, who dwells under the earth, and the loud-crashing Earth-Shaker, and wise Zeus, father of gods and men, by whose thunder the wide earth is shaken. These great Cronos swallowed as each came forth from the womb to his mother's knees with this intent, so that no other of the proud sons of Heaven should hold the lordly office among the immortals.

For he learned from Earth and starry Heaven that he was destined to be overcome by his own son, strong though he was, through the contriving of great Zeus. For this reason he kept no blind vigil, but watched and swallowed his children: and unceasing grief seized Rhea. But when she was about to bear Zeus, the father of gods and men, she besought her own dear parents, Earth and starry Heaven, to devise some plan with her that the birth of her dear child might be concealed, and that Cronos might pay the penalty for what he did to his own father and to his children whom he had swallowed.

And they readily heard and obeyed their dear daughter, and told her all that was destined to happen, both to Cronos the king and his stout-hearted son.

So they sent her to Lyetus, to the rich land of Crete, when she was ready to bear great Zeus, the youngest of her children. Him did vast Earth receive from Rhea in wide Crete to nourish and to bring up. To this place came Earth carrying him swiftly through the black night to Lyctus first, and took him in her arms and hid him in a remote cave beneath the secret places of the holy earth on thick-wooded Mount Aegeum; but to the mightily ruling son of Heaven, the earlier king of the gods, she gave a great stone wrapped in swaddling clothes. Then he took it in his hands and thrust it down into his belly: wretch! He did not know in his heart that in place of the stone his son was left behind, unconquered and untroubled, and that he was soon to overcome him by force and might and drive him from his honours, himself to reign over the deathless gods.

After that, the strength and glorious limbs of the young god increased quickly, and as the years rolled on, great Cronos the wily was troubled by the deep suggestions of Earth, and brought up again his offspring, vanquished by the arts and might of his own son, and he vomited up first the stone which he had swallowed last. And Zeus set it fast in the wide-walked earth at fair Pytho under the glens of Parnassus, to be a sign thenceforth and a marvel to mortal men. And he set free from their deadly bonds the brothers of his father, sons of Heaven whom his father in his foolishness had bound. And they remembered to be grateful to him for his kindness, and gave him thunder and the glowing thunderbolt and lightening: for before that, huge Earth had hidden these. In them he trusts and rules over mortals and immortals.

Now Iapetus wed slender-ankled Clymene, daughter of Ocean, and went up with her into bed. And she bore him a stout-hearted son, Atlas: she also bore glorious Menoetius and clever Prometheus, full of various wiles, and slow-witted Epimetheus who from the beginning was a curse to men who eat bread; for it was he who first took from Zeus the woman, the virgin whom he had formed. But Menoetius was outrageous, and far-seeing Zeus struck him with a bright thunderbolt and sent him down to Erebus because of his mad arrogance and hubris. And Atlas, through hard constraint, holds up the wide heavens with unwearying head and arms, standing at the borders of the earth before the clear-voiced Hesperides; for this lot wise Zeus assigned to him. And clever Prometheus he bound with inextricable bonds, cruel chains, and drove a shaft through his middle, and set against him a wide-winged eagle, which used to eat his immortal liver; but by night the liver grew as much again everyway as the wide-winged eagle devoured in the whole day.

That bird Heracles, the valiant son of slender-ankled Alcmene, slew; and saved the son of Iapetus from the cruel curse, and released him from his affliction—not without the will of Olympian Zeus, who reigns on high, that the glory of Heracles the Theban-born might be yet greater than it was before over the plenteous earth. This, then, he regarded, and honoured his famous son; though he was angry, he ceased from the wrath that he had possessed before because Prometheus matched himself in wit with the almighty son of Cronos. For when the gods and mortal men had a dispute at Mecone, even then Prometheus was bold to cut up a great ox and set portions before them, trying to fool the mind of Zeus. Before the rest he set flesh and inner parts, thick with fat, upon the hide, covering them with an ox stomach; but for Zeus he put the white bones dressed up with cunning art and covered with shining fat. Then the father of men and of gods said to him:

"Son of Iapetus, most glorious of all lords, good son, how unfairly you have divided the portions!" So said Zeus whose wisdom is everlasting, rebuking him. But wily Prometheus answered him, smiling softly and not forgetting his cunning trick: "Zeus, most glorious and greatest of the eternal gods, take whichever of these portions your heart within you bids." So he said, planning trickery. But Zeus, whose wisdom is everlasting, saw and failed not to perceive the trick, and in his heart he planned mischief against mortal men, which also was to be fulfilled. With both hands he picked up the white fat and was angry at heart, and wrath came to his heart when he saw the white ox-bones craftily laid out: and because of this the tribes of men upon earth burn white bones to the deathless gods upon fragrant altars. But Zeus who drives the clouds was greatly vexed and said to him: "Son of Iapetus, clever above all! So, son, you have not yet forgotten your cunning arts!"

So spoke Zeus in anger, whose wisdom is everlasting; and from that time he always remembered the trick, and would not give the power of unwearying fire to the Melian race of mortal men who live on the earth. But the noble son of Iapetus outwitted him and stole the bright gleam of unwearying fire in a hollow reed. And Zeus who thunders on high was stung in spirit, and his dear heart was angered when he saw among men the bright spark of fire. Straightaway he made an evil thing for men as the price of fire; for the very famous Limping God formed of earth the likeness of a shy virgin as the son of Cronos willed it. And the goddess bright-eyed Athene decked her out and clothed her with silvery accessories, and down from her head she spread with her hands a embroidered veil, a wonder to see; and she, Pallas Athena, put about her head lovely garlands, flowers of new-grown herbs.

Also she put upon her head a crown of gold, which the famous Limping God made himself and worked with his own hands as a favour to Zeus his father. On it was much curious work, wonderful to see; for of the many creatures which the land and sea rear up, he put most upon it, wonderful things, like living beings with voices: and great beauty shone out from it. But when he had made the beautiful evil to be the price for the blessing of fire, he brought her out, delighting in the finery which the bright-eyed daughter of a mighty father had given her, to the place where the other gods and men were. And wonder took hold of the deathless gods and mortal men when they saw that which was sheer guile, not to be withstood by men.

For from her is the deadly race and tribe of women who live amongst mortal men to their great trouble, no helper in hateful poverty, but only in wealth. And as in thatched hives bees feed the drones whose nature is to do mischief—by day and throughout the day until the sun goes down the bees are busy and lay the white combs, while the drones stay at home in the covered skeps and reap the toil of others into their own bellies—even so Zeus who thunders on high made women to be an evil to mortal men, with a nature to do evil. And he gave them a second evil to be the price for the good they had: whoever avoids marriage and the sorrows that women cause, and will not wed, reaches deadly old age without anyone to tend his years, and though he at least has no lack of livelihood while he lives, yet, when he is dead, his kin divide his possessions among them. And as for the man who chooses the lot of marriage and takes a good wife suited to his mind, evil continually contends with good; for whoever happens to have mischievous children, lives always with unceasing grief in his spirit and heart within him; and this evil cannot be healed. So it is not possible to deceive or go beyond the will of Zeus; for not even the son of Iapetus, kindly Prometheus, escaped his heavy anger, but by necessity strong chains confined him.

But when first their father was angry at Obriareus and Cottus and Gyes, he bound them in cruel bonds, because he was jealous of their exceeding manhood and beauty and great size: and he made them live beneath the widely-walked earth, where they were afflicted, being set to dwell under the ground, at the end of the earth, at its great borders, in bitter anguish for a long time and with great grief at heart. But the son of Cronos and the other deathless gods whom rich-haired Rhea bore from union with Cronos, brought them up again to the light at Earth's advising. For she herself recounted all things to the gods fully, how that with the help of Heaven's sons they would gain victory and a glorious cause to boast of themselves. For the Titans and as many as sprang from Cronos had for a long time been fighting together in stubborn war with heart-grieving toil, the lordly Titans from high Othrys, and the gods, givers of good, whom rich-haired Rhea bore in union with Cronos, from Olympus. So they, with bitter wrath, were fighting continually with one another at that time for ten full years, and the hard strife had no exit or end for either side, and the issue of the war hung evenly balanced…

Then Zeus no longer held back his might; but immediately his heart was filled with fury and he showed all his strength. From Heaven and from Olympus he came forward, hurling his lightning: the bolts flew thick and fast from his strong hand together with thunder and lightning, whirling an awesome flame. The life-giving earth crashed around in burning, and the vast wood crackled loud with fire all about. All the land seethed, and Ocean's streams and the unfruitful sea. The hot vapour lapped round the earthborn Titans: flame unspeakable rose to the bright upper air: the flashing glare of the thunder-stone and lightning blinded their eyes for all that there were strong. Astounding heat seized Chaos: and to see with eyes and to hear the sound with ears it seemed even as if Earth and wide Heaven above came together; for such a mighty crash would have arisen if Earth were being hurled to ruin, and Heaven from on high were hurling her down; so great a crash was there while the gods were meeting together in strife.

Also the winds brought rumbling earthquake and dust-storm, thunder and lightning and the lurid thunderbolt, which are the shafts of great Zeus, and carried the ringing and the war-cry into the midst of the two hosts. A horrible uproar of terrible strife arose: mighty deeds were shown and the battle inclined. But until then, they kept at one another and fought continually in cruel war. And amongs the front ranks Cottus and Briareos and Gyes insatiable for war, raised fierce the war-cry and were fighting: three hundred rocks, one upon another, they launched from their strong hands and overshadowed the Titans with their missiles, and buried them beneath the widely-walked earth, and bound them in bitter chains when they had conquered them by their strength for all their great spirit, as far beneath the earth to Tartarus.

For a great anvil falling down from heaven nine nights and days would reach the earth upon the tenth: and again, a great anvil falling from earth nine nights and days would reach Tartarus upon the tenth. Round it runs a fence of bronze, and night spreads in triple line all about it like a neck-circlet, while above grow the roots of the earth and unfruitful sea. There by the counsel of Zeus who drives the clouds the Titan gods are hidden under misty gloom, in a dank place where are the ends of the huge earth. And they may not leave; for Poseidon fixed gates of bronze upon it, and a wall runs all round it on every side. There Gyes and Cottus and great-souled Obriareus live, trusty warders of Zeus who holds the aegis.

And there the children of dark Night have their dwellings, Sleep and Death, awful gods. The glowing Sun never looks upon them with his beams, neither as he goes up into heaven, nor as he comes down from heaven. And the former of them roams peacefully over the earth and the sea's broad back and is kindly to men; but the other has a heart of iron, and his spirit within him is pitiless as bronze: whomsoever of men he has once seized he holds fast: and he is hateful even to the deathless gods. There, in front, stand the echoing halls of the god of the Underworld, strong Hades, and awful Persephone. A fearful hound, Three-headed Cerberus, guards the house in front, pitiless, and he has a cruel trick. On those who go in he fawns with his tail and both is ears, but allows them not to go out back again, but keeps watch and devours whomsoever he catches going out of the gates of strong Hades and awful Persephone.

But when Zeus had driven the Titans from heaven, huge Earth bore her youngest child Typhoeus, by the love of Tartarus, and with the aid of golden Aphrodite. He had strength in his hands in all that he did and the feet of the strong god were untiring. From his shoulders grew an hundred heads of a snake, a fearful dragon, with dark, flickering tongues, and from under the brows of his eyes in his marvellous heads flashed fire, and fire burned from his heads as he glared. And there were voices in all his dreadful heads which uttered every kind of unspeakable sound; for at one time they made sounds such that the gods understood, but at another, the noise of a bull bellowing aloud in proud, ungovernable fury; and at another, the sound of a lion, relentless of heart; and at another, sounds like dogs, wondrous to hear; and again, at another, he would hiss, so that the high mountains echoed.

And truly an even beyond help might have happened on that day, and he would have come to reign over mortals and immortals, had not the father of men and gods been quick to notice it. But he thundered hard and mightily: and the earth around resounded terribly and the wide heaven above, and the sea and Ocean's streams and the nether parts of the earth. Great Olympus reeled beneath the divine feet of Zeus as he arose and earth groaned. And through the two of them heat seized the dark-blue sea, through the thunder and lightning, and through the fire from the monster, and the scorching winds and blazing thunderbolt. The whole earth seethed, and sky and sea: and the long waves raged along the beaches round and about, at the rush of the deathless gods: and there arose an endless shaking.

Hades trembled where he rules over the dead below, and the Titans under Tartarus who live with Cronos, because of the unending clamour and the fearful strife. So when Zeus had raised up his might and seized his arms, thunder and lightning and bright thunderbolt, he leaped from Olympus and struck him, and burned all the marvellous heads of the monster about him. But when Zeus had conquered him and lashed him with strokes, Typhoeus was hurled down, a maimed wreck, so that the huge earth groaned. And flame shot forth from the thunder-stricken lord in the dim rugged glens of the mount, when he was destroyed. A great part of huge earth was scorched by the terrible vapour and melted as tin melts when heated by men's art in channelled crucibles; or as iron, which is hardest of all things, is softened by glowing fire in mountain glens and melts in the divine earth through the strength of Hephaestus28. Even so, then, the earth melted in the glow of the blazing fire. And in the bitterness of his anger Zeus cast him into wide Tartarus.

Now Zeus, king of the gods, made Metis his wife first, and she was wisest among gods and mortal men. But when she was about to bring forth the goddess bright-eyed Athena, Zeus craftily deceived her with cunning words and swallowed her in his own belly, as Earth and starry Heaven advised. For they advised him so, to the end that no other should hold royal sway over the eternal gods in place of Zeus; for very wise children were destined to be born of her, first the maiden bright-eyed Tritogeneia, equal to her father in strength and in wise understanding; but afterwards she was to bear a son of overbearing spirit, king of gods and men. But Zeus put her into his own belly first, that the goddess might devise for him both good and evil.

Next he married bright Themis who bore the Hours, and Order, Justice, and blooming Peace, who mind the works of mortal men, and the Fates to whom wise Zeus gave the greatest honour, Clotho, and Lachesis, and Atropos who give mortal men evil and good to have. And Eurynome, the daughter of Ocean, beautiful in form, bare him three fair-cheeked Graces, Aglaea, and Euphrosyne, and lovely Thalia, from whose eyes as they glanced flowed love that unnerves the limbs: and beautiful is their glance beneath their brows. Also he came to the bed of all-nourishing Demeter, and she bare white-armed Persephone whom Aidoneus carried off from her mother; but wise Zeus gave her to him. And again, he loved Mnemosyne with the beautiful hair: and of her the nine gold-crowned Muses were born who delight in feasts and the pleasures of song.

3b) Works and Days (Hesiod, Works and Days, 1-705, passim)

Muses of Pieria who give glory through song, come to me, tell of Zeus your father and chant his praise. Through him mortal men are famed or unknown, sung or unsung alike, as great Zeus wills. For easily he makes a man strong, and easily he brings the strong man low; easily he humbles the proud and raises the obscure, and easily he straightens the crooked and blasts the proud, Zeus who thunders aloft and has his dwelling most high. Attend with eyes and ears, and make judgements straight with righteousness. And I would tell you, my brother Perses, of true things.

There was not one kind of Strife alone, but all over the earth there are two. As for the one, a man would praise her when he came to understand her; but the other is blameworthy: and they are wholly different in nature. For one fosters evil war and battle, being cruel: her no man loves; but inevitably, through the will of the deathless gods, men pay harsh Strife her honour due. But the other is the elder daughter of dark Night, and the son of Cronos who sits above and dwells in the aether, set her in the roots of the earth: and she is far kinder to men. She stirs up even the lazy to toil; for a man grows eager to work when he considers his neighbour, a rich man who hastens to plough and plant and put his house in good order; and neighbour vies with is neighbour as he hurries after wealth. This Strife is wholesome for men. And potter is angry with potter, and craftsman with craftsman, and beggar is jealous of beggar, and minstrel of minstrel.

Perses, let go of these things in your heart, and do not let that Strife who delights in mischief hold your heart back from work, while you peep and peer and listen to the arguments of the courthouse. Little concern has one with quarrels and courts who has not a year's provisions laid up early, even that which the earth offers, Demeter's grain. When you have got plenty of that, you can raise disputes and strive to get another's goods. But you shall have no second chance to deal so again: No, let us settle our dispute here with true judgement, which is of Zeus and is perfect. For we had already divided our inheritance, but you seized the greater share and carried it off, greatly swelling the glory of our bribe-swallowing lords who love to judge such a cause as this. Fools! They do not know how much more the half is than the whole, nor what great advantage there is in weeds and greens.

For the gods keep hidden from men the means of life. Otherwise you would easily do work enough in a day to supply you for a full year even without working; soon would you put away your rudder over the smoke, and the fields worked by ox and sturdy mule would run to waste. But Zeus in the anger of his heart hid it, because crafty Prometheus deceived him; therefore he planned sorrow and mischief against men. He hid fire, but the noble son of Iapetus stole it again for men from Zeus the counsellor in a hollow reed, so that Zeus who delights in thunder did not see it. But afterwards Zeus who gathers the clouds said to him in anger: "Son of Iapetus, surpassing all in cunning, you are glad that you have outwitted me and stolen fire—a great plague to you yourself and to men that shall be. But I will give men as the price for fire an evil thing in which they may all be glad of heart while they embrace their own destruction."

So said the father of men and gods, and laughed aloud. And he ordered Hephaestus make haste and mix earth with water and to put in it the voice and strength of human kind, and fashion a sweet, lovely woman-shape, like the immortal goddesses in face; and Athena to teach her needlework and the weaving of the varied web; and golden Aphrodite to shed grace upon her head and cruel longing and cares that weary the limbs. And he charged Hermes the guide, the Slayer of Argus, to put in her a shameless mind and a deceitful nature.

But when he had finished the sheer, hopeless snare, the Father sent glorious Argus-Slayer, the swift messenger of the gods, Hermes, to take it to Epimetheus as a gift. And Epimetheus did not think about what Prometheus had said to him, bidding him never take a gift of Olympian Zeus, but to send it back for fear it might prove to be something harmful to men. But he took the gift, and afterwards, when the evil thing was already his, he understood. For before this the tribes of men lived on earth remote and free from ills and hard toil and heavy sickness which bring the Fates upon men; for in misery men grow old quickly.

But the woman took off the great lid of the jar with her hands and scattered all these and her thought caused sorrow and mischief to men. Only Hope remained there in an unbreakable home within under the rim of the great jar, and did not fly out at the door; for before that, the lid of the jar stopped her, by the will of Aegis-holding Zeus who gathers the clouds. But the rest, countless plagues, wander amongst men. For earth is full of evils and the sea is full. Of themselves diseases come upon men continually by day and by night, bringing mischief to mortals silently; for wise Zeus took away speech from them. So is there no way to escape the will of Zeus. Or if you will, I will sum you up another tale well and skilfully—and remember it in your heart, how the gods and mortal men sprang from one source.

First of all the deathless gods who dwell on Olympus made a golden race of mortal men who lived in the time of Cronos when he was reigning in heaven. And they lived like gods without sorrow, remote and free from toil and grief: miserable age did not afflict them, but with legs and arms never failing, they enjoyed themselves with feasting beyond the reach of all evils. When they died, it was as though they were overcome with sleep, and they had all good things; for the fruitful earth unforced bare them fruit abundantly and without stint. They dwelled in ease and peace upon their lands with many good things, rich in flocks and loved by the blessed gods. But after earth had covered this generation—they are called pure spirits dwelling on the earth, and are kindly, delivering from harm, and guardians of mortal men; for they roam everywhere over the earth, clothed in mist and keep watch on judgements and cruel deeds, givers of wealth; for this royal right also they received.

Then they who dwell on Olympus made a second generation which was of silver and less noble by far. It was like the golden race neither in body nor in spirit. A child was brought up at his good mother's side an hundred years, an utter simpleton, playing childishly in his own home. But when they were full grown and were come to the full measure of their prime, they lived only a little time in sorrow because of their foolishness, for they could not keep from sinning and from wronging one another, nor would they serve the immortals, nor sacrifice on the holy altars of the blessed ones as it is right for men to do wherever they dwell. Then Zeus the son of Cronos was angry and put them away, because they would not give honour to the blessed gods who live on Olympus.

But when earth had covered this generation also—they are called blessed spirits of the underworld by men, and, though they are of second order, yet honour attends them also —Zeus the Father made a third generation of mortal men, a brazen race, sprung from ash-trees; and it was in no way equal to the silver age, but was terrible and strong. They loved the lamentable works of Ares and deeds of violence; they ate no bread, but were hard of heart like stone, fearful men. Great was their strength and unconquerable the arms which grew from their shoulders on their strong limbs. Their armour was of bronze, and their houses of bronze, and of bronze were their implements: there was no black iron. These were destroyed by their own hands and passed to the dank house of chill Hades, and left no name: terrible though they were, black Death seized them, and they left the bright light of the sun.

But when earth had covered this generation also, Zeus the son of Cronos made yet another, the fourth, upon the fruitful earth, which was nobler and more righteous, a god-like race of heroes who are called demigods, the race before our own, throughout the boundless earth. Grim war and dread battle destroyed a part of them, some in the land of Cadmus at seven-gated Thebe when they fought for the flocks of Oedipus, and some, when it had brought them in ships over the great sea gulf to Troy for rich-haired Helen's sake: there death's end enshrouded a part of them. But to the others father Zeus the son of Cronos gave a living and an abode apart from men, and made them dwell at the ends of earth. And they live untouched by sorrow in the islands of the blessed along the shore of deep swirling Ocean, happy heroes for whom the grain-giving earth bears honey-sweet fruit flourishing thrice a year, far from the deathless gods, and Cronos rules over them; for the father of men and gods released him from his bonds. And these last equally have honour and glory. And again far-seeing Zeus made yet another generation, the fifth, of men who are upon the bounteous earth.

If only I were not among the men of the fifth generation, but either had died before or been born afterwards. For now truly is the race of iron, and men never rest from labour and sorrow by day, and from perishing by night; and the gods shall lay sore trouble upon them. But, notwithstanding, even these shall have some good mingled with their evils. And Zeus will destroy this race of mortal men also when they come to have grey hair on the temples at their birth. The father will not agree with his children, nor the children with their father, nor guest with his host, nor comrade with comrade; nor will brother be dear to brother as before. Men will dishonour their parents as they grow old quickly, and will grumble at them, blame them with bitter words, hard-hearted, not knowing the fear of the gods. They will not repay their aged parents the cost of their nurture, for might shall be their right: and one man will sack another's city.

There will be no favour for the man who keeps his oath or for the just or for the good; but rather men will praise the evil-doer and his violent act. Strength will be right and reverence will cease to exist; and the wicked will hurt the worthy man, speaking false words against him, and will swear an oath upon them. Envy, foul-mouthed, delighting in evil, with scowling face, will go along with wretched men one and all. And then Shame and Nemesis, with their sweet forms wrapped in white robes, will go from the widely-walked earth and forsake mankind to join the company of the immortal gods: and bitter sorrows will be left for mortal men, and there will be no help against evil.

And now I will tell a story for princes who themselves understand. Thus said the hawk to the nightingale with the speckled neck, while he carried her high up among the clouds, gripped fast in his talons, and she, pierced by his curved talons, cried pitifully. In reply, he spoke spitefully: "Wretched creature, why do you cry out? One far stronger than you now grasps you, and you must go wherever I take you, songstress as you are. And if I please I will eat you, or let you go. One is a fool who tries to withstand the stronger, for one does not get the mastery and suffers pain in addition to shame." So said the swiftly flying hawk, the long-winged bird.

But you, Perses, listen to right and do not foster violence; for violence is bad for a poor man. Even the prosperous cannot easily bear its burden, but he is weighed down under it when he has fallen into delusion. The better path is to go by on the other side towards justice; for Justice outruns Outrage when she comes at length to the end of the race. But only when he has suffered does the fool learn this. For Oath keeps pace with wrong judgements. There is a noise when Justice is being dragged in the way where those who swallow bribes and give sentence with crooked judgements, take her. And she, wrapped in mist, follows to the city and haunts of the people, weeping, and bringing mischief to men, even to such as have driven her forth in that they did not deal straight with her.

But they who give straight judgements to strangers and to the men of the land, and go not aside from what is just, their city flourishes, and the people prosper in it: Peace, the nurse of children, is abroad in their land, and all-seeing Zeus never decrees cruel war against them. Neither famine nor disaster ever haunt men who do true justice; but light-heartedly they tend the fields which are all their care. The earth bears them supplies in plenty, and on the mountains the oak bears acorns upon the top and bees in the midst. Their woolly sheep are laden with fleeces; their women bear children like their parents. They flourish continually with good things, and do not travel on ships, for the grain-giving earth bears them fruit. But for those who practise violence and cruel deeds far-seeing Zeus, the son of Cronos, ordains a punishment.

Often even a whole city suffers for a bad man who sins and devises presumptuous deeds, and the son of Cronos lays great trouble upon the people, famine and plague together, so that the men perish away, and their women do not bear children, and their houses become few, through the contriving of Olympian Zeus. And again, at another time, the son of Cronos either destroys their wide army, or their walls, or else makes an end of their ships on the sea. You princes, mark well this punishment you also; for the deathless gods are near among men and mark all those who oppress their fellows with crooked judgements, and do not ignore the anger of the gods. For upon the bounteous earth Zeus has thousands of spirits, watchers of mortal men, and these keep watch on judgements and deeds of wrong as they roam, clothed in mist, all over the earth.

And there is maiden Justice, the daughter of Zeus, who is honoured and revered among the gods who dwell on Olympus, and whenever anyone hurts her with lying slander, she sits beside her father, Zeus the son of Cronos, and tells him of men's wicked heart, until the people pay for the mad folly of their princes who, evilly minded, pervert judgement and give sentence crookedly. Keep watch against this, you princes, and make straight your judgements, you who devour bribes; put crooked judgements altogether from your thoughts.

To you, foolish Perses, I will speak good sense. Wickedness can be acquired easily and in abundance: the road to her is smooth, and she lives very near us. But between us and Goodness the gods have placed the sweat of our brows: long and steep is the path that leads to her, and it is rough at the first; but when a man has reached the top, then is she easy to reach, though before that she was hard…

Do not let a flaunting woman coax and cozen and deceive you: she is after your barn. The man who trusts womankind trust deceivers… Bring home a wife to your house when you are of the right age, while you are not far short of thirty years nor much above; this is the right age for marriage. Let your wife have been grown up four years, and marry her in the fifth. Marry a maiden, so that you can teach her careful ways, and especially marry one who lives near you, but look well about you and see that your marriage will not be a joke to your neighbours. For a man wins nothing better than a good wife, and, again, nothing worse than a bad one, a greedy soul who roasts her man without fire, strong though he may be, and brings him to a raw old age.

Adapted from Hugh G. Evelyn-White, Hesiod. Theogony, and Works and Days (Cambridge, MA: Harvard University Press; London: William Heinemann Ltd., 1914)

READING 4:

Ovid's *Metamorphoses*

Publius Ovidius Naso (Ovid) was born in 43 BCE in Italy. These were tumultuous times. Civil wars had ripped the Roman Republic apart for decades until, in 30, Caesar Octavian (later called Augustus) defeated Mark Antony and became sole master of the Roman world. Ovid came from a prosperous family and influential members among Augustus' associates eventually noticed his gift in poetry. By the turn of the millennium, he had become one of the premier poets in the Roman world. Among his works, which include elegiac poems on love and the art of loving (*Amores, Ars Amatoria*) was his epic *Metamorphoses*. Sometimes amusing and sometimes dreadful, it always offers a brilliant reinterpretation of many Greek and Roman myths, in which gods, humans, animals, plants and even the stars interact and transform themselves into one another. Scholars of Greek and Roman myth have often read the *Metamorphoses* with suspicion, criticizing Ovid for his playful or apparently irreverent attitude towards stories and characters that should be "serious" and described with solemnity. More recently, *Metamorphoses* has come to be seen as one of the finest works in Roman literature, and Ovid's versions of the myths are indispensible to our study of them today.

4a) Creation and the Four Ages of Man (1. 1-144, passim)

My soul is led to sing of forms transformed to bodies new and strange! Immortal Gods, inspire my heart, for you have changed yourselves and all things! Lead my song in smooth and measured strains, from older days when earth began to this present time!

Before the ocean and the earth appeared, before the skies had overspread them all, the face of Nature in a vast expanse was nothing but Chaos, uniformly waste. It was a crude and undeveloped mass, nothing except a ponderous weight; and all jarring elements were confused and congested in a shapeless heap. The sun did not yet offer earth any light, nor did the moon renew her crescent horns; the earth was not suspended in the air exactly balanced by her heavy weight. Not far along the margin of the shores had Amphitrite stretched her lengthened arms, for all the land was mixed with sea and air. The land was soft, the sea unfit to sail, the atmosphere opaque, nothing had a proper form, strife was in everything, and all was mingled in a seething mass—heat conflicted with cold, and wet with dry and soft with hard, and mass with empty void.

Some god, or kindly Nature, ended strife - he separated the land from skies, the sea from land, the ethereal heavens from material air; and when were all evolved from that dark mass he bound the fractious parts in tranquil peace. The fiery and massless heaven leaped from the void to the heavenly summit, to which the air was next in place. The denser earth attracted greater parts and moved by its gravity sank underneath; and last of all the wide surrounding waves in deeper channels rolled around the globe.

And when this God - which one is still unknown - had carved apart that discordant mass, had reduced it to its elements, so that every part should equally combine, he rounded out the earth and molded it into a mighty globe. Then he poured forth the deeps and commanded that they should swell in the rapid winds, that they should compass every shore of earth. He also added fountains, pools and lakes, and bound with rising banks the meandering streams, which partly are absorbed and partly join the boundless ocean. Thus received into the wide expanse of uncontrolled waves, they lapped the shores instead of crooked banks. At his command the boundless plains were extended, the valleys depressed, the woods clothed in green, the stony mountains risen. And as the heavens are intersected by two broad zones on the right and two on the left, and by a central zone, consumed with fiery heat, by such a number did the careful god mark the measured weight, and thus the earth received as many climates—such heat consumes the middle zone that none may dwell in it; and two extremes are covered with deep snow; and two are placed between the hot and cold, which mixed together give a temperate climate; and over all the atmosphere suspends the air, proportioned to be heavier to ether, exactly as the weight of earth compares with that of water.

And he ordered mist to gather in the air and spread the clouds. He set the thunder that disturbs our souls, and brought the lightning on destructive winds that also blow the cold. Nor did the great designer permit these mighty winds to blow unbounded in the pathless skies, but each discordant brother fixed in their space, although his power can barely restrain their rage to rip apart the universe. At his command to far Aurora, Eurus took his way, to Nabath, Persia, and that mountain range first lit by the dawn; and Zephyr's flight was towards the evening star and peaceful shores, warm with the setting sun; and Boreas invaded Scythia and the northern snows; and Auster wafted to the distant south where clouds and rain encompass his abode. and over these he fixed the liquid sky, devoid of weight and free from earthly waste.

And scarcely had he separated these and fixed their certain bounds, when all the stars, which for a long time were pressed and hidden in the mass, began to gleam out from the heavens, and travelled, with the Gods, over bright fields of ether: and so that no part might be bereft of life the gleaming waves were filled with twinkling fish; the earth was covered with wild animals; the fluttering air was filled with birds.

But one more perfect and more blessed, a being capable of thought, intelligence to rule, was needed – man was created! Did the unknown god designing a better world make man of divine seed? Or did Prometheus take the new soil of earth (that still contained some godly element of heaven) and use it to create the race of man, first mingling it with water of new streams; so that his new creation, upright man, was made in image of commanding gods? On earth the brute creation bends its gaze, but man was given a higher expression and was commanded to behold the skies; and with an upright face may view the stars. And so it was that shapeless clay put in the form of man until then unknown to earth.

First was the Golden Age. Then goodness was natural to their hearts, as was faith. No fear of punishment was seen, for laws were neither known nor needed. No harsh decrees were fixed on brazen plates, no throng of suppliants trembled before the face of Justice. No lofty pines were cut from their heights, chopped down and braced for travelling the waves to foreign alien shores – no distant realms were known to wandering men. The towns were not entrenched for war; they had no sounding trumpets, nor horns of curving bronze, nor helmets, shields nor swords. There was no thought of martial glory - secure, a happy multitude enjoyed tranquility. Then, of her own accord, the earth produced a store of every fruit. The plough did not touch her, nor did the plowshare wound her soil. Man was content with the food given without effort, and gathered arbute fruits and wild strawberries on the mountain sides, and ripe blackberries clinging to the bush, and cherries and sweet acorns on the ground, fallen from the spreading tree of Jove. Eternal Spring! Soft-breathing Zephyrs soothed and warmly cherished buds and blooms, produced without a seed. The valleys though unplowed gave many fruits; the fields though not resown glistened white with the heavy bearded wheat: rivers flowed milk and nectar, and the trees, the very oak trees, then gave honey by themselves.

When Saturn had been banished into night and all the world was ruled by Jove supreme, the Silver Age, though not so good as gold but still surpassing yellow bronze, prevailed. Jove first reduced to years the Primal Spring, by him divided into four, unequal periods: summer, autumn, winter, spring. Then glowed with orange heat the parched air, or dangling icicles in winter froze and man stopped crouching in crude caves, while he built his homes of trees, bark entwined. Then were the grains planted in long rows, and oxen groaned beneath the heavy yoke.

The Third Age followed, called The Age of Bronze, when cruel people were inclined to arms but not to impious crimes. And last of all the ruthless and hard Age of Iron prevailed, from which malignant vein great evil sprung; and modesty and faith and truth fled, and in their place deceit and snares and frauds and violence and wicked greed, succeeded. Then the sailor spread his sails to winds unknown, and timber that long had stood on lofty mountains pierced uncharted waves. Surveyors marked anxiously with measurements the land, created free as light and air: no longer did the rich ground furnish only crops, and give due nourishment as required, men penetrated the bowels of earth and dug up wealth, the cause of all our ills – rich ores which long ago the earth had hid and removed to gloomy Stygian caves. And soon destructive iron and harmful gold were brought to light; and War, which uses both, came forth and shook with bloody grip his clashing arms. Greed burst loose—the guest was not protected from his host, the father-in-law from his own son-in-law; even brothers seldom could abide in peace. The husband threatened to destroy his wife, and she her husband: horrid stepmothers mixed the deadly poison: eager sons thought about their fathers' age. Piety was lost, and last of all the virgin deity, Astraea, vanished from the blood-stained earth.

4b) The Flood, Deucalion and Pyrrha (1. 163-415, passim)

When, from his high throne, the Son of Saturn viewed their deeds, he groaned deeply, and calling to his mind the loathsome feast Lycaon had prepared, a recent deed not commonly reported, the heart of Wondrous Jove burned with great anger and he convened a council. No delay detained the chosen gods.

When skies are clear a path is well seen on high, which men, because it is so white, have named the Milky Way. It marks a passage for the gods and leads to palace of the Thunder God, to Jove's imperial home. On either side of its wide way the noble gods are seen, inferior gods in other parts dwell, but there the potent and renowned of Heaven have fixed their homes. It is a glorious place, our most courageous verse might designate the "Palace of High Heaven."

When the Gods were seated, therefore, in its marble halls the King of all above the throng sat high, and leaning on his ivory scepter, three times and once again he shook his awful locks, an in doing so he moved the earth, and seas and stars, and thus indignantly began to speak: "The time when serpent-footed giants strove to fix their hundred arms on captive Heaven, not more than this event could cause alarm for my dominion of the universe. Although it was a savage enemy, yet we warred with a unity derived of one. Now must I utterly destroy this mortal race wherever Nereus roars around the world. Indeed, by the Infernal Streams that glide through Stygian groves beneath the world, I swear it. Every method has been tried. The knife must cut immedicable wounds, so that disease does not infect untainted parts. Beneath my sway are lesser gods and fauns, nymphs, rustic deities, sylvans of the hills, satyrs; all these, unworthy of Heaven's abodes, we should at least permit to dwell on earth that we gave to them. What do you think, gods?"

With shouts some approved the words of Jove and added fuel to his wrath, while others gave assent: but all lamented and questioned the idea of earth deprived of mortals. Who could offer frankincense upon the altars? Would he suffer earth to be despoiled by hungry beasts of prey? Such idle questions of the state of man the King of Gods did not allow, but granted soon to people earth with a miraculous race, unlike the first. And now his thunderbolts Jove scattered far and wide, but he feared the flames, unnumbered, sacred ether might ignite and burn the center of the universe, and he remembered in the scroll of fate, that there is a time appointed when the sea and earth and Heavens shall melt, and fire destroy the universe built of great labour. Such weapons forged by the skill of Cyclops he laid aside for different punishment— for straightway he preferred to overwhelm the mortal race beneath deep waves and storms from every raining sky.

And instantly he shut the Northwind in Aeolian caves, and every other wind that might dispel the gathering clouds. He ordered the Southwind blow – the Southwind flew abroad with dripping wings, concealing in the gloom his awful face: the drenching rain descended from his wet beard and hoary locks; dark clouds were on his brows and from his wings and garments dripped the dews: his great hands pressed the overhanging clouds; loudly the thunders rolled, the torrents poured; Iris, the messenger of Juno, clad in many-coloured clothes, drew upward the steaming moisture to renew the clouds. The standing grain was beaten to the ground, the farmer's crops were scattered in the mire, and he bewailed the long year's fruitless toil. The wrath of Jove was not content with powers that emanate from Heaven; he brought to aid his bluish brother, lord of flowing waves, who called upon the Rivers and the Streams: and when they entered his pearled abode, Neptune, their ancient ruler, thus began; "A long appeal is not needed, pour forth in a rage of power, open up your fountains, rush over obstacles, let every stream pour forth in boundless floods." Thus he commanded, and with none dissenting, all the River gods returned, and opened up their fountains rolled tumultuous to the deep unfruitful sea.

And Neptune with his trident struck the Earth, which trembling with unexpected throes heaved up the sources of her bare waters, and through her open plains the rapid irresistible rivers rushed onward, bearing the waving grain, the budding groves, the houses, sheep and men, and holy temples, with their sacred urns. The mansions that remained, resisting vast and total ruin, deepening waves concealed and overwhelmed their tottering towers in the flood and whirling gulf. And now in one vast expanse, the land and sea were mingled in the waste of endless waves—a sea without a shore.

One desperate man seized on the nearest hill; another sat in his curved boat, plying the long oar where he might have plowed. Another sailed above his grain, above his hidden dwelling; and another hooked a fish that sported a leafy elm. Possibly an anchor dropped in green fields, or curving keels were pushed through tangled vines; and where the graceful goat enjoyed the green, unsightly seals now rested. Beneath the waves were wondering Nereids, viewing cities, groves and houses. Dolphins darting between the trees, meshed in the twisted branches, beat against the shaken oak trees. There the sheep swim with the frightened wolf, the surging waves float tigers and lions. His lightning shock the wild boar, nor the stag's fleet footed speed resist it. The wandering bird, seeking shady groves and hidden vales, with wearied trap droops into the sea. The waves increasingly surge above the hills, and rising waters dash on mountain tops. Thousands are swept away by the waves, and those the waters spare, for lack of food, starvation slowly overcomes at last.

When Jupiter beheld the globe in ruin, swept with wasting waves, and when he saw one man of thousands left, one helpless woman left of thousands alone, both innocent and worshiping the gods, he scattered all the clouds; he blew away the great storms by the cold northwind. Once more the earth appeared to heaven and the skies appeared to earth. The fury of the seas abated, for the Ocean-ruler laid his trident down and pacified the waves, and called on azure Triton. Triton arose above the waves, his shoulders mailed in purple shells. He bade the Triton blow, blow in his echoing shell the known signal, to recall the wandering streams and rivers: a hollow wreathed trumpet, tapering wide and slender stemmed, the Triton took the seas and wound the pearly shell at midmost sea. Between the rising and the setting suns the wild notes echoed from shore to shore, and as it touched his lips, wet with the brine beneath his dripping beard, it sounded retreat: and all the waters of the land and sea obeyed. The fountains heard and ceased to flow, the waves subsided, hidden hills rose, the shores of ocean emerged, channels filled with flowing streams, the soil appeared, the land increased its surface as the waves decreased, and after several days the trees showed forth, with ooze on bending boughs and naked tops.

And all the wasted globe was now restored, but as he viewed the vast and silent world Deucalion wept and said to Pyrrha, "O sister! Wife! Alone of woman left! My kindred in descent and origin! Dearest companion of my marriage bed, doubly joined by common danger – of all the dawn and evening of earth, only you and I are left, for the deep sea has taken the rest! And what prevents the tide from overwhelming us? Remaining clouds frighten us. How could you endure your fears if you alone were rescued by this fate, and who would then console your bitter grief? Rest assured, if you were buried beneath the waves, I would follow you and be with you! Oh if only by my father's art I might restore the people, and inspire this clay to take the form of man. Alas, thus the gods decreed and we alone are living!"

Thus Deucalion's lamented to Pyrrha, and they wept. And after he had spoken, they resolved to ask the aid of sacred oracles, and so they hastened to Cephissian waves which was filled with mud in its known channels. To this place, when their robes and brows were well sprinkled with libation, they turned their footsteps to the sacred shrine of Themis. Its gables were fouled with reeking moss and on its altars every fire was cold. But when the two of them had reached the temple steps they fell upon the earth, inspired with awe, and kissed the cold stone with their trembling lips, and said: "If righteous prayers appease the Gods, and if the wrath of high celestial powers may be turned away, declare, O Themis! How might humanity be raised from destruction? O gentle goddess, help this dying world!"

Moved by their supplications, she replied: "Depart from me and veil your brows; take off your robes, and cast behind you as you go, the bones of your great mother." Long they stood in dumbfounded: Pyrrha, the first to recall her voice, refused the command and with trembling lips implored the goddess to forgive – she feared to violate her mother's bones and displease her sacred spirit. They often pondered the words involved in such obscurity, repeating them often: and thus Deucalion spoke to Epimetheus' daughter with soothing seriousness: "Oracles are just and do not urge evil deeds. Our "mother" must be the Earth, and I may guess that the stones of earth are bones that we should cast behind us as we go."

And although Pyrrha was moved by his words, she hesitated to complym and both doubted the purpose of the oracle, but thought no harm could come from trying. They, descending from the temple, veiled their heads and loosed their robes and threw some stones behind them. Beyond belief, if earlier ages had not witnessed it, the hard and rigid stones assumed a softer form, becoming larger as their brittle nature changed to milder substance, until the shape of man appeared, imperfect, faintly outlined first, as a marble statue chiseled in the rough. The soft moist parts were changed to softer flesh, the hard and brittle substance into bones, the veins retained their ancient name. And now the supreme gods ordained that every stone Deucalion threw should take the form of man, and those cast by Pyrrha should assume woman's form: so are we tough in endurance, and we prove by our labour and our deeds from what source we sprung.

4c) Jupiter and Io (1. 567-746, passim)

There is a grove in Thessaly, enclosed on every side with precipitous crags, on which a forest grows—and this is called the Vale of Tempe. Through this valley flows the River Peneus, white with foaming waves, that issue from the foot of Pindus, whence with sudden fall up gather steamy clouds that sprinkle mist upon the circling trees, and far away with mighty roar resound. It is the abode, the solitary home, that mighty River Peneus, where deep in the gloom of his rocky cavern, he resides and rules the flowing waters and the water nymphs abiding there. Inachus alone is absent, hidden in his obscure cave, deepening his waters with his tears—most wretchedly bewailing, for he believes his daughter, Io, is lost. Whether she yet lives or roam as a spirit in the netherworld he dares not even guess but dreads.

For Jove not long before had seen her while returning from her father's stream, and said; "Maiden, worthy of immortal Jove, although some happy mortal's chosen bride, behold these shades of overhanging trees, and seek their cool shadows while the sun is glowing in the height of middle skies…" and as he spoke he pointed out the groves, "But if the dens of wild beasts frighten you, with safety you may enter the deep woods, conducted by a god—not a god of small repute, indeed, but in the care of him who holds the heavenly scepter in his hand and throws the thunder bolts. Reject me not!" For while he spoke she fled, and swiftly left behind the fields of Lerna, and Lyrcea's arbours, where the trees are planted thickly. But the God called forth a heavy shadow, which covered the wide extended earth, and stopped her flight, and he ravished in that cloud.

Meanwhile, the goddess Juno gazed down on earth's expanse, and with wonder saw the clouds as dark as night enfold those middle fields while day was bright above. She was convinced the clouds were not composed by river mist nor raised from marshy fens. Suspicious now, for she often detected the affairs of her spouse, she glanced around to find her absent husband, and quite convinced that he was far from heaven, she thus exclaimed; "This cloud deceives my mind, or Jove has wronged me." From the dome of heaven she glided down and stood upon the earth, and commanded the clouds to recede. But Jove perceived the coming of his queen. He had transformed the lovely Io, so that she appeared as a milk-white heifer—formed so beautiful and fair that envious Juno gazed on her. She asked: "From whose land do you come? What fields?" As if she guessed no knowledge of the truth. And Jupiter, false hearted, said the cow was born of the earth, for he feared his queen might question the owner's name. Juno asked for the heifer as a gift – what then was the Father of the Gods to do? It would be cruel to sacrifice his own beloved to a rival's wrath. Although refusal must imply his guilt, the shame and love of her almost prevailed. But if a present of such little worth were now denied to the sharer of his bed, the partner of his birth, it would prove that the earth born heifer was other than she seemed—and so he gave his mistress up to Juno.

Juno, mindful of Jove's cunning art, so that he would not change her to her human form, gave the unhappy heifer to the charge of Argus, the watchman, whose head was circled with a hundred glowing eyes; of which but two did slumber in their turn while all the others kept on watch and guard. Whichever way he stood his gaze was fixed on Io—even if he turned away, his watchful eyes still remained on Io. He let her feed by day; but when the sun was under the deep world he shut her up, and tied a rope around her tender neck. She fed upon green leaves and bitter herbs and slept on the cold ground—too often bare, she could not rest upon a cushioned couch. She drank the troubled waters. Hoping for aid, she tried to stretch imploring arms to Argus, but all in vain, for now no arms remained; the sound of bellowing was all she heard, and she was frightened by her own voice. While in former days she loved to roam and sport, she wandered by the banks of Inachus: there reflected in the stream she saw her horns and, startled, turned and fled. And Inachus and all her sister Naiads did not recognize her, although she followed them, although she allowed them to touch her sides and praise her. When the ancient Inachus gathered sweet herbs and offered them to her, she licked his hands, kissing her father's palms, nor could she restrain her falling tears. If only words as well as tears would flow, she might implore his aid and tell her name and all her sad misfortune; but, instead, she traced in dust the letters of her name with cloven hoof; and thus her sad status was known.

"Ah wretched me! " her father cried, and as he clung around her horns and neck repeated while she groaned, "Ah wretched me! Are you my daughter, searched for in all lands? When you were lost I could not grieve for you as now that you are found; your sighs instead of words heave up from your deep breast, your longings answer give me. I once prepared for you the wedding and bridal chamber, in my ignorance, since my first hope was for a son in law, and then I dreamed of children from the match. But now the herd must provide you with a mate, and all your children will be of that herd. Oh, if only a righteous death would end my grief! It is a dreadful thing to be a river god! Behold, the lethal gate of death is shut against me, and my growing grief must last throughout eternity." While he moaned, starry Argus came there, and took Io from her lamenting father. From there he led his charge to other pastures; and took her away to a lofty mountain, where he could always watch her, undisturbed.

Jupiter could no longer endure to witness Io's suffering. He called his son, whom Maia, brightest of the Pleiades brought forth, and commanded him slay the star-eyed guard, Argus. He seized his sleep-compelling wand and fastened wings on his swift feet, and deftly fixed his brimmed hat on his head: Mercury, the favoured son of Jove, descending to the earth from heaven's plains, took off his cap and wings, although he still retained his wand with which he drove through pathless wilds some stray she goats, and as a shepherd, piping on reeds melodious tunes. Argus, delighted with the charming sound of this new art said; "Whoever you are, sit with me on this stone beneath the trees in cooling shade, while we watch the tended flock and abundant herbs; for you can see the shade is fit for shepherds."

In response, Mercury sat down beside the guardian and spoke of various things—passing the slow hours. Then, he softly piped on the reeds to lull those ever-watchful eyes asleep. Now perceiving that Argus' eyes were dimmed in sleepy doze, he hushed his voice and touched the drooping eyelids with his magic wand, compelling slumber. Then without delay he struck the sleeper with his crescent sword, where neck and head are joined, and hurled his head, blood dripping, down the rocks and rugged cliff. Argus was laid low, his hundred eyes dark, his many orbed lights extinguished in the universal gloom that night surrounds. But Saturn's daughter spread his eyes on the feathers of her bird, the peacock, decorating its tail with starry gems.

Juno hastened, inflamed with towering rage, to vent her wrath on Io, and she raised in thought and vision of the girl a dreadful Fury. She planted in her breast invisible and pitiless stings, and drove her wandering throughout the world. The furthest limit of her toiling way, O Nile, you remained. When she reached this river, and placed her tired knees on that river's edge, she laid there, and as she raised her neck and looked upward to the stars, and groaned and wept and mournfully bellowed: trying to plead, by all the means she had, that Jupiter might end her miseries. Remorseful Jove embraced his wife, and begged her to end the punishment: "Fear not," he said, "For she shall trouble you no more." He spoke, and called on bitter Styx to hear his oath.

And now regal Juno, pacified, permitted Io to resume her form – at once the hair fell from her snowy sides; the horns subsided, her dilate pupils decreased, the opening of her jaws contracted; hands appeared and shoulders, and each transformed hoof became five nails. And every mark or form that gave the appearance of a heifer changed, except her fair white skin; and the glad Nymph was raised erect and stood upon her feet. But long the very thought of speech, that she might bellow as a heifer, filled her mind with terror, till the words so long forgot for some sufficient cause were tried once more.

4d) Jupiter and Europa (2. 844-865; 3.1-3)

Erotic love cannot abide the majesty of kings, not can love dwell for long in the same place. Upon a throne Jove laid aside his glorious dignity, for he assumed the form of a bull and mingled with the bulls in the groves, his colour white as virgin snow, unblemished, untainted by the watery Southern Wind. His neck was thick with muscles, dew hung between his shoulders; and his polished horns, so small and beautifully set, appeared to be formed by the artifice of man – fashioned as fair and more transparent than a clear gem. His forehead was not lowered for attack, nor was there fury in his open eyes, the love of peace was in his countenance. When Europa beheld his beauty and mild eyes, the daughter of Agenor was amazed, but, daring not to touch him, she stood apart from him until her virgin fears were quieted. Then, near him, she offered fragrant flowers in her hand, tempting his gentle mouth. And then the loving god in his great joy kissed her sweet hands, and could not abide his own will.

Jove then began to frisk upon the grass, or laid his snow-white side on the smooth sand, yellow and golden. As her courage grew he gave his breast one moment for caress, or bent his head for garlands, wreathed for his polished horns. The royal maid, unaware of what she was doing, at last sat down upon the bull's broad back. Then, slowly, the god moved from the land and from the shore, and placed his feet, that seemed but shining hoofs, in shallow water by the sandy beach; and without a moment resting, he bore her from there, across the surface of the Sea, while she, frightened gazed upon the shore so quickly receding. And she held his horn with her right hand, and, steadied by the left, held on his muscular back—and in the breeze her waving garments fluttered as they went. Now Jupiter had not revealed himself, nor thrown aside the form of a bull, until they stood upon the fields of Crete.

4e) Actaeon and Diana (3. 133-250, passim)

Nor should we say, "He leads a happy life," until after death the funeral rites are paid. There is a valley called Gargaphia; sacred to Diana, dense with pine trees and cypress, where, deep in the woods that fringed the valley's edge, was hollowed in frail sandstone and the soft white pumice of the hills an arch, so perfect it seemed the art of man, for Nature's ingenious touch had so fairly formed the stone, making the entrance of a grotto. Upon the right a clear fountain flowed and babbled, as its lucid channel spread into a pure pool edged with tender grass. Here, when wearied by exciting sport, the Forest goddess loved to come and bathe her virgin beauty in the crystal pool. After Diana entered with her nymphs, she gave her javelin, quiver and her bow to one accustomed to the care of arms; she gave her mantle to another nymph who stood near by her as she took it off, and two others loosed the sandals from her feet. And while they bathed Diana in their streams, Actaeon, wandering through the unknown woods, entered the area of that sacred grove, with uncertain steps wandered he as fate had directed. As soon as he entered where the clear springs welled or trickled from the grotto's walls, the nymphs, now ready for the bath, beheld him, struck at their breasts, and made the woods echo, suddenly shrieking. Quickly they gathered to shield Diana with their naked forms, but she stood head and shoulders taller than her guards, as clouds bright-tinted by the slanting sun, or purple-dyed Aurora, so appeared Diana's body when she was seen.

Oh, how she wished her arrows were at hand! But only having water, this she took and threw it at him, and sprinkled with avenging stream his hair, and said these words, foreshadowing his future woe; "Go tell, if your tongue can tell the tale, how your bold eyes saw me stripped of all my robes." She threatened no more, but she fixed the horns of a great stag firmly on his sprinkled brows, she lengthened out his neck; she made his ears sharp at the top, she changed his hands and feet, lengthened his arms, and covered him with dappled hair—his courage turned to fear. The brave son of Autonoe fled, and marveled that he ran so swiftly. He saw his horns reflected in a stream and would have said, "Ah, wretched me!" but now he had no voice, and could only groan: large tears ran trickling down his face, transformed in every feature. Yet, his human understanding remained clear, and he wondered what he should attempt to do: should he return to his ancestral palace, or plunge into vast depths of forest wilds? Fear made him hesitate to trust the woods, and shame deterred him from going homeward.

While pondering in this way, his own dogs spotted him there. All eager for their prey, the pack climbs rocks, cliffs and crags, where paths are steep, where there are no roads. He flees by routes so often pursued but now, alas, his flight is from his own! He would have cried, "Behold your master! It is I, Actaeon!" Words failed him.

The yelping pack pressed on. First Blackmane seized and tore his master's back, Savage the next, then Rover's teeth were clinched deep in his shoulder. These, though late, cut through a by-path and arriving first clung to their master till the pack arrived. The whole pack fastened on their master's flesh until there was no place for others. Groaning, he made frightful sounds that no human voice could utter, nor a stag, and filled the hills with dismal moans. And just like a suppliant, he fell down to the ground upon his trembling knees, and turned his stricken eyes on his own dogs, entreating them to spare him from their fangs.

But his companions, oblivious to his plight, urged on the swift pack with their hunting cries. They sought Actaeon and they vainly called, "Actaeon! Hey, Actaeon!" just as though he was away from them. Each time they called he turned his head. And when they made fun of him, whose absence denied him the joys of sport, how much he wished laziness had held him from his ravenous pack. Oh, how much! Better it is to see the hunt, and the fierce dogs, than to feel their savage deeds! They gathered round him, and they fixed their snouts deep in his flesh: tore him to pieces, he whose features only resembled a stag. It is said Diana's fury raged with no end until the torn flesh ceased to live.

4f) Tireisias (3. 317-338, passim)

It is said that Jupiter, in a careless mood, indulged too freely in the nectar cup; and having laid aside all weighty thoughts, joked with Juno as she sat beside him. A little too freely the god said; "Who doubts the truth? A female's sexual pleasure is a great delight, much greater than the sexual pleasure of a male." Juno refuted this, and it was then agreed to ask Tiresias to declare the truth, since he was alone in knowing both male and female joys. For wandering in a green wood he had seen two serpents coupling, and he took his staff and sharply struck them, until they broke and fled. 'Tis marvelous, that instant he became a woman from a man, and so remained while seven autumns passed. When eight were told, again he saw them in their former plight, and thus he spoke; "Since such a power was wrought, by one stroke of a staff my sex was changed—again I strike!" And even as he struck the same two snakes, his former sex returned; his manhood was restored.—as both agreed to choose him umpire of the sportive strife, he gave decision in support of Jove; from this the disappointment Juno felt surpassed all reason, and enraged, decreed eternal night should seal Tiresias' eyes.—immortal Deities may never turn decrees and deeds of other Gods to naught, but Jove, to recompense his loss of sight, endowed him with the gift of prophecy.

4g) Arachne (6. 10-145, passim)

Arachne in a mountain town had grown by skill so famous in the Land of Lydia, that unnumbered, curious nymphs eager to witness her dexterity deserted the lush vineyards of Timolus; or even left the cool and flowing streams of bright Pactolus, to admire the cloth, or to observe her deftly spinning wool. So graceful was her motion then, that one might well believe how much Minerva had instructed her. But this Arachne always would deny, displeased to share her fame, and she said, "Let her contend in art with me; and if her skill prevails, I then will forfeit my claim!"

Minerva heard about this, and came to her, disguised with long grey hair, and with a staff to steady her weak limbs. She seemed a feeble woman, very old, and quavered as she said, "Old age is not the cause of every ill – experience comes with lengthened years. Therefore, you should not despise my words. It is no harm in you to long for praise of mortals, when your nimble hands are spinning the soft wool, but you should not deny Minerva's skill and you should pray that she may pardon you, for she will grant you pardon if you ask." Arachne, scowling with an scornful face, looked at the goddess as she dropped her thread. She hardly could restrain her threatening hand, and, trembling in her anger, she replied to disguised Minerva: "Silly fool, worn out and witless in your senility, a great age is your great misfortune! Let your daughter and your son's wife – if the Gods have blessed you – let them profit by your words. My knowledge is sufficient, and you need not believe that your advice does any good, for I am quite unchanged in my opinion. Be gone! Advise your goddess to come here herself, and not avoid the contest!" Instantly, the goddess said, "Minerva comes to you!" And with those brief words, put aside the shape of the old woman, and revealed herself as divine Minerva. All the other Nymphs and matrons of Mygdonia worshiped her, but not Arachne, who stood defiant, although at first she flushed up, then went pale, then blushed again, reluctant. Just as, at first, Aurora rises and, quickly when the glorious sun comes up, the sky pales into white. She even rushed upon her own destruction, for she would not give up her desire to gain victory. Nor did the daughter of almighty Jove decline, disdaining to delay with words, she did not hesitate.

Minerva wove the Athenian Hill of Mars, where ancient Cecrops built his citadel, and showed the old contest for which it would be named. Twelve celestial Gods surrounded Jupiter, on lofty thrones, and all their features were so nicely drawn, that each could be distinguished: Jupiter appeared as king of those judging gods, Neptune, guardian of the sea, was shown contending with Minerva. As he struck the Rock with his long trident, a wild horse sprang forth which he bequeathed to man. He claimed his right to name the city for that gift. And then she wove a portrait of herself, bearing a shield, and in her hand a lance, sharp-pointed, and a helmet on her head – her breast well-guarded by her Aegis – there she struck her spear into the fertile earth, from which a branch of olive seemed to sprout, pale with new clustered fruits. And those twelve Gods, appeared to judge, that olive as a gift surpassed the horse which Neptune gave to man.

And, so that Arachne, rival of her fame, might learn the madness of her attempt by seeing the great deeds of ancient tales and what award hubris must receive, Minerva wove four corners with life scenes of contest, brightly colored, but small in size. In one of these was shown the snow-clad mountains, Rhodope, and Haemus, which for punishment were changed from human beings to those rigid forms, when they aspired to rival the gods. And in another corner she described that Pygmy, whom the angry Juno changed from queen to a crane. Because she thought herself an equal of the living gods, she was commanded to wage cruel wars upon her former subjects. In the third, she wove the story of Antigone, who dared compare herself to Juno, queen of Jupiter, and showed her as she was transformed into a silly chattering stork, that praised her beauty, with her ugly beak. Despite the powers of Troy and her lord Laomedon, her shoulders fledged white wings. And so, the third part finished, there was lone corner left, where Minerva deftly worked the story of the father, Cinyras, as he was weeping on the temple steps, which once had been his daughter's living limbs. And she adorned the border with designs of peaceful olive – her devoted tree – which having shown it, she completed the work.

Arachne, of Maeonia, wove at first the story of Europa, as the bull deceived her, and so perfect was her art that it seemed a real bull in real waves. Europa seemed to look back towards the land which she had left, and call in her alarm to her companions, and as if she feared the touch of dashing waters, to draw up her timid feet, while she was sitting on the bull's back. And she wove Asteria seized by the assaulting eagle, and beneath the swan's white wings showed Leda lying by the stream, and showed Jove dancing as a Satyr, when he sought the beautiful Antiope, whom was given twins. And how he appeared as Amphitryon when he deceived Alcmena, and how he courted lovely Danae, luring her as a gleaming shower of gold, and poor Aegina, hidden in his flame, Jove as a shepherd with Mnemosyne, and beautiful Proserpina, deceived by a spotted snake. And in her web, Arachne wove the scenes of Neptune, who was shown first as a bull, when he was deep in love with virgin Arne, then as Enipeus when the giant twins, the Aloidae, were bor, and as the ram, the deceiving Theophane, as a horse loved by the fruitful Ceres, golden haired, all-fruitful mother of the yellow grain, and as the bird that hovered round snake-haired Medusa, mother of the winged horse, and as the dolphin, playing with the Nymph, Melantho. All of these were woven true to life, in proper shades. And there she showed Apollo, when disguised in various forms: as when he seemed a farmer, and as when he wore hawk-wings, and then the orange skin of a great lion, and once more when he deluded Isse, as a shepherd boy. And there was Bacchus, when he was disguised as a large cluster of fictitious grapes, deluding by that wile the beautiful Erigone. And Saturn, as a steed, begetter of the dual-natured Chiron. And then Arachne, to complete her work, wove all around the web a patterned edge of interlacing flowers and ivy leaves.

Minerva could not find a fleck or flaw – even Envy cannot censure perfect art – and enraged because Arachne had such skill, she ripped apart her weaving, and ruined all the scenes that showed those wicked actions of the Gods, and with her boxwood shuttle in her hand, struck the unhappy mortal on her head – struck sharply three times, and even once again. Arachne's spirit, pretending not to suffer such and insult, brooded, till she tied a cord around her neck, and hung herself. Minerva, moved to pity at the sight, sustained and saved her from that bitter death, but, still angry, pronounced another doom: "Although I grant you life, most wicked one, your fate shall be to dangle on a cord, and your posterity forever shall take your example, so that your punishment may last forever!" Even as she spoke, before withdrawing from her victim's sight, she sprinkled her with an extract of herbs of Hecate. At once all hair fell off, her nose and ears remained not, and her head shrunk rapidly in size, as well as all her body, leaving her tiny. Her slender fingers gathered to her sides as long thin legs, and all her other parts were quickly absorbed in her abdomen, from where she vented a fine thread, and ever since, Arachne, as a spider, weaves her web.

4h) Niobe (6. 146-312, passim)

Niobe had known Arachne long before, when in Maeonia near to Mount Sipylus, but the sad fate which overtook Arachne, was lost on her. She never ceased her own boasting and refused to honor the great gods. So many things increased her pride: She loved to boast of her husband's skill, their noble family, the rising grandeur of their kingdom. Such facts were great delights to her, but nothing could exceed the arrogant way she boasted of her children, and in truth, Niobe might have been judged on earth the happiest mother of mankind, if pride had not destroyed her mind.

And while they worship, Niobe comes there, surrounded with a troup that follow her, and most conspicuous in her purple robe, bright with inwoven threads of yellow gold. "Madness" she said, "has incited you to worship some imagined gods of Heaven, which you have only heard of. Come, explain to me, why Latona is worshiped and adored, while frankincense is not offered to me? For my divinity is known to you. "Tantalus was my father, who alone approached the tables of the Gods in heaven. My mother, sister of the Pleiades, was daughter of huge Atlas, who supports the world upon his shoulders! I can boast of Jupiter as father of my husband, I count him also as my father-in-law. We rule together all the people that our walls encompass and defend. In my features you can see the beauty of a goddess, but above that majesty is all the glory due to me, the mother of my seven sons and daughters seven. And the time will come when by their marriage they will magnify the circle of my invincible power. But, suppose a few of my fair children should be taken! Even deprived in such a way, I could not be reduced to only two, as this Latona, who, might quite as well be childless! Forget this sacrifice. Make haste! Cast off the wreathing laurels from your brows!" They plucked the garlands from their hair, and left the sacrifice, obedient to her will, although in gentle murmurs they adored the goddess Niobe had so defamed.

Latona, furious when she heard the speech, flew swiftly to the highest peak of Cynthus, and spoke to her two children in these words: "Behold your mother, proud of having borne such glorious children! I will yield prestige before no goddess, except immortal Juno alone! I have been insulted, and driven for all ages from my own altars, devoted to me by tradition, and so must languish through eternity, unless sustained by you. Nor is this all; that daughter of Tantalus, bold Niobe, has added curses to her evil deeds, and with a tongue as wicked as her husband's, has raised her base children over mine. She has even called me childless! A sad fate more surely should be hers! Oh, I beg" – but Phoebus answered her, "No more complaint is necessary, for it only serves to hinder the swift action of her doom." And with the same words Phoebe answered her. And having spoken, they descended through the shielding shadows of surrounding clouds, and hovered on the citadel of Cadmus.

There, far below them, was a level plain that swept around those walls, where trampling horses, with horny hoofs, and multiple wheels, had beaten a wide track. And on the field the older sons of Niobe on steeds decorated with bright dyes and rich harnesses with studded gold, were circling. One of these, Ismenus, first-born of his mother, while controlling his fleet courser's foaming mouth, cried out, "Ah wretched me!" A shaft had pierced the middle of his breast; and as the reins dropped slowly on the rapid horse's neck, his drooping form fell forward to the ground. Not far from him, his brother, Sipylus, could hear the whistling of a fatal shaft, and in his fright urged on the racing steed: as when the watchful pilot, sensible of storms approaching, crowds on sail, hoping to catch a momentary breeze, just so he fled, urging an impetuous flight. But while he fled, the unerring shaft flew, transfixed him with its quivering death; struck where the neck supports the head and the sharp point protruded from his throat. In his swift flight, as he was leaning forward, he was struck, and, rolling over the wild horse's neck, he pitched to the ground and stained it with his blood.

The rumors of an awful tragedy, the wailings of sad Niobe's loved friends, the terror of her grieving relatives, all gave some knowledge of her sudden loss. But so bewildered and enraged was her mind, that she could hardly realize that the gods had privilege to dare against her power. Nor would she, until her lord, Amphion, thrust his sword deep in his own breast, by which his life and anguish both were ended in dark night. Alas, proud Niobe, once arrogant queen! Proud Niobe, she fell upon the bodies of her sons, and in a frenzy of maternal grief, kissed their unfeeling lips. Then to Heaven with accusing arms, railed against her enemy: "Enjoy your revenge! Latona, enjoy your rage! Yes, let my lamentations be your joy! Go, satiate your hard heart with death! Are not my seven sons all dead? Am I not waiting to be carried to my grave? Exult and triumph, my victorious foe! Victorious? No! Much more remains to me in all my utmost sorrow, than to you, you gloater upon vengeance – undismayed, I stand victorious in my Field of Woe!"

No sooner had she spoken, than the cord twanged from the ever-ready bow, and all who heard the fatal sound again were filled with fear, except fo Niobe, bold in her misery, defiant in misfortune. Clothed in black, the sisters of the stricken brothers stood, with hair disheveled, by the funeral biers. And one, while plucking from her brother's heart a shaft, swooned unto death, and fell on her face, on her dear brother's corpse. Another girl, while she consoled her mother, suddenly was stricken with an unseen, deadly wound, and doubled over in convulsions, closed her lips, held them tight, until both breath and life were gone. Another vainly rushed away from death – she met it, and pitched head-first to the ground. And still another died upon her corpse, while another vainly sought a secret death, and,then another slipped beyond's life's boundary. So, altogether, six of seven died, each victim stricken in a different way. One child remained. Then, in a frenzy, the mother, as she covered her with all her garments and her body, wailed, "Oh, leave me this one child, the youngest of them all! My darling daughter, only leave me one!" But even while she was entreating for its life, the life was taken from her only child.

Childless, she crouched beside her slaughtered sons, her lifeless daughters, and her husband's corpse. The breeze not even moved her fallen hair, a chill of marble spread upon her flesh, beneath her pale, set brows, her eyes did not move, her bitter tongue turned stiff in her hard jaws, her lovely veins congealed, and her stiff neck and rigid hands could neither bend nor move. Her limbs and body, all were changed to stone. Yet forever would she weep, and as her tears were falling, she was carried from the place, enveloped in a storm and mighty wind, far, to her native land, where fixed upon a mountain summit she dissolves in tears, and to this day the marble drips with tears.

4i) Marsyas (6. 383-400, passim)

The Satyr Marsyas, when he played the flute in rivalry against Apollo's lyre, lost that audacious contest and, alas! His life was forfeited, for, they had agreed that the one who lost should be the victor's prey. And, as Apollo punished him, he cried, "Ahh! why are you now tearing me apart? A flute has not the value of my life!" Even as he shrieked out in his agony, his living skin was ripped off from his limbs, till his whole body was a gaping wound, with nerves and veins and viscera exposed. But all the weeping people of that land, and all the Fauns and Sylvan Deities, and all the Satyrs, and Olympus, his loved pupil – even then renowned in song – and all the Nymphs, lamented his sad fate. And all the shepherds, roaming on the hills, lamented as they tended fleecy flocks. And all those falling tears, on fruitful Earth, descended to her deepest veins, as drip the moistening dews,—and, gathering as a fount, turned upward from her secret-winding caves, to rise, sparkling, in the sun-kissed air, the clearest river in the land of Phrygia, through which it swiftly flows between steep banks down to the sea. And, therefore, from his name, it is called "The Marsyas" to this very day.

4k) Jason and Medea (7. 1-158, passim)

Over the storm-tossed waves, the Argonauts had sailed in the Argo, their long ship to where King Phineus, needy in his old age, reigned, deprived of sight and feeble. When the sons of Boreas had landed on the shore, and seen the Harpies snatching from the king his nourishment, befouling it with obscene beaks, they drove those human-vultures away. And having suffered hardships and great toils, after the day they rescued the sad king from the vile Harpies, those twin valiant youths, Zetes and Calais came with their chief, the mighty Jason, where the River Phasis flows. From the green margin of that river, all the crew of Argonauts led by Jason went to the king Aeetes and asked for the Golden Fleece, that he received from Phryxus. When they had bargained with him, full of tricks he offered to restore the Golden Fleece only to those who might to him return, victorious from hard labors of great risk.

Medea, the king's daughter, near his throne, saw Jason, leader of the Argonauts, as he was pressing to secure the prize, and loved at first sight with a consuming flame. Although she struggled to suppress her love, she was unable to restrain herself. And she says to herself, "But why should I cry out to the gods to save him from such suffering, when, by my actions and my power, I myself may shield him from all such evils? Such a decision would wreck the kingdom of my father, and through me the wily stranger would escape from him, and spreading to the wind his sails he would forget and leave me to my fate. Oh, if he should forget my sacrifice, and prefer those who neglected him, let him then perish in his treachery! But these are idle thoughts: his bearing reveals innate nobility and grace, that should dispel all fear of treachery, and guarantee his ever-faithful heart. The Gods will witness our united souls, and he shall pledge his faith. Secure with it, my fear will be removed. Be ready, then, and make a virtue of necessity: your Jason owes himself to you; and he must join you in true wedlock. Then you shall be celebrated through the land of Greece, by mobs of women, for the man you saved."

Then, to an ancient altar of the goddess named Hecate, Perse's daughter made her way in the deep shadows of a forest. She was confident in her purpose now, and all the flames of vanquished passion had died down, but when she saw the son of Jason, dying flames leaped up again. Her cheeks grew red, then all her face went pale again, as a small spark when, hid beneath the ashes, if fed by a breath of wind grows and regains its strength, as it is fanned to life, so now her love that had been smoldering, and which you would have thought was almost dead, when she had see again his manly youth, blazed up once more. For on that day his graceful person seemed as glorious as a god, and as she gazed, and fixed her eyes upon his expression, her frenzy so conquered, that she was convinced that he was not a mortal. And her eyes were fascinated, and she could not turn away from him. But when he spoke to her, and promised marriage, grasping her right hand, she answered, as her eyes filled with tears; "I see what I will do, and ignorance of truth will not be my undoing now, but love itself. By my assistance you shall be preserved, but when preserved, fulfill your promise." He swore that she could trust in him. Then by the goddess of the triple form, called Diana, Trivia, or Luna, and by her sacred groves and temples, he vowed, and by the hallowed Sun that sees all things, and by his own adventures, and his life, on these the youthful Jason took his oath. With this she was assured and quickly gave to him the magic herbs: he learnt their use and full of joy withdrew into his house.

Now, when the dawn had dimmed the glittering stars, the people moved to the sacred field of Mars, and on the hills stood waiting. Arrayed in purple, and in majesty distinguished by his ivory sceptre, sat the king, surrounded by a crowd. Below them on the Field of Mars, huge bronze-footed bulls were breathing from adamantine nostrils living flames, blasting the green plants in their path! The son of Aeson went to meet them. As he came to meet them, the fierce animals turned against him their terrible faces and sharp horns tipped with iron, and they pawed the dusty earth with cloven feet, and filled the place with fiery bellows. The Minyans were struck with fear. Jason went up to the bulls, not feeling their hot breath at all, so great was the power of his charmed drugs, and while he was stroking their down-hanging necks with a fearless hand, he placed the yoke down on their necks and made them draw the heavy plow, and cut through fields that never felt the steel before. The Colchians were amazed and silent, but the loud shouting of the Minyans increased their hero's courage.

Taking then the serpent's teeth out of a bronze helmet, he sowed them in the newly-plowed field. The moist earth softened these seeds that were steeped in virulent poison and the teeth swelled up and took new forms. And just as in its mother an infant gradually assumes the form of man, and is perfected through all parts within, and does not come forth to the light till fully formed, just so, when the forms of men had been completed in the womb of the pregnant earth, they rose up from it, and what is yet more amazing, each one clashed weapons that had been brought forth with him. When his companions saw the warriors turn as if with one accord, to hurl their spears, sharp-pointed, at the head of Jason, fear unnerved the boldest and their courage failed. So, too, the young woman whose sorcery had saved him from much danger, when she saw the youth encompassed by those raging enemies, and he alone against so many. Struck with sudden panic, she turned ashen white, her bloodless cheeks were blanched, and chilled with fear she wilted to the ground, and so that the herbs, so lately given him, might not fail his need, she added incantations and invoked mysterious arts. While she protected him, he seized a heavy stone and hurled it in the midst of his new enemies. Distracted by this cast, and murderous, they turned from him, and clashing their new arms, those earth-born brothers fought among themselves till all were slaughtered in blood-thirsty strife. Gladly the Greeks acclaimed him conqueror, and pressed around him for the first embrace. Then, too, Medea, barbarous Colchian maid, although her modesty restrained her heart, eagerly longed to fold him in her arms, but careful of her good name, held back, rejoicing in deep, silent love, and she acknowledged to the Gods her mighty gift of incantations.

But the dragon, still alert, magnificent and terrible with gorgeous crest and triple tongue, and fangs barbed as a javelin, guards the Golden Fleece. Jason can obtain that quest only if slumber may seal up the monster's eyes. Jason, successful, sprinkled on his crest Lethean juices of a magic herb, and then recited three times the words which bring deep slumber, potent words which would calm the storm-tossed ocean, and would stop the flow of the most rapid rivers of our earth: and slowly sleep sealed the dragon's eyes. While that great monster slept, the hero took the Golden Fleece, and proudly sailed away, bearing his treasure and the willing girl, (whose aid had saved him) to his native port Iolcus, victorious with the Argonauts.

41) Minos and the Minotaur (7. 152-182, passim)

King Minos, when he reached the land of Crete and left his ships, remembered he had made a vow to Jupiter, and offered up a hundred bulls, and the splendid spoils of war later adorned his palace. Now the infamous scandal of Crete had grown, now that his wife's adultery was exposed by the beastly child of both bull and. So, Minos, moved to cover his disgrace, resolved to hide the monster in a prison, and he built it with intricate design created by Daedalus, a famous architect of wonderful ability. He planned confusion by labyrinthine passages that deceived the eyes. Daedalus contrived innumerous paths, and vague windings so intricate that he, the architect, hardly could retrace his own steps.

In this structure the Minotaur was hidden, and there he devoured Athenian victims sent every nine seasons, until on the third occasion, Theseus, son of Aegeus, slew him and retraced his way, finding the path by Ariadne's thread. Without delay the victor fled from Crete, together with the loving daughter, and sailed for the Island of Naxos, where he left her abandoned. Lamenting and deserted, Bacchus found her and for his love immortalized her name. He set in the dark heavens the bright crown that rested on her brows. Through the soft air it whirled, while all the sparkling jewels changed to flashing fires, assuming in the sky between the Serpent-holder and Hercules the well-known shape of Ariadne's Crown.

4m) Pygmalion, Venus, and Adonis (10. 243-733, passim)

Pygmalion saw these women waste their lives in wretched shame and critical of faults that nature had so deeply planted through their female hearts. He lived preferring to remain unmarried for many years. But while he was single, with consummate skill, he carved a statue out of snow-white ivory, and gave to it exquisite beauty, which no woman of the world has ever equaled. She was so beautiful, he fell in love with his creation. It appeared in truth a perfect virgin with the grace of life, but in the expression of such modesty all motion was restrained, and so his art concealed his art. Pygmalion gazed, inflamed with love and admiration for the form of a woman he had carved. He lifts up both his hands to feel the work, and wonders if it can be ivory, because it seems to him more truly flesh. His mind refuses to see it as ivory, and he kisses it and feels his kisses are returned. And speaking love, caresses it with loving hands that seem to make an impression on the parts they touch so real that he fears he then may bruise her by his eager pressing. He uses the softest tones each time he speaks to her. He brings to her such presents as are surely prized by sweet girls, such as smooth round pebbles, shells, and birds, and fragrant flowers of many hues, lilies, and painted balls, and amber tears of Heliads, which distill from far off trees. He drapes her in rich clothing and in gems, rings on her fingers, a rich necklace round her neck, pearl pendants on her graceful ears, and golden ornaments adorn her breast. All these are beautiful, and she appears most lovable, if carefully attired, or perfect as a statue, unadorned. He lays her on a luxurious bed, spread with coverlets of Tyrian purple dye, and naming her the consort of his bed, lays her reclining head on the most soft and downy pillows, believing she could feel them.

The festival of Venus, known throughout all Cyprus, now had come, and crowds were there to celebrate. Heifers with spreading horns, all gold-tipped, fell when given the stroke of death upon their snow-white necks, and frankincense was smoking on the altars. There, intent, Pygmalion stood before an altar, when his offering had been made. And although he feared the result, he prayed: "If it is true, O gods, that you can give all things, I pray to have as my wife..." – but, he did not dare to add "my ivory statue-maid," and said, "One like my ivory..." Golden Venus heard him, for she was present at her festival, and she knew clearly what the prayer had meant. She gave a sign that her Divinity favored his plea: three times the flame leaped high and brightly in the air. When he returned, he went directly to his image, bent over her, and kissed her many times while she was on her bed, and as he kissed, she seemed to gather some warmth from his lips. Again he kissed her, and he felt her breast. The ivory seemed to soften at the touch, and its firm texture yielded to his hand, as honey-wax of Mount Hymettus turns to many shapes when handled in the sun, and surely softens from each gentle touch. He is amazed, but stands rejoicing in his doubt, while fearful that there is some mistake, again and yet again, gives tests his hopes by touching her with his hand. It must be flesh! The veins pulsate beneath the careful test of his directed finger. Then, indeed, the astonished hero poured out lavish thanks to Venus, pressing with his raptured lips his statue's lips. Now real, true to life, the maiden felt the kisses given to her, and blushing, lifted up her timid eyes, so that she saw the light and sky above, as well as her rapt lover while he leaned gazing beside her – and all this at once. The goddess graced the marriage she had willed, and when nine times a crescent moon had changed, increasing to the full, the statue-bride gave birth to her dear daughter Paphos. From which famed event the island takes its name.

Once, while the goddess' son, Cupid, with quiver held on shoulder, was kissing his loved mother, by chance he grazed her breast with a projecting arrow. Instantly the wounded goddess pushed her son away, but the scratch had pierced her deeper than she thought and even Venus was at first deceived. Delighted with the beauty of the youth, she does not think of her Cytherian shores and does not care for Paphos, which is girt by the deep sea, nor Cnidos, haunts of fish, nor Amathus far-famed for precious ores. Venus, neglecting heaven, prefers Adonis to heaven, and so she holds close to his ways as his companion, and forgets to rest at noon in the shade, neglecting care of her sweet beauty. She goes through the woods and over mountain ridges and wild fields, rocky and covered with thorns, bare to her white knees like Diana. And she cheers the hounds, intent to hunt for harmless prey, such as the leaping hare, or the wild stag, high-crowned with branching antlers, or the doe. She keeps away from fierce wild boars, away from ravenous wolves, and she avoids the bears of frightful claws, and lions glutted with the blood of slaughtered cattle.

"My dear Adonis," she warns him, "keep away from all such savage animals, and avoid all those who do not turn their fearful backs in flight but offer their bold breasts to your attack, so that courage should not be fatal to both of us." Thus she warned him, and harnessing her swans, she traveled swiftly through the thin air, but his rash courage would not listen to advice. By chance, his dogs, which followed a certain track, aroused a wild boar from his hiding place, and, as he rushed out from his forest lair, Adonis pierced him with a glancing stroke. In a frenzy, the fierce boar's curved horns first struck the spear-shaft from his bleeding side and, while the trembling youth was seeking where to find a safe retreat, the savage beast raced after him, until at last he sank his deadly tusk deep in Adonis' groin, and stretched him dying on the yellow sand.

Sweet Aphrodite, borne through air in her light chariot, had not yet arrived at Cyprus, on the wings of her white swans. From afar she recognized his dying groans, and turned her white birds towards the sound. And when down looking from the lofty sky she saw him nearly dead, his body bathed in blood, she leaped down, tore her garment, tore her hair, and beat her breast with distracted hands. And blaming Fate, she said, "But not everything is at the mercy of your cruel power. My sorrow for Adonis will remain, enduring as a lasting monument. Each passing year the memory of his death shall cause an imitation of my grief. Your blood, Adonis, will become a perennial flower. Was it not allowed to you Persephone, to transform Menthe's limbs into sweet fragrant mint? And can this change of my loved hero be denied to me?" Her grief declared, she sprinkled his blood with sweet-smelling nectar, and his blood as soon as it was touched by it began to boil, just as transparent bubbles always rise in rainy weather. From Adonis' blood, exactly of its color, a loved flower sprang up in less than an hour, of a colour such as pomegranates give to us, small trees which later hide their seeds beneath a tough rind. But the joy it gives to man is short-lived, for the winds which give the flower its name, Anemone, shake it right down, because its slender stem, always so weak, lets it fall to the ground.

4n) Orpheus and Dionysos (10. 1-84, passim)

While with his songs, Orpheus, the bard of Thrace, allured the trees, the savage animals, and even the insensitive rocks, to follow him, Ciconian matrons, with their raving breasts concealed in skins of leopards, from the summit of a hill observed him there, attuning love songs to a sounding harp. One of those women, as her tangled hair was tossed upon the light breeze shouted, "See! Here is the poet who has scorned our love!" Then hurled her spear at the melodious mouth of great Apollo's bard, but the spear's point, trailing in flight a garland of fresh leaves, made only a harmless bruise and did not wound him. The weapon of another was a stone, which in the very air was overpowered by the true harmony of his voice and lyre, and so disabled lay before his feet, as if asking pardon for that vain attempt. The madness of such warfare then increased. All moderation is entirely lost, and a wild Fury overcomes reason. Although their weapons would have lost all force, subjected to the power of Orpheus' harp, the clamorous discord of their boxwood pipes, the blaring of their horns, their tambourines and clapping hands and Bacchanalian yells, with hideous discord drowned his voice and harp. At last the stones that heard his song no more became crimson with the Thracian poet's blood. Before his life was taken, the maenads turned their threatening hands upon the many birds, which still were charmed by Orpheus as he sang, the serpents, and the company of beasts—fabulous audience of that worshipped bard. And then they turned on him their blood-stained hands, and flocked together swiftly, as wild birds, which, by some chance, may see the bird of night beneath the sun. And as the savage dogs rush on the doomed stag, loosed some bright fore-noon, on blood-sand of the amphitheatre, just so they rushed against the bard, with swift hurled thyrsi which, adorned with emerald leaves had not till then been used for cruelty.

And some threw clods, and others branches torn from trees, and others threw flint stones at him, and, so that no lack of weapons might restrain their savage fury then, not far from there by chance they found some oxen which turned up the soil with ploughshares, and in fields nearby were strong-armed peasants, who with eager sweat worked for the harvest as they dug hard fields, and all those peasants, when they saw the troop of frantic women, ran away and left their implements of labor strewn upon deserted fields – harrows and heavy rakes and their long spades. After the savage mob had seized those implements, and torn to pieces oxen armed with threatening horns, they hastened to destroy the harmless bard, devoted Orpheus; and with impious hate, murdered him, while his out-stretched hands implored their mercy – the first and only time his voice could not persuade. O great Jupiter! Through those same lips which had controlled the rocks and which had overcome ferocious beasts, his life breathed forth, departed in the air.

Meanwhile, the fleeting shade of Orpheus had descended under earth, and remembering now those regions that he saw when there before, he sought Eurydice through fields frequented by the blessed; and when he found her, folded her in eager arms. Then lovingly they wandered side by side, or he would follow when she chose to lead, or at another time he walked in front, looking back – safely – at Eurydice.

Bacchus would not permit the wickedness of those who slaughtered Orpheus to remain unpunished. Grieving for the loss of his loved bard of sacred rites, at once he bound with twisted roots the feet of everyone of those Edonian women who had caused the crime of Orpheus' death. Their toes grew long. He thrust the sharp points in the solid earth. As when a bird entangled in a snare, hid by the cunning hunter, knows too late that it is held, then vainly beats its wings, and fluttering only makes more tight the noose with every struggle, so each woman whose feet were sinking in the soil, when she attempted flight, was held by deepening roots. And while she looks down where her toes and nails and feet should be, she sees wood growing up from them and covering all her graceful legs. Full of delirious grief, endeavoring to kill with right hand on her changing thigh, she strikes on solid oak. Her tender breast and shoulders are transformed to rigid oak. You would declare that her extended arms are real branches of a tree, and such a thought would be the very truth.

4o) Polyphemus, Galatea, Acis; Scylla and Glaucis (13. 724-968; 14. 1-74, passim)

Favored by the tide, and active oars, by nightfall all of Aeneas' fleet arrived together on Zanclaean sands. Scylla upon the right infests the shore, Charybdis, restless on the left, destroying. Charybdis swallows and then vomits out unlucky ships that she has taken down, while Scylla's dark waist is decorated with savage dogs. She has a maiden's face, and, if we may believe what poets tell, she was once a maiden. Many suitors courted her, but she repulsed them and, because she was so much beloved by all the Nereids, she sought these nymphs and used to tell how she escaped from the love-stricken youths.

But Galatea, while her loosened locks were being combed, said to her visitor, "Truly, O maiden, a gentle race of men courts you, and so you can, and do, refuse all without punishment. But I, whose father is Nereus, and whom the azure Doris bore, though guarded by so many sister nymphs, escaped the Cyclops' love with tragic loss." And, sobbing, she was choked with tears. When with her fingers, marble white and smooth, Scylla had wiped away the rising tears of sorrow and had comforted the nymph, she said, "Tell me, dear goddess, and do not conceal from me (for I am true to you) the cause of your great sorrows." And the nymph, daughter of Nereus, thus begand her tale.

Acis, the son of Faunus and the nymph Symaethis, was a great delight to his dear father and his mother, but even more to me, for he alone had won my love. While I pursued him with a constant love, the Cyclops followed me as constantly. And, should you ask me, I could not declare whether my hatred of him, or my love of Acis was the stronger.—They were equal. O gentle Venus! What power equals yours! That savage, dreaded by the forest trees, feared by the stranger who beholds his face, filled with contempt of Olympus and the gods, now he can feel what love is. He is filled with passion for me. He burns hot for me, forgetful of his cattle and his caves. Now, Polyphemus, wretched Cyclops, you are careful of appearance, and you try the art of pleasing. You have even combed your stiffened hair with rakes: it pleases you to trim your shaggy beard with scythes, while you gaze at your fierce features in a pool so earnest to compose them. Love of flesh, ferocity and your keen thirst for blood have ceased. The ships may safely come and go!

A wedge-formed hill projects far in the sea and either side there flow the salty waves. To this the giant savage climbed and sat upon the highest point. The wooly flock, no longer guided by him, followed him. There, after he had laid his pine tree down, which served him for a staff, although so tall it seemed best fitted for a ship's high mast, he played his shepherd pipes. All this time I was hidden by a rock, reclining on the bosom of my own dear Acis and, although far away, I heard such words as these, which I can not forget:

"O Galatea, fairer than the flower of snow-white privet, and more blooming than the meadows, and more slender than the tall delightful alder, brighter than smooth glass, more skittish than the tender kid, smoother than shells worn by continual floods, more pleasing than the winter sun, or than the summer shade, more beautiful than fruit of apple trees, more pleasing to the sight than lofty plane tree, clearer than pure ice, and sweeter than the ripe grape, softer than soft swan-feathers and the softest curdled milk, alas, and if you did not fly from me, I would declare you are more beautiful than any watered garden of this world.

"And yet, O Galatea, I must say, that you are wilder than all untrained bulls, harder than seasoned oak, more treacherous than tumbled waters, tougher than the twigs of osier and the white vine, harder to move than cliffs that face these waves, more violent than any torrent, you are prouder than the flattered peacock, fiercer than hot fire, rougher than thistles, and more cruel than the pregnant mother-bear, deafer than the waves of stormy seas, more savage than the water-snake, and, (if only I could deprive you of it) your speed is quicker than the deer pursued by frightful howls, and more swift than rapid storm-winds and the flitting air. But Galatea, if you knew me well you would regret your hasty flight from me, and you would even blame your own delay, and strive for my affection. I now hold the choice part of this mountain for my cave, roofed over with the native rock. The sun is not felt in the heat of middle day, nor is the winter felt there. Apples load the bending boughs and luscious grapes hang on the lengthened vines, resembling gold, and purple grapes as rich – I keep for you those two delicious fruits. With your own hands, you shall yourself uncover strawberries, growing so soft beneath the woodland shade, and you shall pluck corners in the autumn ripening, and plums, not only darkened with black juice but larger kinds as yellow as new wax. If I may be your mate, you shall have chestnuts, fruits of the arbute shall be always near, and every tree shall yield at your desire.

Come Galatea come! And do not scorn my presents. Certainly, I know myself, for only recently I saw my own reflection pictured clear in limpid water, and my features pleased and charmed me when I saw it. See how huge I am. Not even Jove in his high heaven is larger than my body! this I say because you tell me how royal Jove surpasses all. Who is he? I never knew. My long hair plentifully hangs to hide unpleasant features, as a grove of trees overshadowing my shoulders. Never think my body is ugly, although rough, thick set with wiry bristles. Every tree without leaves is unseemly, every horse, unless a mane hangs on his tawny neck. Feathers must cover birds, and their soft wool is ornamental on the best formed sheep. Therefore a beard, and rough hair spread upon the body is becoming to all men. I have but one eye centered perfectly within my forehead, so it seems most like a mighty buckler. Ha! Does not the Sun see everything from heaven? Yet it has but one eye!

"Why reject the Cyclops for the love that Acis gives? And why prefer his smiles to my embraces, but let him please himself, and let him please you, Galatea, though against my will. If I am given an opportunity he will be shown that I have every strength proportioned to a body vast as mine: I will pull out his palpitating entrails, and scatter his torn limbs about the fields and over and throughout your salty waves, and then let him unite himself to you. I burn so much, and my slighted passion raves with greater fury, and I seem to hold and carry Etna in my breast, transferred there with its flames. Oh Galatea! Can you listen to my passion thus unmoved!"

I saw all this and, after he in vain had uttered such complaints, he stood up like a raging bull whose heifer has been lost and cannot stand still, but must wander on through brush and forests that he knows so well. When that fierce monster saw me and my Acis, we neither knew nor guessed our fate, he roared: "I see you and you never will again parade your love before me," in such a voice as matched his giant size. All Etna shook and trembled at the noise. I, amazed with horror, plunged into the nearby sea. My beloved, Acis, turned his back and fled and cried out, "Help me Galatea, help! O, let your parents help me, and admit me safe within their realm, for I am nearing my destruction!" But the Cyclops rushed at him and hurled a fragment, he had torn out from the mountain, and although the extreme edge only of the rock could reach him there, it buried him entirely.

Then I did the only thing the Fates permitted me: I let my Acis take ancestral power of river deities. The purple blood flowed from beneath the rock, but soon the red richness faded and became at first the color of a stream, disturbed and muddied by a shower, and then became clear. The rock that had been thrown then split in two, and through the fissure a reed, proud and strong, arose to life. And soon the hollow mouth in the great rock resounded with the waters gushing forth. And wonderful to tell, a youth emerged, the water flowing clear about his waist, his new horns circled with entwining reeds, and the youth certainly was Acis, though he was of larger stature and his face and features all were blue. Acis changed into a stream which ever since that time has flowed there and retained its former name…

Glaucus, swimming with his huge hands through those Tyrrhenian seas, drew near the hills so rich in magic herbs and halls of Circe, daughter of the Sun –halls filled with men in guise of animals. After due greetings had been given and received by her as kindly, Glaucus said, "You as a goddess, certainly should have compassion upon me, a god, for you alone (if I am worthy of it) can relieve my passion. What the power of herbs can be, Titania, none knows more than me, for by their power I was myself transformed. To make the cause of my strange madness known, I have found Scylla on Italian shores, directly opposite Messenian walls. It shames me to recount my promises, begging, and caresses, and at last rejection of my suit. If you have known a power of incantation, I implore you now repeat that incantation here, with sacred lips. If herbs have greater power, use the tried power of herbs. But I would not request a cure for the healing of this wound. Much better than an end of pain, let her share, and feel with me my impassioned flame."

But Circe was more quick than any other to burn with passion's flame. "You might do better," she replied, "to court one who is willing, one who wants your love, and feels a similar desire. You did deserve to win her love, yes, to be wooed yourself. In fact you might be. If you give some hope, you have my word, you shall indeed be wooed. So that you may have no doubt, and so keep all confidence in your attraction's power, behold! I am a goddess, and I am the daughter also, of the radiant Sun! And I who am so potent with my charms, and I who am so potent with my herbs, wish only to be yours. Despise her who despises you, and her who is attached to you repay with similar attachment, so by one act offer each her just reward." But Glaucus answered her attempt of love, "The trees will sooner grow in ocean waves, the sea-weed sooner grow on mountain tops, than I shall change my love for graceful Scylla."

The goddess in her jealous rage could not and would not injure him, whom she still loved, but turned her wrath upon the one preferred. She bruised immediately the many herbs most infamous for horrid juices, which, when bruised, she mingled with most artful care and incantations given by Hecate. Then, clothed in blue clothing, she passed through her troop of fawning savage animals, and left from the center of her hall. Pacing from there to Rhegium, opposite the dangerous rocks of Zancle, she at once entered the tossed waves boiling up with tides, and on these, as if she walked on the firm shore, she set her feet and, hastening on dry sandals, she skimmed along the surface of the deep. Not far away there was a cove, round as a bent bow, which was often used by Scylla as a favorite retreat. There, she withdrew from heat of sea and sky when in the sun in its zenith blazed and cast the shortest shadows on the ground. Circe infected it before that hour, polluting it with monster-breeding drugs. She sprinkled juices over it, distilled from an obnoxious root, and twenty-seven times she muttered over it with magic lips, her most mysterious charm involved in words of strangest meaning and of dubious thought. Scylla came there and waded in waist deep, then saw her loins defiled with barking shapes. Believing they could be no part of her, she ran and tried to drive them back and feared the boisterous canine jaws. But what she fled she carried with her. And, feeling for her thighs, her legs, and feet, she found Cerberian jaws instead. She rises from a rage of dogs, and shaggy backs encircle her shortened loins.

The lover Glaucus wept. He fled the embrace of Circe and her hostile power of herbs and magic spells. But Scylla did not leave the place of her disaster and, as soon as she had opportunity, for hate of Circe, she robbed Ulysses of his men. She would have wrecked the Trojan ships, if she had not been changed beforehand to a rock, which to this day reveals a craggy rim. And even the rock awakes the sailors' dread.

Adapted from Brookes More, Ovid. Metamorphoses (Boston: Cornhill Publishing Co. 1922)

READING 5:

Vergil's *Aeneid*

Publius Vergilius Maro (Vergil) was born in 70 BCE in Italy. Like his younger contemporary, Ovid, he too lived during a period of civil strife and violence in the Roman Republic, marked by confiscations of farmland, banditry, and civil war. Also like Ovid, his great talent in poetry won him a reputation among the Roman elite, and caught the eye of the newly-minted Emperor, Augustus. *Aeneid* was Vergil's last, and greatest poem. It is a sprawling epic of the trials and tribulations of Aeneas, son of Venus and a prince of Troy, and the Trojan refugees whom he guided from the ruin of their city to a new, divinely ordained home in Italy. Tales of Aeneas' connection to the Roman people were old in Italy, but it was Vergil who produced the definitive version of the tale and made the divine connection between Aeneas the Julian clan, represented by Augustus. Sometimes described as propaganda for the new "Golden Age" proclaimed by Augustus, the poem nonetheless reflects the weariness of the previous period of civil wars, to whom Augustus himself had contributed.

Like Odysseus and his comrades, Aeneas and his Trojan exiles encounter many obstacles and endure much suffering before reaching their destination, including some of the very same monsters. Like Odysseus, Aeneas must journey to the Underworld to speak with ghosts and learn of his destiny. Like Odysseus, the end of his journey only leads to more violence, as the Trojans must fight a brutal war before being accepted in Italy. It is Aeneas' relationship with Queen Dido of Carthage, however, which truly distinguishes the poem. Dido shelters the exiles, and hearing Aeneas' tale of the destruction of Troy, she and Aeneas fall in love, only for it to end disastrous consequences, both for Dido and for Aeneas' descendants.

5a) A Roman Hero (Vergil, Aeneid, 1. 1-417, passim)

Of arms and the man I sing, who first made his way, destined for exile, from the Trojan shore to Italy, the blessed Lavinian shore. Smitten of storms he was on land and sea By violence of Heaven he was Beaten by storms on land and sea by the violence of the gods, all to satisfy stern Juno's sleepless wrath. And he suffered much in war, seeking at the last to found the City, and bring over his fathers' gods to dwell safely in Latium. From what source sprung the Latin race, old Alba's reverend lords, and from her hills, wide-walled, imperial Rome.

O Muse, speak of the causes! What sacrilege or vengeful sorrow moved the heavenly Queen to thrust dark dangers and endless toil against a man whose greatest honor in men's eyes was serving Heaven? Can the gods feel such anger? In ages gone stood an ancient city: Carthage, a colony of Tyre, which from afar made would bring war upon Italy and the mouth of the Tiber. Its wealth and riches were vast, and ruthless was its quest of war.

It is said that Juno, of all lands she loved, she most cherished this – not dear Samos. Here were her arms, her chariot; even then, if Fate had not opposed it, it was her dearest hope to establish here a throne of power over nations far and wide. But anxiously she heard that from Trojan blood a new people was rising, which upon the destined day would utterly overwhelm her Tyrian towers; a people of wide power, proud in victory, would bring Libya's doom. Such was the web the Fatal Sisters spun.

And Aeneas' men were overwhelmed in the combined shock of wave and wind. Saturnian Juno's vengeful plan, however, did not go unseen by her majestic brother's. And calling loud east and west, he voiced this word…and swifter than his word the swelling of the floods was subdued, dispersed the assembled clouds were dispersed, and light was brought back to heaven.

Aeneas' wave-worn crew now made for land, and took the nearest passage: the coast of Libya. A haven was there, walled in by stark walls of a rocky island, offering a spacious and secure retreat. To this place sailed Aeneas with only seven ships left of his scattered fleet. With a passionate longing for the touch of land, out leapt the Trojans to the welcoming shore, and they fling their dripping limbs along the ground.

And with these words Aeneas consoled their grief: "My companions, we have not failed to feel calamity. You have borne far heavier sorrow, and to this Jove will make an end. You sailed a hard course through furious Scylla's howling cliffs and caves. You remember the Cyclops' crags. Lift up your hearts! No more complaint and fear! It may well be that some happier hour will find this moment a good one. Through chance and transformation and hazard without end, our goal is Latium; where our destinies beckon us to blessed dwellings, and which have ordained that Troy shall rise new-born! Have patience! And live hopefully for that golden day." Such were his words, but sick with grief and care, he pretends hope on his firm face, and locks his pain within his heart.

After these things were past, exalted Jove, from his ethereal sky surveying the seas all winged with sails, lands widely spread and populous nations from shore to shore, he paused on the peak of heaven, and fixed his gaze on Libya. But while he anxiously mused, near him, her radiant eyes all dim with tears nor smiling any more, Venus approached, and complained: "You who controls mortal and divine affairs by changeless laws, enthroned in awful thunder!

What great wrong could my Aeneas and his few Trojans achieve against your power? For they have borne unnumbered deaths, and, failing Italy, the gates of all the world close against them."

Smiling with such a look as clears the skies of storm, the lord of gods and men modestly kissed his daughter kissed, and replied: "Let Cytherean Venus cast her fears away! Irrevocably blessed are the fortunes of you and yours. Nor shall you fail to see that City, and the proud predestined walls encompassing Lavinium. Your son in Italy shall wage great war and subdue its wild peoples. His city-walls and sacred laws shall be a mighty bond around his gathered people. In three summers Lavinium shll call him king. His heir, Ascanius (now called Iulus) shall reign for a full thirty months, then move the throne from the Lavinian citadel, and build for Alba Longa its enduring walls. Here for three full centuries Hector's race shall have kingly power, until a priestess queen shall conceive and bear by Mars her twin offspring. Then Romulus, nursed by a wolf, shall receive the sceptre of his people. He shall raise the war-god's citadel and lofty walls, and he shall bestow on the Romans his own name."

"To these people I give no limit of time or power, but an empire without end. Yes, even my Queen, Juno, who now assaults land and sea with her dread face, will find a different way, and at my sovereign side she will protect and bless the Romans, masters of the whole round world, who, clad in the peaceful toga, shall judge mankind. Such is my decree!" These words he gave, and he summoned Maia's son, the messenger Mercury, who, flying earthward, should order the Tyrian realms and new-built towers to welcome the Trojan exiles, so that Dido, blind to Fate's decree, should not thrust him from the land.

5b) The Fall of Troy (Vergil, Aeneid, 2. 1-1080, passim)

A general silence fell; and all listened while from his noble place at the feast, Aeneas began with these words:

Weary of the war, And by crushed ill-fortune, year after year, the kings of Greece, by Minerva' divine skill, built a huge horse, a thing of mountainous size, with wooden ribs of fir. They falsely say it has been vowed to Heaven for their safe return, and spread this lie abroad. Then they conceal a selected band of warriors in the deep, dark side, and fill the caverns of that monstrous womb with weapons and soldiers. In sight of Troy lies Tenedos, a beautiful and widely famed island, before Priam's kingdom fell, but a poor haven now, with anchorage not even half as secure. It was there they sailed, and lurked unseen by that abandoned shore. We thought that they were away and sailing far, bound for home – Mycenae.

Then out from the citadel indignantly hurried Laocoön with all his associates, and from afar he hailed the people: "O unhappy men! What madness is this? Who believes our enemies have fled? Do you think the gifts of Greece lack deception? Do you not remember Ulysses? Do not trust this horse, Trojans! I fear the Greeks, even when they bear gifts." So saying, he hurled a heavy javelin and struck straight at the rounded side of the great, wooden beast. A tremor struck its towering form, and through the cavernous womb rolled a loud reverberating rumble, deep and long. If heaven's decree, if our own wills, at that hour had not been fixed on grief, his spear might have brought a bloody slaughter on our ambushed foe, and Troy would be standing this day!

But now a greater spectacle of fear burst over us, to trouble our startled souls. Laocoön, on that day by lot was Priest of Neptune, and was to slay a huge bull at the god's appointed sanctuary. But then, over the tranquil deep from Tenedos appeared a pair (I shudder to tell) of giant, coiling serpents, side by side, stretching along the waves, and slithering a swift course to the shore; their necks were lifted high, their gory dragon-crests skimmed the waves, while the rest of them, half seen, trailed low along the sea. Soon they reached the land, their furious bright eyes glowed with blood-red fire, their quivering tongues lapped hungrily their hissing, gruesome jaws. All pale with terror, we fled.

Unswerving then, the monsters went after Laocoön. First around the tender limbs of his two sons each serpent coiled, and on their shrinking flesh they held fast. Then they seized on the father, who flew to his sons' aid, a javelin in his hand, embracing close in bondage twice around his waist, and twice around his neck, and over him they grimly peered with their lifted heads and crests. All the while, his body fouled with venomous blood, he tore at his bonds with a desperate hand, And lifted up such agonizing voice, as when a bull with a deadly wound seeks to flee the sacrificial altar, and thrusts back from his doomed head the ill-aimed, glancing blade. Then swiftly the dragon-pair slithered away to the templed height, and in the shrine of cruel Pallas found asylum beneath the goddess' feet and orbed shield.

Such trembling horror as we had never known seized all of our hearts. "For his terrible guilt," they say, "Laocoön receives his just reward. "For he abominably struck and violated the blessed wood with his spear. Bring this statue to the temple! Ask the grace of glorious Pallas!" So the people cried In general acclaim. We ourselves made a breach within our walls and opened wide the ramparts of our city. The skies rolled on, and over the ocean fell the veil of night, until utmost earth and heaven and all their Greek stratagems were cloaked darkly over. In silent sleep the Trojan city lay, and dull slumber chained Its weary life.

O, then my slumbering senses seemed to see Hector, with woeful face and teary eyes. I seemed to see him trailing from the chariot, foul with dark dust and gore, his swollen feet Pierced with a cruel thong. Silent he stood, nor would he await my vain lament, but he groaned and spoke: "Make haste, goddess-born, out of the flames. Make flight! Our foes have scaled the wall. Exalted Troy is falling. The fatherland and Priam ask no more of you. If human action could profit Troy, my own would have kept her free. Her Lares and her people Troy commends to your hands. Let them be companions of all your fortunes. Let them share your quest for that wide realm, which, after wandering far, you shall find, at last, beyond the sea."

Now shrieks and loud confusion swept the city, and although my father's dwelling stood apart, deep in trees, the increasing din drew nearer, and the battle-thunder swelled. I woke suddenly, and raising myself, I scaled the roof, the tower, then stood with listening ear. It was like a harvest burning, when wild winds rouse the flames; it was like a mountain stream that bursts in flood and ruinously overwhelms sweet fields and farms and all the ploughman's toil, whirling whole groves along, while dumb with fear, from some far cliff, the shepherd hears the sound. Now the Greek plot was made clear, the stratagem at last laid bare. Shrill trumpets blared, loud, shouting voices roared. Wildly I armed myself – when the battle calls, how dimly reason shines! I burned to join the rally of my comrades, and to gather at the heights. Frenzy and a great rage seized my soul. With sword in hand, I only sought some way to die a noble death.

Straightway the roar and chaos summoned us to Priam's palace, where a battle raged, as if to save this place no other conflict were needed, and all Troy's dying brave were mustered there. Now at the threshold of the outer court Pyrrhus stood triumphant with glittering arms and a helm of burnished bronze. He glittered like some swollen viper fed on poisoned leaves, whom chilling winter shelters underground until, fresh and strong, he sheds his scales, and crawling out rejuvenated, he uncoils his slimy length.

Confusion, groans, and piteous turmoil were in that house – women shrieked and wailed from many a dark corners, and their loud cries rang to the golden stars. Through those vast halls the panic-stricken mothers wildly roved and clung with frantic kisses and embraces onto the cold columns. Fierce as his father, Pyrrhus strides on, neither bar nor guard may stop him. Down tumbles the great door beneath the battering beam, and with it fall hinges and torn frames – force bursts all bars. The assaulting Greeks break in, begin their butchery, and with soldiers possess whatever place they wish. With barely a similar rage does a foaming river, when its dykes are knocked down, overwhelms its mounded shores, and over the plains it rolls mountain-high, while from the ravaged farms its fierce flood sweeps along both flock and fold.

Within Priam's walls stood a lofty altar beneath the wide and open sky, an old laurel-tree leaned over it, and embraced in sacred shade the statues of the ancestral powers. Here Hecuba and all the princesses took vain refuge within the place of prayer. Like panic-stricken doves in some dark storm, gathering they stand close, and embraced their graven gods in despair. But when the Queen saw Priam with his youthful armour on, she cried "What madness, my wretched lord set you in such arms? Where are you going now? The moment does not need such defences or such an arm as yours. Yield, I beg you! This altar now shall save us one and all, or we must die together!" With these words She drew him to her side, and near the shrine found a place to cling for her aged husband. But suddenly, trying to escape Pyrrhus' murderous hand, Polites, one of Priam's sons, fled fast along the corridors, through mobs of soldiers and a thick rain of spears. Wildly he gazed across the desolate halls, wounded to death. Fierce Pyrrhus pursued, pressing hard with a mortal blow, and now his hand and spear were close: just when the doomed youth leaped into his father's sight, and lay there dying, while his life-blood ebbed away.

Then Priam, although death was everywhere, would not back away from strife or revenge: "May the gods justly reward and properly repay your crime and impious hubris! You have made me see my own son's murder!" With these proud words the old warrior hurled his ineffectual spear with a weak arm, and it hoarsely rang, rebounding on the bronze shield, and hung piercing the midmost boss – but all in vain. Then Pyrrhus replied: "Take these tidings, and convey a message to my father, Peleus' son! Tell him of my wicked deeds! Be sure and say how I have shamed his ancestors. Now, die!" With this, he dragged the trembling King before the shrines, and Priam's feet slipped in the stream of his own son's blood. Then Pyrrhus' left hand clutched his old, grey hair, while his right hand lifted high a glittering sword, and buried it as far as the hilt in that defenseless heart. So Priam's story ceased. Such final doom fell on him, while his dying eyes surveyed Troy burning, and her altars overthrown, though once the great lord of many eastern lands and peoples. His severed body lies tombless on the shore In huge piles, the head torn from shoulder, the corpse unknown.

Then wild horror struck my soul and dazed me utterly. A vision rose of my own cherished father, as I saw the King, his old peer, wounded and lying in mortal agony. I saw a vision too of my lost Creusa at my ravaged hearth, and young Iulus' peril. Then my eyes looked round me, seeking aid. But all were fleeing, war-wearied and undone, and some leaped down to the earth from wall or tower, others in despair yielded their suffering bodies to the flame. I stood there, the sole survivor.

Then with clear vision (never had I seen her presence so unclouded) I beheld, In golden beams that pierced the midnight gloom, my gracious mother, visibly divine, and with that expression of majesty she wears when seen in heaven. She touched me with her hand, and from her lips of rose she gave this counsel: "Son, what sorrow stirs your boundless rage? What madness is this? Or where has your love of me vanished? Will you not seek to know where Anchises is, you abandoned father, now weak with age? Or if Creusa lives and young Ascanius, who are surrounded by ranks of Greek foes, and long before this, if my love had not shielded and defended them would have fallen on flame or have been fed to some hungry sword? It is not Helen's hated beauty that brings this woe, nor oft-maligned Paris. The cruelty of gods, of gods alone, overwhelms your country's power, and casts Troy down from its lofty height. Behold, I take away the cloud that dims your mortal eyes, with murk and mist. Do not fear to obey your mother's word, nor let your heart refuse obedience to her counsel. Amid these trembling ruins, where you see stone torn from stone, with dust and rising smoke, Neptune strikes the wall! His vast trident makes her foundation tremble, and unseats the city from her throne. Fierce Juno leads resistless assaults on the Scaean gate, and summons from the ships the league of powers, wearing her wrathful sword. The gods themselves are against the Trojan arms. Fly, my son! Give up the war's wild work! I will be always near and will make you safe upon your father's threshold." Having said this, she fled into the dark night.

I left the citadel and, led by Heaven, threaded the maze of deadly enemies and fires, through spears that glanced aside and flames that fell. Soon I reached came my family's ancient home, our house and heritage. And higher over the blazing walls leaped the loud fire, while ever nearer drew The rolling surges of tumultuous flame. "Haste, father," I shouted, "climb on my bending shoulders! This back is ready, and the burden light. One danger will kill us both, whatever happens, or both will find one refuge. Let young Iulus run close to my side, and my wife, Creusa follows and hears what way we will go. Father, hold onto our household gods and sacred objects!"

So instructing, I bowed my neck and broad shoulders and lifted up my load. Close at my side little Iulus slipped his hand in mine and followed me with unequal step. My wife followed just behind We rushed onward, creeping through shadows. With feverish anxiety, fearing both for him whom I bore and him who clasped my hand. Now we drew near the gates, and thought our flight was now safely at end, when suddenly I heard the sound of many warriors that seemed right nearby, while my father peered through the murky night and shouted, "My son, away, away! For surely all our enemies are after us, and my eyes see the shine of glittering shields and flash of arms."

O, then some evil-working, nameless god clouded my senses: for while I sped along our pathless way, and left behind all known paths and places – wretched me! Creusa had fallen into some dark disaster! She stopped, or wandered, or sank down – I never knew what – and never again did I see her alive. Yet I did not know my loss, nor turned backward a single look or thought until we came near that hallowed hill to which we promised to gather – she alone did not come, while husband, friends, and son searched in vain. I rushed back to that doomed city and put on glittering arms. I was determined to renew all the dangers, to search all of Troy, and once again offer my life to endless peril.

My voice rang out again and again through the gloom. From street to street I cried in vain and anguish, and calling piteously for Creusa, I echoed laments over and over. And while I roamed through the city in this pursuit, somehow, there rose upon my sight – o shape of sorrow! My Creusa's ghost, hers truly. I quailed, my hair rose, and I gasped for fear, but she spoke to me and soothed my grief: "Why are you bending your soul to such such frenzied sorrows, my dearest husband! The will of Heaven has brought all this to pass. Fate does not send me on the long journeys you shall take, nor has the Olympian King given such a decree. Long will be your banishment, your ship must plough the vast, far-spreading sea. Then you will come to Hesperia, whose fruitful plains are watered by the Tiber. You shall obtain good fortunes, and a throne and royal bride. For your beloved Creusa weep no more! No Greek's proud palace waits me now. On these beloved shores the Mother of the Gods compels me to stay. Farewell! Farewell! Cherish forever your son and mine!"

Her utterance had scarcely when, as I strove through tears to reply, she left me and dissolved in empty air. Three times my frustrated arms tried to embrace her, three times from my grasp that vision fled, like wafted winds and a fleeting dream. The night had passed, and to my friends once more I made my way, and was amazed to find a mighty host assembled there of friends who had just come – women, men-at-arms, and youth bound for exile bound – a grievous crowd. From far and near they drew, their hearts prepared and their possessions gathered, to sail to unknown lands, wherever over the waves I ordered them to follow. Now above the crest of highest Ida rose the morning-star, chief in the beginning of day. The Greeks held fast the captive gates of Troy. No help or hope was ours any more. Then, yielding everything, and lifting once again my old father, we fled for refuge to the distant hills.

5c) Aeneas and Dido (Vergil, Aeneid, 4. 1-629, passim)

Now felt the Queen the sharp, slow-gathering pangs of love, and out of every pulsing vein love nourished the wound and fed its hidden fire. Her hero's virtues and his lordly line keep calling to her soul, and his words, his glance cling to her heart like lingering, barbed steel, and both rest and peace desert her troubled body. She guides Aeneas around her city's walls she guides to show off Sidon's gold, and what her realm can boast. Often her voice tries to speak but slowly dies away. Or, when the daylight fades, she lays out a royal banquet, and once more will plead, mad that she is, to hear the Trojan sorrow, and with oblivious ravishment once more, she hangs on his lips when he tells it.

For Dido did not heed the importance of honour and a good name, nor did she mean her love to hide, but she called the lawlessness a marriage, and with phrases tried to cover her shame. Swift through the Libyan cities sped

Rumor. Rumor! What evil can surpass her speed? In movement she grows mighty, and achieves strength and dominion as she flies swifter.

She now with varied stories filled men's ears, joyful, whether false or true she continued to sing: how Trojan-born Aeneas had come, and how Dido, the lovely widow, gazed at him, eager to wed; how all winter long they passed time in revel and pleasure, given over to leisure, failing to heed either crown or kingdom – shameless! Enslaved by lust! Such stories the filthy goddess spread, broadcast through the lips of men.

The Jove turned his gaze upon the royal dwelling, where for love the passionate duo had forgotten their place and name. Then to Mercury he gave this command: "Hasten, my son, upon the west wind and make your winged way! Bring my command to that prince of Troy who delays now in Tyrian Carthage, heedless utterly of an empire fated by Heaven. Not for this did his mother shield him twice from the Greeks in arms, but so that he might rule Italy, a land filled with thrones and echoing with war, and that he, of Teucer's seed, should found a race and bring beneath its law the whole wide world.

Mercury observed his great lord's command with prompt obedience. He fastened first those sandals of bright gold, which carry him aloft over land or sea, with airy wings that race along fleeting wind, and then lifted his wand, with which he summons from the grave pale ghosts, or, if he chooses, assigns to grievous Tartarus, or by its power brings or dispels sleep. With these, he rips through the winds or cleaves the obscurity of stormy clouds. When first his winged feet came near the clay-built Punic huts, he saw Aeneas building a citadel and founding walls and towers. Straightaway the god said: "Do you labour to building strong foundations for lofty Carthage? Do you, a woman's weak slave, build her proud city? Have you forgot your kingdom and divine task? If the proud reward of your destined journey does not move your heart, if all the arduous toil does not speak to your own honor, Iook upon Iulus in his youth, your hope and heir, Ascanius. It is his rightful place to reign over Roman lands in Italy."

Aeneas at the sight stood, struck dumb with a choking voice and rising hair. He desired to flee at once and leave that lovely land, wondering at Heaven's wrathful word. Alas! What cunning argument could he plead to the Queen? How to break such news? Flashing this way and that, his startled mind produces many possibilities, and he considers them all.

But that unclean tongue of Rumor informed Dido and fevered her heart, that the fleet was being made fit to depart, and was hastening to embark. Finding Aeneas, she chastised him and poured out her heart: "Did you hope to hide it, liar, that such crime was in your heart, to steal away, without farewell, out of my kingdom? Did our mutual love not move you, nor your own true promise given once upon a time? Do I, who will die a death of sorrow, not move you? Why compel your ships to brave the winter stars? Why off to sea so fast through stormy skies? O, cruelty!"

But he, obeying Jove's decree, gazed consistently away, and he repressed the crushing, cruel pain in his heart. He broke his silence: "My Queen, hear my brief plea! It was not my hope to hide this flight, as you have dreamed. No, I never lit a bridegroom's torch, nor did I give you the vow of marriage. Had my destiny decreed that I should shape life to my heart's desire, and at my own will put away the weight of trouble and pain, my place would now be found in Troy, among the cherished homes of my own kin, and

Priam's mansion, proud and still standing. But now to Italy Apollo's power commands me to go, and his Lycian oracles are loud for Italy. My heart is there, and there my fatherland. If the towers of Carthage and your Libyan colony delight your Tyrian eyes, would you refuse to Trojan exiles their haven shore?"

She, with averted eyes and a glance that rolled speechless this way and that, had listened long to his reply, till her rage finally broke: "No goddess gave birth to you! No Dardanian produced your ancestors! But on its breast of stone Caucasus bore you, and the tigresses of hellish Hyrcania gave their udders to your infant lips. That orphan and castaway I found in beggary and gave him a share – fool that I was – in my own royal glory. His lost fleet and his sorry crews I steered away from death. Begone! Sail on to Italy, your throne, through wind and wave! I pray that, if there be any just gods of power, you may drink down death on the rocks of the sea, and often call with dying gasps on Dido's name, while I pursue with vengeful fire. When cold death rips the body from the breath, my ghost shall sit forever in your path. Your stubborn heart shall pay full punishment. They'll never bring me never into that deep gulf of death of all your woe!" She ceased her rant abruptly, and sick at heart, she fled the light of day, as if to shrink from human eyes, and left Aeneas there irresolute with horror, while his soul conceived of many vain replies.

From her walls the watchful Queen gazed at the brightened sky, and she saw the sails push forth to sea, till all of her port and shore held not an oar or keel. Thrice and four times she smote her lovely breast with wrathful hand, and tore her golden hair. "O avenging furies," she cries, "O gods that guard Queen Dido's dying breath! Listen, and extend your power to my guiltless misery. Hear what I pray! O you Tyrians, I sting with your hatred all his seed and people forever. This is the offering my ashes ask. No love between our two peoples! No truce or friendship! Arise, out of my dust, unknown Avenger, rise to aggravate and lay waste with sword and flame those Dardan settlers, and to trouble them today, tomorrow, and as long as power is yours to use! My dying curse deploys shore against shore and the opposing seas in shock of arms with arms. May living enemies pass down from father to son insatiable war!"

5d) Aeneas in the Underworld (Vergil, Aeneid, 6. 1-853, passim)

Aeneas sailed the fleet along the waves to the old, sacred shores of Euboean Cumae. They turn all the prows toward sea, and anchor the ships in a line along the lengthy beaches. The young, eager warriors leap to shore, upon Hesperian soil. Aeneas, servant of the gods, ascends the hill where lofty Apollo reigns, and that far-off, deep cave of the fearsome Sibyl, in stupendous cave, into whose mind Delian Apollo breathes prophesies, unfolding things to come…

The Sibyl spoke to Aeneas: "Offspring of the gods, Anchises' son, the downward path to death is easy – all the night and day dark Pluto's door stands open for a guest – remounting to the world of light, this is a task indeed, a supreme challenge. Few, very few, whom righteous Jove did blessed, or with constnat virtue carried to the stars, children of gods, have won such a victory. Grim forests block the way. Slow, gliding Cocytus circles through the sightless gloom. But if it is your dream and fond wish to travel twice over the Stygian gulf, twice to set your eyes upon the glooms of Tartarus, if a such mad quest is your pleasure, hear what must be first fulfilled . A certain tree hides in the darkest shade a golden bough of pliable stems and many leaves of gold, sacred to Proserpine, infernal Queen. Far in the grove it hides, in sunless vale is keeps deep shadows keep in captivity. No pilgrim to that underworld can pass except him who who plucks this flourished, golden leaf; for beautiful Proserpine has ordained that this is her chosen gift. Whenever it is picked, the golden fruit never fails to spring another shoot. Therefore, seek it with uplifted eyes, and when by will of the gods you find it, reach forward and pluck it, for at a touch it yields a free and willing gift – if Fate commands it. But otherwise no mortal strength can help you, nor strong, sharp steel, to cut it from the tree. Another task awaits…

Then Aeneas dedicated a dark altar to Pluto, Stygian King, and he piled upon the flames the heavy entrails of the bulls, and poured oil over the burning flesh. Then, suddenly, at sunrise, the ground groaned beneath their feet. The forests and hills shook, and it seemed the hounds of hell howled through the shade to hail their Queen. "Away, you irreverent spirits! Stand far away!" the priestess shrieked, "do not dare to come to this sacred grove! Come, Aeneas! Begin your journey! Draw your sheathed blade! Now, keep your courage!" So she spoke, and she bursts into the yawning cave with frenzied steps, while he follows where she leads and strides with unfaltering feet by her side. Gods! who rule the spirits of the dead!

In the first courts and entrances of Hell sorrows and vengeful Cares lay on couches: there dwells sad, Old Age, pale Disease, and Fear, and Hunger, temptress to all crime; Want, base and vile, and, two fearsome shapes to see, Slavery and Death; then Sleep, Death's next of kin, and dreams of guilty joy. Death-dealing War is always at the door, and nearby are the terrible Furies' beds of steel, united to wild-eyed Strife, and her snaky hair with blood-stained skin. There in the middle court a shadowy elm spreads its ancient branches, and in its leaves deluding visions haunt and seize. Then come strange prodigies of beasts: Centaurs are stabled there, and double shapes like Scylla, or the dragon bred by Lerna with its hideous scream; Briareus, clutching with his hundred hands, the Chimaera, wreathed with flame, a crowd of Gorgons, Harpies with foul wings, and giant Geryon's triple-monstered body draws its shadow.

Aeneas, shuddering with sudden fear, drew his sword and faced them with naked steel. If it were not for his wise guide, who told him that these were only shapes and shadows sweeping by, his stroke would have swept the vacant air in vain. From there the path leads to that Tartarean stream of Acheron, whose fierce and foul torrent spills all of its sands into Cocytus. A ferryman, gruesome in appearance, keeps guard. This was Charon, clothed in foul garments with an unkempt, thick gray beard upon his chin, and staring eyes of flame. A tattered cloak, all stained and knotted, falls from his shoulder, and he guides his craft with a pole, and in the black boat ferries over the dead. He is old, but a god's old age looks fresh and strong.

To those dim shores the crowd of shades stream on, husbands and wives, and pale, un-breathing forms of great heroes, fair boys and virgins, and strong youth at whose graves dear parents mourned. As numberless a throng of souls as leaves that fall when autumn's early frost is on the grove, or like vast flocks of birds sent flying over wide seas to lands of flowers by winter's chill. All stood begging to begin their voyage across that river, and reached out pale hands, in passionate yearning for its distant shore. But the grim boatman takes now these, now those, or thrusts them away without pity.

Aeneas, moved to wonder and deep awe, gazed at the chaos, and cried: "Virgin seer, why do the mob of ghosts move toward that stream? What are they seeking there? Or what judge decides that these linger unwillingly, while their peers sweep forward over the leaden waves?" The Sibyl replied:

"Son of Anchises, offspring of the gods, in that direction lie Cocytus and the Stygian stream, by whose terrible power the gods themselves fear to take an oath in vain. Here far and wide you see the hapless horde of people that have no grave. Those buried with proper rites the boatman Charon bears across the deep. But over that loud flood and dreadful shore no traveller may be borne, until his gathered ashes rest in peace For a hundred years around this dark borderland some ghosts haunt and roam, then win late passage over the long-desired waves."

At last the hero and his guide arrived safely across the river, and were moored amid sea-green grasses in the formless mire. Here Cerberus, with triple-throated bark, made all the region echo, as he lay there at full length in his cave. Seeing the serpents writhe around his neck, the Sibyl threw down a loaf with of honeyed herbs and a drowsy fragrance, and he, ravenous, opened his mouth wide with his three fierce jaws and snatched the bait, then crouched with his large back loose upon the ground, and filled his cavern floor from end to end.

Aeneas walked through Hell's gate, while its guard slept, then he fled those shores of the Stygian river, from where travellers never return. Now he suddenly hears sobs, and piteous, lisping cries of souls of infants upon the threshold, whom, before they had taken their portion of sweet life, dark Fate had torn from their nursing breast and plunged into the bitterness of death. Nor far from these lay the throng of dead slain by unjust judgment. Not without judge or law did these very realms exist: wise Minos holds the urn of justice there, and maintains assembly of the silent shades, hearing the stories of their lives and deeds. Close to this place dwell those miserable ghosts who, not because of crime, but for hating life and light had seized death by their own hands, and cast away the vital essence of their life – alas – willingly! Now, they would suffer any need or bear any burden if only they might regain their former life! But Fate forbids it. Around them wind the sad, unlovely waves of the Styx: nine times it coils and flows into itself. Not far from here, spread out on every side, lie the Fields of Sorrow – such a name do they bear. Here all were wasted away for ruthless love wander in unseen paths, or in the gloom of a dark myrtle grove. Not even in death have they forgotten their grief of so long ago.

Here Tyrian Dido, her wound still unhealed, roamed through a mighty forest. The Trojan prince's eyes saw her near him through the murky gloom…down fell his tears, and he fondly spoke: "Poor, suffering Dido! Were the tidings true that you flung yourself on the fatal sword? Your death, ah me! I produced it. But I swear by stars above us, by the powers in Heaven, or whatever oath you dead believe, that not by choice did I flee your shores! Divine decrees compelled me, even as now among these ghosts I pass, and thread my way along this gulf of night and loathsome land. How could I think that my cruel departure would bring you at last to all this end? Stay! Why ignore me? Why run away? Our last farewell! Our doom! I speak it now!" Thus, though she glared with fierce, relentless gaze, Aeneas, with loving words and tear-filled pleas, tried to soothe her angry soul. But on the ground she fixed her averted eyes. For all he spoke moved her no more than if her frowning brow were unchanging flint or carved in Parian stone. Then, after a pause, she fled away in wrath and took refuge within the cool, dark grove where her first spouse, Sichaeus, mingled his own tears with hers in mutual love.

Aeneas, still recognized her guiltless suffering with his own anguish, watched with dimmed eyes her departure, and pitied from afar the fallen Queen.

But now he must keep going along his fated way, now the last regions lie around the travellers, where famous warriors dwell in the darkness. Here Tydeus comes into view, with renowned Parthenopaeus and pale Adrastus pale. Here are those mourned in the world above with many moans, those who have fallen in battle, the Trojans, whose long line Aeneas groans to see…but Sibyl spoke a warning: "Night speeds by, Aeneas, and we lose it in lamenting here. Now comes the place where the paths separate. Your road, on the right, goes toward Pluto's dwelling, and leads us to Elysium. But the left speeds sinful souls to doom, and is their path to Tartarus the land of the accursed."

Aeneas immediately saw by the cliff on the left a spreading tower, dominated by a triple-wall, and around it circled a raging river of flood of flame, Infernal Phlegethon, which whirls along Loud-thundering rocks. A mighty columned gate of adamant is there – no human power, not even that of the gods, can destroy this gate. It has a tall tower of steel, and seated there Tisiphone, flecked in blood, sleepless forever, guards the entrance. Here groans are heard, fierce cracks of the whip and scourge, loud-clanking iron links and trailing chains. Aeneas, motionless with horror, stood overwhelmed at such an uproar.

"Virgin priestess," Aeneid asked, "What shapes of guilty are these? What punishment pursudes them in this way? What wailing splits the air?" The Sibyl replied, "Far-famed prince of Troy, the feet of innocence may never pass into this house of the wicked. But Hecate, when she gave me power over the Avernian groves, taught me what penalties the gods decree, and showed me all. There Cretan Rhadamanthys keeps his kingdom, and from his unpitying throne he punishes and lays bare the secret crimes of mortals who, exulting in their vain cunning, elude due punishment until their death. There, armed forever with her vengeful whip, Tisiphone pursues with menace and outrages the guilty swarm, and in her left hand she lifts her angered serpents, while she calls a troop of her sister-furies as fierce as she is."

"Here in a prison-house, awaiting their doom, are men who hated their entire life their brothers, or maltreated their gray fathers, or tricked a humble friend. The men who grasped at hoarded riches, never sharing them with their friends and family. Here now are slain adulterers, and men who dared to fight in unjust cause, and broke all faith with their own lords. Do not seek to know what forms of woe they feel, what fateful shape of punishment have overwhelmed them there. Some roll huge boulders up, some hang on wheels, lashed to the whirling spokes. In his sad seat Theseus is sitting, never again to rise, while unhappy Phlegyas uplifts his voice in warning through the darkness, calling loud, "Learn to bow to justice, never scorn the gods!"

Now, with every rite fulfilled, and due tribute paid to the sovereign power of Proserpine, at last their journey led to a land of joy, the home of the blessed among fortunate groves and green fields. A full sky bestows a rose light on the bright land, where cloudless rays of the sun and planets beam in a manner unknown to those who dwell on earth. On smooth green graases, contending limb with limb, immortal athletes play, and wrestle against friend or rival on the yellow sand, with echoing footsteps and ecstatic song, some perform the divine dance, and among them walks the bard of Thrace, in clad lowing clothes, playing a seven-noted melody, sweeping the numbered strings with nimble hand, or striking with ivory point his golden lyre…

From that vantage point they saw a broad, shining land, and walking down to this place. And far below in a pleasant vale stood Anchises, pondering, while his eyes and mind perceived a host of imprisoned spirits, who were waiting there for their entrance to terrestrial air…Soon he noticed Aeneas coming to him over the green slope, and, lifting both his hands in eager welcome, spread them swiftly forward. Tears fell from his eyes, and he said: "Are you here at last? Has your proven love of me, your father, overcome this difficult way? Will Heaven, beloved son, once more allow us look eye to eye? And shall I hear your kindred voice mingling with my own? I cherished for a long time this hope. My soul counted the elapse of days, and did my thought did not deceive me. Over what lands and seas were you driven to my embrace! What varied perils assaulted you, my son, on every side! How long I feared that that Libyan throne would bring suffering upon you!"

Aeneas replied: "Your own image, Father, your sorrowful shade, often came to me in a vision, and compelled me to journey here. Our fleet of ships lies safe at anchor in the Tuscan seas. Come, take my hand! Come, father, I beg you, and accept my loving embrace, your heart to mine!" So spoke Aeneas, his eyes filled with tears. Three times he tried in vain to embrace his father with his arms, three times the shade fled from the touch of his hand, like wispy winds or hovering dreams. Afterwards, Aeneas noticed the solemn groves in a deep, distant valey, where trees were whispering, and forever flowed the river Lethe, through its land of calm.

Innumerable peoples roamed and haunted there, just as when, upon a still summer morning, as the bees taste blooming, rainbow-coloured flowers in the field, or pour out in a busy swarm around the white lilies, although dispersed, their murmured songs from all the meadows still hum. Aeneas views them in amazement, and fearfully inquires of where they come from and why they are here – what are those rivers, and what people press themselves, line after line, along those dim shores. Anchises told him, "Those crowding souls prepare to be reborn in their destined form. Here, at the river Lethe's waves, they drink waters that quell all worries and oblivion. I shall explain this to you, and show you the number and groups of my posterity. In doing so, your heart will rejoice in the thought of Italy, you new-found home."

"Father," said Aeneas, "should I guess that it is from this very place that joyful souls rise to the upper air, and shall once more return to burdened flesh? Why do they feel, these wretched spirits, such a fatal lust to live a mortal life?" Anchises responded, "I will speak to this, my son, so that you shall have no doubts." And so he laid out the truth in ordered words, unfolding from point to point:

"Know first that heaven and earth and ocean's plain, the moon's bright orb, and stars born of Titans are all nourished by one Life. One primal Mind, entwined with the vast and general universe, fills every part and stirs the mighty whole. In it, man and beast, creatures of the air, and all the swarming monsters that can be found beneath the marbled sea. The seeds of them all are retained in a fiery virtue, a celestial power. But crude bodies, with limbs of clay and parts born to die, encumber and overcloud this divine seed. It is from this energy that terrors and passions also spring, and suffering and joy. For from deep darkness and captivity all gaze blindly on the radiant world. Nor when they bid farewell to life's last beam, may those suffering strop their pain, nor will they be freed from all their sickness of the flesh, but by a fixed law, the strange, hardened disease works deeply into the each one's spirit. The punishment of past evils is suffered here, and full penalty is paid. Some hang on high, outstretched to viewless winds. For others, the contagion of their wickedness must be purged in vast cleansing of deep-rolling seas, or burned away in fire. Each man receives his ghostly portion in the world of dark.

But afterwards we go free to the realm of Elysium, where for a time we abide by these dwellings of bliss, until time's long interval is fulfilled, and all impurities are removed, restoring the pure, ethereal soul of virginal fire. At last, when thousands of years have passed, God calls them forth to this Lethaean stream, in a great host, and, completely oblivious, they may now behold once more the vaulted sky, and willingly return to shapes of flesh." So spoke Anchises, and he then led his son forward, the Sibyl with him, to the shades assembled there, and they stopped on a lofty hill from where they could clearly see long procession and discern each face.

"Pay attention now," Anchises said, "for I will now show you the future glory of our Dardanian blood, of our sons' sons to be born in Italy, who shall be mighty spirits, and prolong our names, their own heritage. I will unfold their story, and reveal the destined years. Look there! In that line of lords, is the son of Mars, great Romulus, given birth to by Ilia, from a long line of Trojan kings! Notice his helmet with the upright, double-crest, while his celestial father shows the appearance of his divine birth! From him, my son, great Rome shall rise, and, favored by his star, will have power around the world and men of godlike mind.

"Let your own visionary glance now look at your people, the Romans. Here is Caesar, of Iulus' glorious seed. Behold him ascending to the world of light! Now behold, at last, that man, for this is he, so often foretold to your listening ears, Augustus Caesar, kindred of Jove! He brings a golden age, and he shall restore old Saturn's sceptre to our Latin land, and his sway shall extend from remotest Africa to India. This fair dominion outruns the horizon – indeed, beyond the sun's bright path, where Atlas' shoulder bears the dome of heaven thick with burning stars.

"Let others forge and mold the bronze to forms more fair, and sculpt living features out of marble, let them plead cases well, or trace the cycled heaven with a pointed wand, and hail the constellations as they rise! But you, Roman, learn to rule the nations with sovereign authority. Your great art shall be to keep the world in lasting peace, to spare the humbled foe, and to trample the proud underfoot." So did Anchises speak.

Adapted from Theodore C. Williams, Vergil. Aeneid (Boston: Houghton Mifflin Co. 1910)

READING 6:

VERGIL'S *GEORGICS*

In Book IV of *Georgics*, Vergil retells the story of the Thracian poet, Orpheus, and his tragic wife, Eurydice. Eurydice is killed by a poisonous snake while attempting to outrun a lustful satyr. Orpheus immediately decides to rescue his love by making a journey to the Underworld (katabasis) to retrieve her. As the greatest poet and musician among mortals, he performs before Pluto (Roman Hades) and Proserpina (Persephone), moves all souls about him. He is granted his wish by Proserpina, and can bring Eurydice back – on one condition: that he not look back at Eurydice as he leads her back to life. Orpheus leads her almost to the world above, but sneaks one last look to see if she is there. Eurydice is immediately sucked back down to Tartarus, and Orpheus comes up empty-handed.

In his mourning, he refuses to play music anymore, and is ripped apart by frenzied Maenads who happen to pass by. For much of *Georgics*, Vergil offers an instructional (didactic) poem on farming. This myth of Orpheus and Eurydice, however, is just one example of the work's greater themes, including the virtue of labour, the rural, peaceful life of a farmer, Epicurean and Stoic philosophy. In explaining to his readers the fleeting nature of fate and the struggles of toil, Vergil's version of the Orpheus and Eurydice myth has become the most famous.

6a) Orpheus and Eurydice (Vergil, Georgics, 4. 453-527, passim)

"Do not doubt that it is divine wrath that plagues you, nor light the debt that you pay. It is the same as of Orpheus, who, similarly unhappy by no fault of his, madly raged for his ravished bride. She in her haste to shun thy hot pursuit along the stream, did not see the coming death, where at her feet upon the bank in the tall grass lay a monstrous water-snake.

But with their cries her band of Dryads filled the mountains to their proudest peaks. they wailed for her fate to the heights of Rhodope, and tall Pangaea, and, beloved of Mars, the land that bowed to Rhesus – Thrace no less, with Hebrus' stream. And Orithyia wept, daughter of old Acte. But Orpheus himself, soothing his love-pain with the hollow shell,

To his sweet wife on the lone shore alone, when day dawned and when it died he sang. Indeed, to the jaws of Taenarus too he came, to Dis, the infernal palace, and a grove grim with a horror of great darkness – he came, entered, and faced the Manes and the King of terrors, whose stone heart no prayer can persuade.

Then from the deepest depths of Erebus, lifted by his skill, the hollow shades came loping, ghostly semblances of forms lost to the light, as birds in thousands come here to greenwood boughs for cover, when twilight-hour or storms of winter chase them from the hills. Wives and men, and great heroic shapes done with life's service; boys, unwedded girls, youths placed on a pyre before their fathers' eyes.

Around them, choked with black slime and hideous weeds, Cocytus winds, and there lies the unlovely swamp of dull dead water, and, to hold them fast, Styx with her ninefold barrier poured between. No, even the deep Tartarean Halls of death stood lost in wonder, and the Furies, their brows with livid locks of serpents entwined; even Cerberus held his triple jaws agape, and, the wind hushed, Ixion's wheel stood still…

And now with homeward steps he had passed all perils unscathed, and, finally restored, had almost brought to realms of upper air Eurydice, following behind him following – for so had Proserpina commanded – when his heart was suddenly seized by a mad desire – a fault to be forgiven, one that even Hell might forgive.

For at the very threshold of the day, heedless, alas, his resolve became vanquished, and he stopped, turned, looked upon Eurydice, his own once more. But even with that look, all his labour became wasted, the bond of that evil tyrant broken, and a crash was heard three times like thunder in the meres of hell…

"Orpheus! What ruin has your madness brought ypon me, alas! And you? No! Once again the unpitying fates recall me, and dark sleep closes my swimming eyes. And now farewell: covered by enormous night, I am borne away, outstretching these helpless hands toward you, yours, alas, no more!"

Thus she spoke, and suddenly, like smoke dissolving into empty air, passed and was taken from his sight. Nor could he, clutching vain shadows, yearning sorely to speak, ever again behold her, nor could he a second time be allowed by Hell's boatman to pass the watery boundary. What should he do? Where could he go, twice aggrieved?

With what tears might he move the Manes, with what voice the Powers of darkness? She indeed even now, cold as death, was floating on the Stygian boat. for seven whole months unceasingly, men say, beneath a high crag, by the lone waves of Strymon, he wept, and in the chill caverns he unrolled his story, melting tigers' hearts, and leading along with his song the oak trees.

As in the poplar-shade a nightingale mourns her lost young, which some relentless predator, spying, has torn unfledged from the nest, but she wails all long night, and perched upon a sprig, with sad insistence she pipes her grievous song, till the whole region overflows with her wrongs. No love, no new desire compelled his soul:

By snow-bound Tanais and the icy north, forever wed to the Far steppes of frosty Rhipaean, alone he wandered, lamenting lost Eurydice, and the ungiven gifts of Dis. Scorned by this tribute the Ciconian women, amid their awful Bacchanalian rites and midnight revellings, tore him limb from limb, and strewed his fragments over the wide fields.

Then too, even then, for a long time along the Hebrus stream, Oeagrian Hebrus, rolled down his drifting head, ripped from his marble neck,the death-chilled tongue still finding a voice to cry "Eurydice! Ah! Poor Eurydice!" With parting breath he called her, and the banks from the broad stream echoed "Eurydice!"

Adapted from J. B. Greenough, Vergil. Georgics (Boston: Ginn & Co., 1900).

READING 7:

THE *HOMERIC HYMNS*

Although called the *Homeric Hymns*, these poems were not written by Homer, but by many anonymous authors over a period of several hundred years. Each of the thirty-three surviving hymns is devoted to an individual god or goddess. In varied length and style, they tell of the deity's origins, powers, associations, and inventions. They range in style from formal and solemn to playful and irreverent. For classicists, they provide a simple but often insightful look into characterizations of the Greek deities in a context beyond Homer and the tragic playwrights.

7a) Athena (Homeric Hymns 11 & 28, passim)

Of Pallas Athena, guardian of the city, I begin to sing. Dread is she, and with Ares she loves deeds of war, the sack of cities and the shouting and the battle. It is she who saves the people as they go out to war and come back. Pallas Athena, the glorious goddess, bright-eyed, inventive, unbending of heart, pure virgin (Parthenos), saviour of cities, courageous, Tritogeneia. Wise Zeus himself bore her from his remarkable head, arrayed in warlike weapons of flashing gold, and awe seized all the gods as they gazed. But Athena sprang quickly from his immortal head and stood before Zeus who holds the aegis, shaking a sharp spear: great Olympus began to shake horribly at the might of the bright-eyed goddess, and the earth cried fearfully, and the sea was moved and tossed with dark waves, while foam burst forth suddenly. The bright Son of Hyperion stopped his swift-footed horses a long while, until the maiden, Pallas Athena, had stripped the heavenly armour from her immortal shoulders. And wise Zeus was glad. And so hail to you, daughter of Zeus who holds the aegis! Now I will remember you and another song as well.

7b) Apollo (Homeric Hymn 3, passim)

To Delian Apollo

I will remember and not forget Apollo who shoots from afar. As he goes through the house of Zeus, the gods tremble before him and all spring from their seats when he comes near, as he bends his bright bow. But Leto alone stays by the side of Zeus who delights in thunder, and then she unstrings his bow, and closes his quiver, and takes his archery from his strong shoulders in her hands and hangs them on a golden peg against a pillar of his father's house. Then she leads him to a seat and makes him sit. And Fatherly Zeus gives him nectar in a golden cup, welcoming his dear son, while the other gods make him sit down there, and queenly Leto rejoices because she bore a mighty son and an archer. Rejoice, blessed Leto, for you bare glorious children, the lord Apollo and Artemis who delights in arrows…

How, then, shall I sing of you who in all ways are worthy of song? For everywhere, O Phoebus, the whole range of song is given to you, both over the mainland that rears heifers and over the islands. All mountain peaks and high headlands of lofty hills and rivers flowing out to the deep and beaches sloping seawards and havens of the sea are your delight. Shall I sing how at the first Leto bore you to be the joy of men, as she rested against Mount Cynthus in that rocky isle, in sea-girt Delos…Leto roamed far and wide while in labour with the god who shoots from afar, to see if any land would be willing to make a dwelling for her son. But they greatly trembled and feared, and none, not even the richest of them, dared receive Phoebus, until queenly Leto set foot on Delos and uttered winged words and asked: "Delos, if you would be willing to be the home of my son Phoebus Apollo and make him a rich temple, you will find that no other place will touch you. And although you will never be rich in oxen and sheep, nor bear vines or produce crops abundantly, nonetheless, if you have the temple of far-shooting Apollo, all men will bring you sacrifices and gather here, and the unceasing smell of rich sacrifice will always arise, and you will feed those who dwell in you from the hand of strangers…"

Now when Leto had sworn and completed her oath, Delos was very glad at the birth of the far-shooting lord. But Leto was racked nine days and nine nights with labour beyond bear. And there with her were all the chief goddesses: Dione, Rhea, Ichnaea, Themis, loud-moaning Amphitrite, and the other deathless goddesses except white-armed Hera, who sat in the halls of cloud-gathering Zeus. Only Eilithyia, goddess of childbirth, had not heard of Leto's labour, for she sat on the top of Olympus beneath golden clouds by white-armed Hera's plotting, who kept her close through envy, because Leto with the lovely tresses was soon to bear a son faultless and strong.

But the goddesses sent Iris from the well-placed island to bring Eilithyia, promising her a great necklace strung with golden threads, nine cubits long. And they told Iris to call her aside from white-armed Hera, in case she might afterwards change her mind from coming by her words. When swift Iris, swift as the wind, had heard all this, she set to run, and quickly completing the distance she came to the home of the gods, sheer Olympus, and called Eilithyia out from the hall to the door and spoke quick words to her, telling her what the goddesses who dwell on Olympus had told her. So she moved the heart of Eilithyia in her dear breast, and they went their way, like shy wild-doves in their travel. And as soon as Eilithyia the goddess of childbirth set foot on Delos, the pains of birth seized Leto, and she longed to give birth, so she cast her arms about a palm tree and kneeled on the soft meadow while the earth laughed for joy beneath. Then the child leaped forth to the light, and all the goddesses raised a cry. Straightaway, great Phoebus, the goddesses washed you purely and cleanly with sweet water, and swathed you in a white garment of fine texture, new-woven, and fastened a golden band about you.

Now Leto did not give Apollo, bearer of the golden blade, her breast. Themis instead poured nectar and ambrosia with her divine hands, and Leto was glad because she had borne a strong son and an archer. But as soon as you had tasted that divine heavenly food, O Phoebus, you could no longer then be held by golden cords nor confined with bands, but all their ends were undone. And then Phoebus Apollo spoke out among the deathless goddesses: "The lyre and the curved bow shall always be dear to me, and I will declare to men the unfailing will of Zeus." So said Phoebus, the long-haired god who shoots from afar and he began to walk upon the wide earth, and all the goddesses were amazed at him…

To Pythian Apollo

Leto's all-glorious son goes to rocky Pytho, playing upon his hollow lyre, clad in divine, perfumed garments, and his lyre, at the touch of the golden key, sings sweetly. From this place, swift as thought, he speeds from earth to Olympus, to the house of Zeus, to join the gathering of the other gods. Then straightway the undying gods think only of the lyre and song, and all the Muses together, voice sweetly answering voice, a hymn for the unending gifts that the gods enjoy, as well as the sufferings of men and all that they endure at the hands of the deathless gods, and how they live witless and helpless and cannot find healing for death or defense against old age.

And from there you went speeding swiftly to the mountain ridge, and came to Crisa beneath snowy Parnassus, a foothill facing towards the west. A cliff hangs over it from above, and a hollow, rugged glade runs underneath. There the lord Phoebus Apollo resolved to make his lovely temple, and thus he said: "In this place I intend to build a glorious temple to be an oracle for men, and here they will always bring perfect sacrifices, both they who dwell in rich Peloponnesus and the men of Europe and from all the wave-washed islands, coming to question me. And I will deliver to them all advice that cannot fail, answering them in my rich temple." When he had said this, Phoebus Apollo laid out all the wide and long foundations, and upon these the sons of Erginus, Trophonius and Agamedes, dear to the deathless gods, laid a footing of stone. And the countless tribes of men built the whole temple out of wrought stones, to be sung about forever.

But nearby was a sweet flowing spring, and there with his strong bow the lord, the son of Zeus, killed the bloated, terrible she-dragon, a fierce monster that delighted harming men upon earth…for she was a very bloody plague. It was she who before received from gold-throned Hera and brought up evil, cruel Typhoeus to be a plague to men. Once upon a time Hera bore him because she was angry with Father Zeus, when the Son of Cronos bore all-glorious Athena from his head. Because of that Queenly Hera was angry and spoke thus among the assembled gods: "Hear from me, all gods and goddesses, how cloud-gathering Zeus begins to dishonor me on purpose, when he has made me his true-hearted wife. See now, apart from me he has given birth to bright-eyed Athena who is first among all the blessed gods. But my son Hephaestus whom I bore was weakly among all the blessed gods, and lame in his foot, a shame and a disgrace to me in heaven, whom I myself took in my hands and cast out so that he fell in the great sea…

When she had so spoken, she went apart from the gods, being very angry. Then straightway, ox-eyed, Queenly Hera prayed, striking the ground with her hand, and speaking in this way: "Hear now, I pray, Earth and wide Heaven above and you, Titan gods who dwell beneath the earth around great Tartarus, and from whom were born both gods and men! Listen now to me, one and all, and grant that I may bear a child apart from Zeus, no lesser than him in strength — no, let him be as much stronger than Zeus as all-seeing Zeus was compared to Cronos." Thus she cried and lashed the earth with her strong hand. Then the life-giving earth was moved: and when Hera saw it she was glad in heart, for she thought her prayer would be fulfilled.

And when the months and days went by, and the seasons duly came, she bore one neither like the gods nor mortal men: evil, cruel Typhoeus, a plague to men. Straightaway ox-eyed, Queenly Hera took him, and bringing one evil thing to another of such kind, gave him to the dragoness, and she received him. And this Typhoeus used to work great mischief among the famous peoples of men. Whoever met the dragoness, the day of doom would sweep him away, until the lord Apollo, who deals death from afar, shot a strong arrow at her. Then she, ripped apart with bitter pain, collapsed, drawing great gasps for breath and rolling about the place. An awful, unspeakable noise swelled up as she writhed continually this way and that in the wood. And so she left her life, breathing it forth in blood. Then Phoebus Apollo boasted over her:

"Now rot here upon the soil that feeds man. You at least shall live no more to be a terrible bane to men who eat the fruit of the all-nourishing earth, and who will bring here perfect sacrifices. Against cruel death neither Typhoeus shall avail you nor the ill-famed Chimera, but here shall the Earth and shining Sun make you rot." Thus said Phoebus, boasting over her, and darkness covered her eyes. And the holy strength of Helios made her rot away there, for which reason the place is now called Pytho, and men call the lord Apollo by another name: Pythian. For on that spot the power of piercing Helios made the monster rot away.

And so, farewell, son of Zeus and Leto, but I will remember you and another song also.

7c) Aphrodite (Homeric Hymns 5 & 6, passim)

Muse, tell me about the deeds of golden Aphrodite, the Cyprian, who stirs up sweet passion in the gods and subdues mortal men and birds that fly in air and all the many creatures that the dry land and the sea rears: all these love the deeds of rich-crowned Cytherea.

Yet there are three hearts that she cannot bend nor yet ensnare. First is the daughter of Zeus who holds the aegis, bright-eyed Athena, for she has no pleasure in the deeds of golden Aphrodite, but delights in wars and in the work of Ares, in strife and battles and in preparing famous crafts…Nor does laughter-loving Aphrodite ever tame in love Artemis, the huntress with shafts of gold, for she loves archery and the slaying of wild beasts in the mountains, the lyre also, and dancing and thrilling cries and shady woods and the cities of upright men. Nor yet does the pure maiden Hestia love Aphrodite's works. She was the first-born child of wily

Cronos and youngest, by will of Zeus who holds the aegis, a queenly virgin whom both Poseidon and Apollo sought to wed. But she was wholly unwilling – no, she even stubbornly refused, and touching the head of father Zeus who holds the aegis, she, that fair goddess, swore a great oath that has in truth been fulfilled, that she would be a virgin all her days. So Zeus the Father gave her a high honor instead of marriage, and she has her place in the midst of the house and has the richest portion. In all the temples of the gods she has a share of honor, and among all mortal men she is chief of the goddesses.

Aphrodite cannot bend or ensnare the hearts of these three. But of all others there is nothing among the blessed gods or among mortal men that has escaped Aphrodite. Even the heart of Zeus, who delights in thunder, is led astray by her, even though he is greatest of all and has the lot of highest majesty, she beguiles even his wise heart whenever she pleases, and mates him with mortal women, unknown to Hera, his sister and his wife, the grandest by far in beauty among the deathless goddesses —most glorious is she whom wily Cronos with her mother Rhea did produce. And Zeus, whose wisdom is everlasting, made her his chaste and careful wife…

Splendid Aphrodite, gold-crowned and beautiful, whose dominion is the walled cities of Cyprus. There the moist breath of the western wind wafted her over the waves of the loud-moaning sea in soft foam, and there the gold-filleted Hours welcomed her joyously. They clothed her with heavenly garments: on her head they put a fine, well-wrought crown of gold, and in her pierced ears they hung ornaments of orichalcum and precious gold, and they adorned her with golden necklaces over her soft neck and snow-white breasts, jewels which the gold-filleted Hours wear themselves whenever they go to their father's house to join the lovely dances of the gods. And when they had fully decked her out, they brought her to the gods, who welcomed her when they saw her, giving her their hands. Each one of them prayed that he might lead her home to be his wedded wife, so greatly were they amazed at the beauty of violet-crowned Cytherea.

7d) Artemis (Homeric Hymn 27)

I sing of Artemis, whose shafts are made of gold, who cheers on the hounds, the pure virgin, shooter of stags, she who delights in archery, sister to Apollo with the golden sword. Over the shadowy hills and windy peaks she draws her golden bow, rejoicing in the hunt, and sends out grievous arrows. The tops of the high mountains tremble and the tangled wood echoes awesomely with the outcry of beasts. The earth quakes – and the sea also, where fishes shoal. But the goddess with a bold heart turns every way, destroying the race of wild beasts, and when she is satisfied and has cheered her heart, this huntress who delights in arrows slackens her supple bow and goes to the great house of her dear brother Phoebus Apollo, to the rich land of Delphi, there to order the lovely dance of the Muses and Graces. There she hangs up her curved bow and her arrows, and heads and leads the dances, gracefully arrayed, while all they utter their heavenly voice, singing how lovely-ankled Leto bore children supreme among the immortals both in thought and in deed. Hail to you, children of Zeus and rich-haired Leto! And now I will remember you and another song also.

7e) Dionysus (Homeric Hymns 1 & 7, passim)

I will sing of Dionysus, the son of glorious Semele, how he appeared on a jutting peninsula by the shore of the fruitless sea, seeming like a stripling in the first flush of manhood. His rich, dark hair was waving about him, and on his strong shoulders he wore a purple robe. At that time Tyrsenian pirates came swiftly over the sparkling sea on a well-decked ship —a miserable doom led them on. When they saw him they made signals to one another and sprang out quickly, and seizing him, they gleefully put him on board their ship, for they thought that he was the son of heaven-nurtured kings. They sought to bind him with crude bonds, but the bonds would not hold him, and the rope fell far away from his hands and feet, and he sat with a smile in his dark eyes. Then the helmsman understood everything and cried out at once to his fellows and said:

"Madmen! What god is this whom you have taken and bound, strong that he is? Not even the well-built ship can carry him. Surely this is either Zeus or Apollo who has the silver bow, or Poseidon, for he looks not like mortal men but like the gods who dwell on Olympus. Come, then, let us set him free upon the dark shore at once – do not lay hands on him, in case he grows angry and stirs up dangerous winds and heavy squalls." But the shipmaster insulted him with taunting words: "Idiot, watch the wind and help hoist sail on the ship! Catch all the sails! As for this fellow, we men will see to him. I think he is bound for Egypt or for Cyprus or to the Hyperboreans or further still. But in the end he will speak out and tell us his friends and all his wealth and his brothers, now that Fortune has thrown him in our way."

After he had said this, he had the mast and sail hoisted on the ship, the wind filled the sail, and the crew hauled tightly the sheets on either side.

But soon strange things were seen among them. First of all, sweet, fragrant wine ran streaming throughout all the black ship and a heavenly smell arose, so that all the seamen were seized with amazement when they saw it. And all at once a vine spread out both ways along the top of the sail with many clusters hanging down from it, and a dark ivy-plant twined about the mast, blossoming with flowers, and with rich berries growing on it, and all the poles were covered with garlands. When the pirates saw all this, then at last they ordered the helmsman to put the ship to land.

But the god changed into a dreadful lion there on the ship in the bow, and roared loudly. Amidships also he showed his powers and created a shaggy bear which stood up bellowing, while on the forepeak the lion glared fiercely with scowling brows. And so the sailors fled to the stern and crowded around the right-minded helmsman, until suddenly the lion sprang upon the shipmaster and seized him, and when the sailors saw it they leapt overboard one and all into the bright sea, escaping from a miserable fate, and were changed into dolphins. But to the helmsman Dionysus showed mercy and held him back and made him altogether happy, saying to him: "Take courage, good man: you have found favour with my heart. I am loud-crying Dionysus whom Cadmus' daughter, Semele, bore after union with Zeus."

Hail, child of fair-faced Semele! He who forgets you can in no way sing a sweet song.

O Heaven-born, in-sewn god, some say you were born in Dracanum, while others say windy Icarus, or Naxos, and others say it was by the deep-eddying river Alpheus that pregnant Semele bore you to Zeus, who loves thunder. And others yet, lord, say you were born in Thebes. But all these people lie. The Father of men and gods gave birth to you remote from men and secretly from white-armed Hera. There is a certain Nysa, a mountain most high and richly grown with woods, far off in Phoenicia, near the streams of Egypt… Be favorable, O in-sewn god, inspirer of frenzied women! We poets sing of you as we begin and as we end a song, and none forgetting you may call a holy song to mind. And so, farewell, Dionysus, in-sewn god, with your mother Semele, whom men call Thyone.

7f) Hermes (Homeric Hymn 4, passim)

Muse, sing of Hermes, the son of Zeus and Maia, lord of Cyllene and Arcadia rich in flocks, the luck-bringing messenger of the immortals whom Maia bore… For she bore a shifty son, blandly cunning, a robber, a cattle driver, a bringer of dreams, a watcher by night, a thief at the gates, one who was soon to show wonderful deeds among the deathless gods. Born at dawn, at mid-day already he played on the lyre, and in the evening he stole the cattle of far-shooting Apollo… As soon as he had leaped from his mother's heavenly womb, he lay not waiting in his holy cradle, but he sprang up and sought the oxen of Apollo. But as he stepped over the threshold of the high-roofed cave, he found a tortoise there and gained endless delight, for it was Hermes who first made the tortoise a singer. The creature fell in his way at the courtyard gate, where it was feeding on the rich grass before the dwelling, waddling along. When he saw it, the luck-bringing son of Zeus laughed and said:

"An omen of great luck for me so soon! I do not ignore it. Hail, comrade of the feast, lovely in shape, sounding at the dance! With joy I meet you! Where did you get that rich material for covering, that spangled shell —a tortoise living in the mountains? But I will take and carry you inside, and you shall help me, and I will do you no disgrace, though first of all you must profit me. It is better to be at home – harm may come outdoors. Living, you shall be a spell against mischievous witchcraft, but if you die, then you shall make sweetest song." Thus speaking, he picked up the tortoise in both hands and went back into the house carrying his charming toy. Then he cut off its limbs and scooped out the marrow of the mountain-tortoise with a scoop of grey iron…He cut stalks of reed according to measure and fixed them, fastening their ends across the back and through the shell of the tortoise, and then stretched ox hide all over it by his skill. He the put in the horns and fitted a cross-piece upon the two of them, and stretched seven strings of sheep-gut. And when he had made it, he tested each string in turn with the key as he held the lovely thing. At the touch of his hand it sounded marvelous, and, as he tried it, the god sang sweet random notes, even as youths bandy songs at festivals…

But while he was singing this, his heart was focused on other matters. And he took the hollow lyre and laid it in his sacred cradle, and sprang from the sweet-smelling hall to a watch-place, pondering sheer trickery in his heart, deeds such as foolish folk pursue in the dark night-time, for he longed to taste flesh. The Sun was going down beneath the earth towards Ocean with his horses and chariot when Hermes came hurrying to the shadowy mountains of Pieria, where the divine cattle of the blessed gods had their steads and grazed the pleasant, unmown meadows. Of these the Son of Maia, the sharp-eyed slayer of Argus, then cut off from the herd fifty loud-lowing oxen, and drove them straggling away across a sandy place, turning their hoof-prints aside. Also, he produced a crafty trick and reversed the marks of their hoofs, making the front behind and the hind before, while he himself walked the other way. Then he wove sandals with wicker by the sand of the sea, wonderful things, unthought of before. He mixed together tamarisk and myrtle-twigs, fastening together an armful of their fresh, young wood, and tied them, leaves and all securely under his feet as light sandals…

Through many shadowy mountains and echoing gorges and flowery plains glorious Hermes drove the oxen. And now the divine night, his dark ally, was mostly passed, and dawn that sets mortals to work was quickly coming, while bright Selene, daughter of the lord Pallas, Megamedes' son, had just climbed her watch-post, when the strong Son of Zeus drove the wide-browed cattle of Phoebus Apollo to the river Alpheus. And they came unwearied to the high-roofed byres and the drinking-troughs that were in the noble meadow. Then, after he had fed the loud-bellowing cattle with fodder and driven them into the byre, close-packed and chewing lotus and dewy galingal, he gathered a pile of wood and began to seek the art of fire. He chose a stout laurel branch and trimmed it with the knife held firmly in his hand, and the hot smoke rose up. For it was Hermes who first invented fire-sticks and fire. Next he took many dried sticks and piled them thick and plenty in a sunken trench, and flame began to glow, spreading afar the blast of fierce-burning fire.

And while the strength of glorious Hephaestus was beginning to kindle the fire, he dragged out two lowing, horned cows close to the fire, for great strength was with him. He threw them both panting upon their backs on the ground, and rolled them on their sides, bending their necks over, and pierced their vital chord. Then he went on from task to task: first he cut up the rich, fatted meat, and pierced it with wooden spits, and roasted flesh and the honorable chine and the paunch full of dark blood all together…

Then glorious Hermes longed for the sacrificial meat, for the sweet smell wearied him, god though he was. Nevertheless his proud heart was not persuaded to devour the flesh, although he greatly desired it. But he put away in the high-roofed byre the fat and all the flesh, placing them high up to be a token of his youthful theft. And after that he gathered dry sticks and utterly destroyed with fire all the hoofs and all the heads…

Then glorious Hermes went hurriedly to his cradle, wrapping his swaddling clothes about his shoulders as though he were a feeble baby, and lay playing with the covering about his knees. But at his left hand he kept close his sweet lyre. But the god did not pass unseen by the goddess his mother. She said to him: "What now, you rogue! Where did you come from so late at night that you wear shamelessness as a garment? And now I surely believe the son of Leto will soon have you outdoors with unbreakable cords around your ribs, or you will live a rogue's life in the glens, robbing all the while. Get! Your father made you to be a great worry to mortal men and deathless gods."

Then Hermes answered her with crafty words: "Mother, why do you seek to frighten me like a feeble child whose heart knows few words of blame, a fearful infant that fears its mother's scolding? No, but I will try whatever plan is best, and so feed myself and you continually. We will not be content to remain here, as you say, alone of all the gods unfed by offerings and prayers – better to live in fellowship with the deathless gods continually, rich, wealthy, and enjoying stores of grain, than to sit always in a gloomy cave! And, regarding honor, I too will enter upon the rite that Apollo has. If my father will not give it me, I will seek – and I am able – to be a prince of thieves. And if Leto's most glorious son seeks me out, I think another and a greater loss will befall him. For I will go to Pytho to break into his great house, and will plunder from it splendid tripods, and cauldrons, and gold, and plenty of bright iron, and clothing, and you shall see it if you wish."

With such words they spoke together, the son of Zeus who holds the aegis, and the lady Maia. Now Dawn the early born, bringing light to men, was rising from deep-flowing Ocean, when Apollo, as he went, came to Onchestus, the lovely grove and sacred place of the loud-roaring Holder of the Earth…And when Apollo learned of what had happened, he went yet more quickly on his way, and then, seeing a long-winged bird, he knew at once by that omen that the thief was the child of Zeus the son of Cronos. So the lord Apollo, son of Zeus, hurried on to beautiful Pylos, seeking his shambling oxen, and he had his broad shoulders covered with a dark cloud. But when the Far-Shooter perceived the tracks of the oxen, he cried: "Oh, oh! Truly this is a great marvel that my eyes behold! These are indeed the tracks of straight-horned oxen, but they are turned backwards towards the flowery meadow. But these others are not the footprints of man or woman or grey wolves or bears or lions, nor do I think they are the tracks of a rough-maned Centaur – whoever it is that with swift feet makes such monstrous footprints, wonderful are the tracks on this side of the way, but yet more wonderful are those on that."

When he had said this, the lord Apollo, the Son of Zeus hastened onward and came to the forest-clad mountain of Cyllene and the deep-shadowed cave in the rock where the divine nymph had brought forth the child of Zeus who is the son of Cronos. A sweet odor spread over the lovely hill, and many thin-shanked sheep were grazing on the grass. Then far-shooting Apollo himself stepped down in haste over the stone threshold into the dusky cave. Now when the Son of Zeus and Maia saw Apollo in a rage about his cattle, he snuggled down in his fragrant swaddling-clothes, and as wood-ash covers over the deep embers of tree stumps, so Hermes cuddled himself up when he saw the Far-Shooter. He squeezed head and hands and feet together in a small space, like a newborn child seeking sweet sleep, though in truth he was wide awake, and he kept his lyre under his armpit. But the Son of Leto was aware and did not fail to perceive the beautiful mountain-nymph and her dear son, albeit a little child and swathed so craftily. He peered in every corner of the great dwelling and, taking a bright key, he opened three closets full of nectar and lovely ambrosia. And much gold and silver was stored in them, and many garments of the nymph, some purple and some silvery white, such as are kept in the sacred houses of the blessed gods. Then, after the Son of Leto had searched out the recesses of the great house, he spoke to glorious Hermes:

"Child, lying in the cradle, hurry up and tell me about my cattle, or we two will soon fall out angrily. For I will take and cast you into dusky Tartarus and awful, hopeless darkness, and neither your mother nor your father shall free you or bring you up again to the light, but you will wander under the earth and be the leader among little folk." Then Hermes answered him with crafty words: "Son of Leto, what harsh words are these you have spoken? And is it cattle of the field you are come here to seek? I have not seen them – I have not heard of them, since no one has told me of them. I cannot give news of them, nor acquire the reward for news. Am I like a cattle-rustler, a stalwart person? This is no task for me, rather I care for other things: sleep, and milk of my mother's breast, and wrappings round my shoulders, and warm baths. Let no one hear the cause of this dispute, for this would be a great marvel indeed among the deathless gods, that a newborn child should pass in through the forepart of the house with cattle of the field – about this matter you speak extravagantly. I was born yesterday, and my feet are soft and the ground beneath is rough. Nevertheless, if you will have it so, I will swear a great oath by my father's head and vow that neither am I guilty myself, nor have I seen any other who stole your cows – whatever cows may be, for I know them only by hearsay."

So, then, said Hermes, shooting quick glances from his eyes, and he kept raising his brows and looking this way and that, whistling long and listening to Apollo's story as to an idle tale. But far-working Apollo laughed softly and said to him: "O rogue, deceiver, crafty in heart, you talk so innocently that I most surely believe that you have broken into many a well-built house and stripped more than one poor wretch bare this night, gathering his goods together all over the house without noise. You will plague many a lonely herdsman in mountain glades, when you come to herds and thick-fleeced sheep, and have a hankering after flesh. But come now, if you don't want to sleep your last, get out of your cradle, you friend of dark night. Surely hereafter this shall be your title amongst the deathless gods, to be called the prince of thieves continually."

So said Phoebus Apollo, and he took the child and began to carry him. But at that moment the strong slayer of Argus formed this plan and, while Apollo held him in his hands, he sent forth an omen, a hard-worked noise of the belly, a rude messenger, and sneezed directly afterwards. And when Apollo heard it, he dropped glorious Hermes out of his hands on the ground. Then, sitting down before him, though he was eager to go on his way, he spoke mockingly to Hermes: "Fear not, little swaddling baby, son of Zeus and Maia. I shall find the strong cattle now by these omens, and you shall lead the way." When Apollo had said this, Cyllenian Hermes sprang up quickly, starting out haste. With both hands he pushed up to his ears the covering that he had wrapped about his shoulders, and said: "Where are you carrying me, Far-Shooter, hastiest of all the gods? Is it because of your cattle that you are so angry and harass me? O dear, if only all these "oxen" might perish! For it is not I who stole your cows, nor did I see another steal them – whatever they may be, and of that I have only heard report. No, be right and take this matter before Zeus, the Son of Cronos."

Then Hermes and Apollo of the Silver Bow stood at the knees of Zeus, and Zeus who thunders on high spoke to his glorious son and asked him: "Phoebus, from where have you come driving this great spoil, a newborn child that has the look of a herald? This is a serious matter that has come before the council of the gods." Then the lord, far-shooting Apollo, answered him: "O my father, you shall soon hear no trifling tale, although you criticize me that I alone am fond of spoil. Here is a child, a burgling robber, whom I found after a long journey in the hills of Cyllene. For my part, I have never seen one so chirpy, either among the gods or all men that catch folk unawares throughout the world. He stole away my cattle from their meadow and drove them off in the evening along the shore of the loud-roaring sea, making straight for Pylos.

When he had so spoken, Phoebus Apollo sat down. But Hermes on his part answered and said, pointing at the Son of Cronos, the lord of all the gods: "Zeus, my father, indeed I will speak the truth to you, for I am truthful and I cannot tell a lie. He came to our house today looking for his shambling cows, as the sun was newly rising. He brought no witnesses with him nor any of the blessed gods who had seen the theft, but with great violence ordered me to confess, threatening to throw me into wide Tartarus. For he has the rich bloom of glorious youth, while I was born yesterday – as he too knows – nor am I a cattle-rustler, a sturdy fellow…

So spoke the Cyllenian, the Slayer of Argus, while he kept shooting sidelong glances and kept his swaddling-clothes upon his arm, and did not cast them away. But Zeus laughed out loud to see his evil-plotting child well and cunningly denying guilt about the cattle. And he told them both to be of one mind and search for the cattle, and guiding Hermes to lead the way and, without mischievousness of heart, to show the place where now he had hidden the strong cattle. Then the Son of Cronos bowed his head, and wondrous Hermes obeyed him, for the will of Zeus who holds the aegis easily prevailed with him.

Then the two all-glorious children of Zeus hastened both to sandy Pylos, and reached the ford of Alpheus, and came to the fields and the high-roofed byre where the beasts were held at nighttime. Now, while Hermes went to the cave in the rock and began to drive out the strong cattle, the son of Leto, looking aside, saw the cowhides on the sheer rock. And he asked glorious Hermes at once: "How were you able, you crafty rogue, to flay two cows, newborn and babyish as you are? For my part, I dread the strength that will be yours: there is no need that you should keep growing long, Cyllenian, son of Maia!" So saying, Apollo twisted strong ropes with his hands meaning to bind Hermes with firm bonds, but the bonds would not hold him, and the ropes fell from him and began to grow at once from the ground beneath their feet in that very place. And intertwining with one another, they quickly grew and covered all the wild-roving cattle by the will of thievish Hermes, so that Apollo was astonished as he gazed…Very easily he softened the heart of the son of all-glorious Leto as much as he could, stern though the Far-shooter was. He took the lyre upon his left arm and tried each string in turn with the key, so that at his touch it sounded awesomely. And Phoebus Apollo laughed for joy, for the sweet throb of the marvelous music struck his heart, and a soft longing took hold on his soul as he listened.

Apollo was seized with a longing not to be put off, and he opened his mouth and spoke swift words to Hermes: "Slayer of oxen, trickster, busybody, comrade of the feast, this song of yours is worth fifty cows, and I believe that now we shall settle our quarrel peacefully. But come now, tell me this, resourceful son of Maia: has this marvelous thing been with you from your birth, or did some god or mortal man give this noble gift to you and teach you heavenly song? For this new-uttered sound I hear is wondrous, the like of which I vow that no man nor god dwelling on Olympus ever yet has known but you, O thievish son of Maia.

Then Hermes answered him with artful words: "You question me carefully, O Far-shooter, yet I am not jealous that you should learn my art: this day you shall know it. For I wish to be friendly with you both in thought and word. Now you well know all things in your heart, since you sit foremost among the deathless gods, O son of Zeus, and are wondrous and strong. And wise Zeus loves you as all right is, and has given you splendid gifts. And they say that from the utterance of Zeus you have learned both the honors due to the gods, O Far-seer, and oracles from Zeus, even all his ordinances. Of all these I myself have already learned that you have great wealth. Now, you are free to learn whatever you please. But since, as it seems, your heart is so strongly set on playing the lyre, chant, and play upon it, and give yourself to merriment, taking this as a gift from me.

When Hermes had said this, he held out the lyre, and Phoebus Apollo took it, and readily put his shining whip in Hermes' hand, and ordained him keeper of herds. The son of Maia received it joyfully, while the glorious son of Leto, the lord far-seeing Apollo, took the lyre upon his left arm and tried each string with the key. Awesomely it sounded at the touch of the god, while he sang sweetly to its note. Afterwards these two, the all-glorious sons of Zeus turned the cows back towards the sacred meadow, but themselves hastened back to snowy Olympus, delighting in the lyre. Then wise Zeus was glad and made them both friends. And Hermes loved the son of Leto continually, even as he does now, when he had given the lyre as gift to the Far-shooter, who played it skillfully, holding it upon his arm. But for himself Hermes found out another cunning art and made himself the pipes whose sound is heard afar.

And so, farewell, Son of Zeus and Maia, but I will remember you and another song also.

7g) Demeter (Homeric Hymn 2, passim)

I begin to sing of rich-haired Demeter, terrible goddess, of her and her slender-ankled daughter whom Hades took away, given to him by all-seeing Zeus the loud-thunderer.

Away from Demeter, lady of the golden sword and glorious fruits, Persephone was playing with the deep-bosomed daughters of Oceanus and gathering flowers over a soft meadow, roses and crocuses and beautiful violets, irises also and hyacinths and the narcissus, which Earth made to grow at the will of Zeus, and to please the Host of Many, to be a snare for the bloom-like girl – a marvelous, radiant flower. It was a thing of awe whether for deathless gods or mortal men to see: from its root grew a hundred blooms and it smelled most sweetly, so that all wide heaven above and the whole earth and the sea's salty swell laughed for joy. And the girl was amazed and reached out with both hands to take the lovely flower, but the wide earth yawned there in the plain of Nysa, and the lord, Lord of the Dead, Son of Cronos, He who has many names, with his immortal horses sprang out upon her.

He seized her unwilling on his golden car and took her away, weeping. Then she cried out shrilly with her voice, calling upon her father, the Son of Cronos, who is most high and excellent. But no one, either of the deathless gods or of mortal men, heard her voice, nor yet the olive-trees bearing rich fruit. Only tender-hearted Hecate, golden-haired, the daughter of Persaeus, heard the girl from her cave, and the lord Helios, Hyperion's bright son, as she cried to her father, the Son of Cronos. But he was sitting aloof, apart from the gods, in his temple where many pray, and receiving sweet offerings from mortal men. So he, that son of Cronos, of many names, who is Ruler of Many and Master of the Dead, was bearing her away by the leave of Zeus on his immortal chariot – his own brother's child, and utterly unwilling.

And as long as she, the goddess, could still behold earth and starry heaven and the strong-flowing sea where fishes shoal, and the rays of the sun, and still hoped to see her dear mother and the eternal gods, so long hope calmed her great heart for all her trouble…and the heights of the mountains and the depths of the sea rang with her immortal voice: and her queenly mother heard her.

Bitter pain seized her mother's heart, and she ripped the covering upon her divine hair with her dear hands. She cast her dark cloak down from both her shoulders and sped, like a wild bird, over the firm land and yielding sea, seeking her child. But no one would tell her the truth, neither god nor mortal man, and from the birds of omen none came with true news for her. Then for nine days queenly Demeter wandered over the earth with flaming torches in her hands, so aggrieved that she never tasted ambrosia and the sweet draught of nectar, nor sprinkled her body with water. But when the tenth enlightening dawn had come, Hecate, with a torch in her hands, met her, and spoke to her and told her news:

"Queenly Demeter, bringer of seasons and giver of good gifts, what god of heaven or what mortal man has raped Persephone and pierced with sorrow your dear heart? For I heard her voice, yet did not see with my eyes who it was. But I tell you truly and briefly all I know." Thus spoke Hecate. And the daughter of rich-haired Rhea did not answer her, but sped swiftly with her, holding flaming torches in her hands. So they came to Helios, who is watchman of both gods and men, and stood in front of his horses, and the bright goddess enquired of him: "Helios, do you at least respect me, goddess as I am, if ever by word or deed of mine I have cheered your heart and spirit? Through the fruitless air I heard the thrilling cry of my daughter whom I bore, sweet offshoot of my body and lovely in form, as of one seized violently, though with my eyes I saw nothing. But you – for with your beams you look down from the bright upper air over all the earth and sea – tell me truly of my dear child, if you have seen her anywhere, what god or mortal man has violently seized her against her will and mine, and so made off with her"

And the Son of Hyperion answered her: "Queen Demeter, daughter of rich-haired Rhea, I will tell you the truth, for I greatly revere and pity you in your grief for your slender-ankled daughter. None other of the deathless gods is to blame, but only cloud-gathering Zeus who gave her to Hades, her father's brother, to be called his plump wife. And Hades seized her and took her loudly crying in his chariot down to his realm of mist and gloom. Yet, goddess, cease your loud lamenting and do not keep such anger unrelenting anger in vain. Hades, the Ruler of Many, is no unfitting husband among the deathless gods for your child, being your own brother and born of the same stock. Also, for honor, he has that third share which he received when division was made at the first, and is appointed lord of those among whom he dwells." So he spoke, and called to his horses: and at his pushing they quickly whirled the swift chariot along, like long-winged birds.

But grief yet more terrible and savage came into the heart of Demeter, and thereafter she was so angered with the dark-clouded Son of Cronos that she avoided the gathering of the gods and high Olympus, and went to the towns and rich fields of men, disfiguring her form a long while. And no men or deep-bosomed women knew her when they saw her, until she came to the house of wise Celeus who then was lord of fragrant Eleusis. Troubled in her dear heart, she sat near the wayside by the Maiden Well, from which the women of the place used to draw water, in a shady place over which grew an olive shrub. And she was like an ancient woman who is cut off from childbearing and the gifts of garland-loving Aphrodite, like the nurses of kings' children who deal justice, or like the house-keepers in their echoing halls. There the daughters of Celeus, son of Eleusis, saw her, as they were coming for easily-drawn water, to carry it in pitchers of bronze to their dear father's house. There were four, and they were like goddesses in the flower of their girlhood: Callidice and Cleisidice and lovely Demo and Callithoe, who was the eldest. They did not recognize her – for the gods are not easily discerned by mortals. – but standing nearby her they spoke winged words:

"Old mother, whence and who are you of folk born long ago? Why are you gone from the city and do not draw near the houses? For there in the shady halls are women of just such age as you, and others younger, and they would welcome you both by word and by deed." Thus they spoke.

And she, that queen among goddesses answered them saying: "Hail, dear children, whoever you are of woman-kind. I will tell you my story, for it is not improper that I should tell you truly what you ask. Doso is my name, for my dignified mother gave it me. And now I have come from Crete over the sea's wide back, not willingly. But against my desire, by force of strength, pirates brought me there. Afterwards they put in with their swift craft to Thoricus, and there they landed the women on the shore in full throng and the men likewise, and they began to prepare a meal by the stern-cables of the ship. But my heart did not crave pleasant food, and I fled secretly across the dark country and escaped my masters, so that they should not take me, unpurchased, across the sea, and there to win a price for me. And so I wandered and have come here, and I know not at all what land this is or what people are in it. But may all those who dwell on Olympus give you husbands and birth of children as parents desire, so you take pity on me, girls, and show me, dear children, to the house of what man and woman I may go to work for them cheerfully at such tasks as belong to a woman of my age. I could nurse a new born child well, holding him in my arms, or keep a house, or spread my masters' bed in a recess of the well-built chamber, or teach the women their work."

So spoke the goddess. And straightaway the unwed maiden Callidice, prettiest in form of the daughters of Celeus, answered her and said: "Mother, what the gods send us, we mortals must bear, although we suffer, for they are much stronger than us. But now I will teach you clearly, telling you the names of men who have great power and honor here and are chief among the people, guarding our city's circle of towers by their wisdom and true judgments: there is wise Triptolemus and Dioclus and Polyxeinus and blameless Eumolpus and Dolichus and our own brave father. All these have wives who manage in the house, and none of them, as soon as they have seen you, would dishonor you and turn you from the house, but they will welcome you, for indeed you are godlike. But if you will, stay here, and we will go to our father's house and tell Metaneira, our deep-bosomed mother, all this matter fully, that she may bid you to come to our home than search after the houses of others. She has an only son, late-born, who is being nursed in our well-built house, a child born of many prayers and welcome. If you could bring him up until he reached the full measure of youth, any one of womankind who should see you would straightway envy you, such gifts would our mother give for his upbringing."

The goddess bowed her head in assent and they filled their shining vessels with water and carried them off, rejoicing. Quickly they came to their father's great house and straightway told their mother what they had heard and seen. Then she told them to go with all speed and invite the stranger to come for a measureless job...And they found the good goddess near the wayside where they had left her before, and led her to the house of their dear father. And she walked behind, distressed in her dear heart, with her head veiled and wearing a dark cloak which waved about the slender feet of the goddess.

Soon they came to the house of heaven-nurtured Celeus and went through the portico to where their queenly mother sat by a pillar of the close-fitted roof, holding her son, a tender boy, at her bosom. And the girls ran to her, but the goddess walked to the threshold, and her head reached the roof and she filled the doorway with a heavenly radiance. Then awe and reverence and pale fear took hold of Metaneira, and she rose up from her couch before Demeter, and told her to be seated. But Demeter, bringer of seasons and giver of perfect gifts, would not sit on the bright couch, but stayed silent with lovely eyes cast down, until careful Iambe placed a jointed seat for her and threw over it a silvery fleece. Then she sat down and held her veil in her hands before her face. A long time she sat upon the stool without speaking because of her sorrow, and greeted no one by word or by sign, but rested, never smiling, and tasting neither food nor drink, because she pined with longing for her deep-bosomed daughter, until careful Iambe, who pleased her moods in later too, moved the holy lady with many a jibe and joke to smile and laugh and cheer her heart. Then Metaneira filled a cup with sweet wine and offered it to her, but she refused it, for she said it was not lawful for her to drink red wine, but told them to mix meal and water with soft mint and give her to drink…

Demeter took the young child in her fragrant bosom with her divine hands, and his mother was glad in her heart. So the goddess nursed Demophoon in the palace, wise Celeus' handsome son whom fertile Metaneira bore. And the child grew like some immortal being, not fed with food nor nourished at the breast, for by day rich-crowned Demeter would anoint him with ambrosia as if he were the offspring of a god and breathe sweetly upon him as she held him in her bosom. But at night she would hide him like a brand in the heart of the fire, unknown to his dear parents. And it wrought great wonder among them that he grew beyond his age, for he was like the gods face to face. And she would have made him deathless and unageing, had not Metaneira in her heedlessness kept watch by night from her sweet-smelling chamber and once spied her. But she wailed and struck her hips, because she feared for her son and was greatly upset in her heart, so she lamented and uttered quick words: "Demophoon, my son, the strange woman buries you deep in fire and works grief and bitter sorrow for me."

Thus she spoke, mourning. And the bright goddess, lovely-crowned Demeter, heard her, and was furious at her. So with her divine hands she snatched from the fire the dear son whom Metaneira had born, unhoped-for, in the palace, and cast him from her to the ground, for she was terribly angry in her heart. Afterwards she said to Metaneira:

"Witless are you mortals and slow to foresee your lot, whether of good or evil, that comes upon you. For now in your heedlessness you have wrought foolishness beyond fixing, for – be a witness for the oath of the gods, the relentless water of Styx – I would have made your dear son deathless and unageing all his days and would have bestowed on him everlasting honor, but now he can in no way escape death and the fates. Yet shall unfailing honor always rest upon him, because he lay upon my knees and slept in my arms. But, as the years move by and when he is in his prime, the sons of the Eleusinians shall ever wage war and terrible strife with one another continually. Behold! I am that Demeter who has share of honor and is the greatest help and cause of joy to the undying gods and mortal men. But now, let all the people build me a great temple and an altar below it and beneath the city and its sheer wall upon a rising hillock above Callichorus. And I myself will teach my rites, so that hereafter you may reverently perform them, and so win the favour of my heart."

When she had so spoken, the goddess changed her stature and her looks, thrusting old age away from her. Beauty spread round about her and a lovely fragrance was wafted from her sweet-smelling robes, and from the divine body of the goddess a light shone afar, while golden tresses spread down over her shoulders, so that the strong house was filled with brightness as with lightning. And so she went out from the palace. And straightway Metaneira's knees were quaking and she remained speechless for a long while and did not remember to pick up her late-born son from the ground. But his sisters heard his pitiful wailing and sprang down from their well-spread beds. One of them picked up the child in her arms and laid him in her bosom, while another revived the fire, and a third rushed with soft feet to bring their mother from her fragrant chamber. And they gathered around the struggling child and washed him, embracing him lovingly, but he was not comforted, because nurses and handmaids much less skillful were holding him now.

All night long they sought to appease the glorious goddess, quaking with fear. But, as soon as dawn began to arrive, they told powerful Celeus all things without fail, as the lovely-crowned goddess Demeter had commanded them. So Celeus called the countless people to an assembly and told them make a lovely temple for rich-haired Demeter and an altar upon the rising hillock. And they obeyed him speedily and obeyed his voice, doing as he commanded. As for the child, he grew like an immortal being.

Now when they had finished building and had drawn back from their toil, every man went to his house. But golden-haired Demeter sat there apart from all the blessed gods and stayed, wasting with yearning for her deep-bosomed daughter. Then she caused a most dreadful and cruel year for mankind over the all-nourishing earth: the ground would not make the seed sprout, for rich-crowned Demeter kept it hidden. In the fields the oxen drew many a curved plough in vain, and much white barley was cast upon the land without avail. So she would have destroyed the whole race of man with cruel famine and robbed them who dwell on Olympus of their glorious right of gifts and sacrifices, had not Zeus perceived and marked this in his heart. First he sent golden-winged Iris to call rich-haired Demeter, lovely in form. So he commanded. And she obeyed the dark-clouded Son of Cronos, and sped with swift feet across the space between. She came to the stronghold of fragrant Eleusis, and there finding dark-cloaked Demeter in her temple, spoke to her and uttered winged words:

"Demeter, father Zeus, whose wisdom is everlasting, calls you to come join the tribes of the eternal gods: come therefore, and let not the message I bring from Zeus pass unobeyed." Thus spoke Iris, begging her. But Demeter's heart was not moved. Then again the father sent out all the blessed and eternal gods in addition, and they came, one after the other, and kept calling her and offering many very beautiful gifts and whatever rights she might be pleased to choose among the deathless gods. Yet no one was able to persuade her mind and will, so aggrieved was she in her heart. She stubbornly rejected all their words, for she vowed that she would never set foot on fragrant Olympus nor let fruit spring out of the ground, until she beheld with her eyes her own fair-faced daughter.

Now when all-seeing Zeus the loud-thunderer heard this, he sent the Slayer of Argus, whose wand is of gold, to Erebus, so that having won over Hades with soft words, he might lead out chaste Persephone to the light from the misty gloom to join the gods, and that her mother might see her with her eyes and end her anger. And Hermes obeyed, and leaving the house of Olympus, straightaway sprang down with speed to the hidden places of the earth. And he found the lord Hades in his house seated upon a couch, and his shy mate with him, reluctant, because she yearned for her mother...And Hades, ruler over the dead, smiled grimly and obeyed the demand of lordly Zeus. For he straightaway urged wise Persephone, saying:

"Go now, Persephone, to your dark-robed mother. Go, and feel kindly in your heart towards me: be not so exceedingly downtrodden, for I shall be no unfitting husband for you among the deathless gods, I who am brother to father Zeus. And while you are here, you shall rule all that lives and moves and shall have the greatest rights among the deathless gods. Those who defraud you and do not appease your power with offerings, reverently performing rites and paying fit gifts, shall be punished for evermore." When he said this, wise Persephone was filled with joy and hastily sprang up with gladness. But for himself he secretly gave her sweet pomegranate seeds to eat, taking care for himself that she might not remain continually with grave, dark-robed Demeter. Then Hades the Ruler of Many openly got ready his deathless horses beneath the golden chariot. And she mounted the chariot, and the strong Slayer of Argus took the reins and whip in his dear hands and drove from the hall, the horses speeding readily.

And when Demeter saw them, she rushed out as a Maenad does down some thick-wooded mountain, while Persephone on the other side, when she saw her mother's sweet eyes, left the chariot and horses, and leaped down to run to her, and falling upon her neck, embraced her. But while Demeter was still holding her dear child in her arms, her heart suddenly felt some deception, so that she feared greatly and ceased fondling her daughter and asked her at once: "My child, tell me, surely you have not tasted any food while you were below? Speak out and hide nothing, but let us both know. For if you have not, you shall come back from loathly Hades and live with me and your father, the dark-clouded Son of Cronos and be honored by all the deathless gods, but if you have tasted food, you must go back again beneath the secret places of the earth, there to dwell a third part of the seasons every year. Yet for the two parts you shall be with me and the other deathless gods. And when the earth shall bloom with the fragrant flowers of spring in every kind, then from the realm of darkness and gloom thou shalt come up once more to be a wonder for gods and mortal men. But now tell me how he took you away to the realm of darkness and gloom, and by what trick did the strong Host of Many beguile you?"

Then beautiful Persephone answered her: "Mother, I will tell you everything without error. When luck-bringing Hermes came, swift messenger from my father the Son of Cronos and the other Sons of Heaven, bidding me to come back from Erebus so that you might see me with your eyes and so cease from your anger and fearful wrath against the gods, I sprang up at once for joy. But Hades secretly put in my mouth sweet food, a pomegranate seed, and forced me to taste against my will."

And all-seeing Zeus sent a messenger to them, rich-haired Rhea, to bring dark-cloaked Demeter to join the families of the gods, and he promised to give her what rights she should choose among the deathless gods and agreed that her daughter should go down for the third part of the circling year to darkness and gloom, but for the two parts should live with her mother and the other deathless gods. Thus he commanded. And the goddess did not disobey the message of Zeus. Swiftly she rushed down from the peaks of Olympus and came to the plain of Rharus, rich, fertile corn-land once, but then in no way fruitful, for it lay idle and utterly leafless because the white grain was hidden by design of slender-ankled Demeter. But afterwards, as Spring came, it was soon to be bristling with long ears of corn, and its rich furrows to be loaded with grain upon the ground, while others would already be bound in sheaves. There first she landed from the fruitless upper air, and glad were the goddesses to see each other and cheered in heart.

And rich-crowned Demeter did not refuse, but straightaway made fruit spring up from the rich lands, so that the whole wide earth was laden with leaves and flowers. Then she went, and to the kings who deal justice, Triptolemus and Diocles, the horse-driver, and to hardy Eumolpus and Celeus, leader of the people, she showed the conduct of her rites and taught them all her mysteries. To Triptolemus and Polyxeinus and Diocles also, she showed awesome mysteries that no one may in any way transgress or pry into or utter, for deep awe of the gods checks the voice. Happy is he among men upon earth who has seen these mysteries, but he who is not initiated and who has no part in them, never has lot of like good things once he is dead, down in the darkness and gloom.

Adapted from Hugh G. Evelyn-White, Anonymous. Homeric Hymns (Cambridge, MA: Harvard University Press; London, William Heinemann Ltd., 1914)

READING 8:

SAPPHO

Sappho was a lyric poet from the island of Lesbos, and wrote roughly during early sixth century BCE. While she is our earliest female Greek poet, precious little is known of her life. Much of her poetry has been lost, but it is clear that this was not because of its quality; she was greatly admired and very popular in the ancient world. Her most famous surviving lyric poems can be described as what we would call "love poetry" – odes to Aphrodite, her powers, and specific, human loves and relationships. The poem below is an excellent showcase for Sappho's simple, fluid style, and also provides evidence of Aphrodite's perceived role in romantic love.

8a) Sappho, Poem 1

Shimmering-throned immortal Aphrodite, daughter of Zeus, Enchantress, I beg you, spare me, O queen, this agony and anguish, do not crush my spirit. Whenever before you have heard me – my voice calling to you in the distance, and obeying, you have come, leaving your Father's golden dominions,

With chariot yoked to your fleet-winged coursers, fluttering swift pinions over earth's darkness, and bringing you through the infinite space, gliding downwards from heaven, then, soon they arrived and you, blessed goddess, smiling with divine appearance, asked me what new woe had befallen me now and why, thus you asked me:

"What in your mad heart was your greatest desire, who was it now who must feel my allurements, who was the fair one that must be persuaded, who wronged you, Sappho? For if now she flees, quickly she shall follow, and if she spurns gifts, soon shall she offer them, yes, if she knows not love, soon shall she feel it – even reluctantly."

Come then, I pray, grant me an end to sorrow, drive away care, I beg you, O goddess! fulfil for me what I yearn to accomplish, be my ally!

Adapted from E. M. Cox, Sappho. The Poems of Sappho (London: Williams and Norgate, 1924).

READING 9:

AESCHYLUS' *PROMETHEUS BOUND*

Dramatic tragedy was born at Athens, the result of adding actors on a stage to the traditional choral dancing and singing devoted to gods during religious festival for Dionysus. Aeschylus (c. 525-455 BCE) was the earliest, and arguably best of Athens' three great tragic playwrights. Only seven of his ninety plays survive – all tragedies. Typically, a playwright wrote and produced a trilogy of plays for each festival and competed against other playwrights for prizes. While the plays presented in a trilogy did not necessarily relate to one another in plot, Aeschylus favoured this approach. *Prometheus Bound* was the first entry in a trilogy whose sequels survive only in fragments. It tells the story of Prometheus, the titan who stole the secret of fire and gave it to humans. As punishment for this, Zeus had him chained to rock, forever to be tortured. Aeschylus' vision of the story shows only Prometheus discuss his plight with various gods and mortals who visit him. The themes of the play are hallmarks of later work by Aeschylus: the nature of Zeus and the grave divisions between divine powers of the universe.

9a) Aeschylus, Prometheus Bound (1-285; 436-525; 887-1093, passim)

SCENE: *Mountainous country, and in the middle of a deep gorge of rock, towards which "Power" (*KRATOS*) and "Power" (*BIA*) carry the gigantic form of* PROMETHEUS. HEPHAESTUS *follows dejectedly with hammer, nails, and chains.*

KRATOS: Now have we journeyed to a remote spot of Earth – the Scythian wild, a wasteland untrodden. And now, Hephaestus, you must execute the task our father laid on you, and bind this troublemaker to the jagged rocks in adamantine, unbreakable bonds. For your own gift of all-forging fire he stole and gave to mortals – a serious crime for which the Gods have called him to account, so that he may learn to bear Zeus' tyranny and cease to play the lover of mankind.

HEPHAESTUS: Kratos and Bia, for you the request of Zeus is complete. Nothing further for you to do. But to bind a brother god forcibly, in chains, in this deep chasm raked by storms,

I do not have the courage, yet I must draw courage from that which is inevitable, for woe to him who slights the Father's word. O high-souled son of those who are wise in counsel, with a heavy heart I must make your heart heavy,

In bonds of unbreakable bronze, nailing you to this crag where no smith dwells, nor sound of human voice nor shape of man shall visit you, but the blazing sun shall roast your flesh; your fair colour shall suffer change; night will be welcome when she hides with spangled robe the light of day; welcome will be the sun returning to disperse the frosts of dawn. And every hour shall bring its weight of woe to wear away your heart, for yet unborn is he who shall release you from your pain. This is your payment for loving humankind. For, being a god, you dated the gods' ill will, preferring humans to exceeding honour. For which reason your long watch shall be comfortless, stretched on this rock, never to close an eye or bend a knee; and vainly you shall lift, with deep groaning and lamentable cries, your voice; for Zeus is hard to be beg, as a newborn power is ever pitiless.

Prometheus: O divine air breezing on swift wings, you river fountains, and of ocean-waves, the infinite laughter Mother Earth! And you, all-seeing circle of the sun, behold what I, a god, from gods endure! Look down upon my shame, the cruel wrong that racks my frame, the grinding anguish that shall waste my strength, until time's ten thousand years have measured out their length! He has devised these chains, the newly enthroned master who reigns, chief of the chieftains of the gods. Ah me! For the woe which is and that which yet shall be, I wail, and pose questions of these wide skies when shall the star of my deliverance arise? And yet…and yet…I foresee exactly All that shall come to pass – no sharp surprise of pain shall overtake me! What's determined to bear, as I can, I must, knowing the might of strong Necessity is unconquerable. But regarding my fate, silence and speech alike are unsupportable. For gifts bestowed on mortal men I am tied in these bonds. I sought the source of fire in a hollow reed hidden privately, a measureless resource for man, and a mighty teacher of all arts. This is the crime for which I must pay hung here in chains, nailed beneath the open sky.

Ha! Ha! What echo, what odour floats by with no sound? Is its strain wafted from a god or mortal or both, that comes here, to this world's end, this mountain-covered ground, to have a sight of my torment? Or why is he obliged? A god you behold in bondage and pain, the foe of Zeus and one feuding with all the gods that find submissive entry into that tyrant's hall; my fault, too great a love of humankind. Ah me! Ah me! What being is now at hand – a of great birds of prey, is this I hear? The bright air fanned whistles and shrills with rapid beat of wings. Here comes nothing, but to my spirit it brings Horror and fear…

The **Chorus of Daughters of Oceanus** *arrives in mid-air in their chariot.*

Prometheus: Ah me! Ah me! Fair progeny, that many-childed Tethys brought to birth, fathered by old Ocean whose sleepless stream is rolled around the vast shores of earth, look on me! Look upon these chains in which I am hung, held fast on these high-pinnacled rocks, my dungeon and my tower of grief, where over an abyss my soul, sad custodian, sustains her unwearied watch!

Chorus: Proud is your heart, your will undone by not one bitter woe, and all too free is the license of your bold, unshackled tongue. But fear has roused my soul with a piercing cry! And for your fate my heart is doubtful! I tremble to know when through the breakers' roar your keel shall touch again the friendly shore; for not by prayer to Zeus will such a port be won; Cronos' son has an implacable heart.

PROMETHEUS: I know the heart of Zeus is hard, that he has tied Justice to his side; but he shall be fully appeased in this way. And, the implacable wrath by which he raged will be smoothed quite away, neither he nor I will be reluctant to seal a bond of peace and amity.

CHORUS: I pray that all that you have said will unfold, that we may hear soon upon what count Zeus took you and with bitter wrong assaults: instruct us, if the telling does not hurt you.

PROMETHEUS: These things are sorrowful for me to speak, yet silence too is sorrow: all ways are woeful! When first the Blessed Ones were filled with wrath and there arose division in their midst, some ready to hurl Cronos from his throne so that Zeus might be their king, and others, opposed, contending that he should never rule the gods, then I, urging wise counsel to persuade the Titans, sons of Ouranos and Chthon, could not persuade: but, ignoring all arguments, by the strong hand, effortless, still supposed that they might seize supremacy. But to me my mother Themis and Gaia, one form called by many names, not only once with oracular voice had prophesied how power should be distributed, that not by strength nor by violence should the mighty be mastered, but by guile. Truths told by me were scorned, nor did they heed my suggestion with any least regard.

Then, of all the options, I judged it best, taking my mother with me, to support not a backward friend, but the not-less cordial Zeus. And by my wise counsel Tartarus, the bottomless and black, old Cronos hides among his allies. So helped by me, thus does the tyrant of the gods, repay such service rendered with ignominious punishment. But it is a common sickness of tyrannical power never to trust a friend. And now, what you asked for, for what he shamefully entreats me, you shall know. When first upon his high, paternal throne he took his seat, straightaway to different gods he gave different good gifts, and parceled out his empire, but concerning miserable men he had no care at all; Instead, it was his wish to wipe out man and rear another race: and these ideas no one else contravened but me. I risked the bold attempt, and saved mankind from stark destruction and the road to hell. Therefore with this sore penalty am I bowed, grievous to suffer, pitiful to see. But, for this compassion shown to man, I in no way deserved such a fate – rather because of wrath I am to be reformed, and made a ridiculous show to Zeus.

CHORUS: This god has a heart of iron, hewn out of unfeeling rock whom, Prometheus, your sufferings will not rouse to wrath. If only I had never seen them, for, truly, the sight of you has wrung my heart.

PROMETHEUS: Yes, to my friends a woeful sight am I.

CHORUS: Have you not boldly transgressed in any other way?

PROMETHEUS: I took from man expectancy of death.

CHORUS: What medicine did you find for this disease?

PROMETHEUS: I planted blind hope in the heart of him.

CHORUS: A mighty gift, then, did you give to man.

PROMETHEUS: Moreover, I conferred the gift of fire.

CHORUS: And have frail mortals now the flame-bright fire?

PROMETHEUS: Yes, and shall master many arts because of it.

CHORUS: And Zeus with such unlawfulness charges you –

PROMETHEUS: He Torments me with the greatest anguish.

CHORUS: And is there no end in prospect to your pains?

PROMETHEUS: None, except when he shall choose to end them.

CHORUS: How should he choose? What hope do you have? Do you not see that you hast erred? But how you erred is a small pleasure for me to tell; indeed, it is great sorrow. Let it go then: instead, seek some deliverance from your woes.

PROMETHEUS: He who stands free with an unrestricted foot is quick to counsel and advise a friend in trouble. But all these things I know well. Of my free will, my own free will, I erred, and freely do I here acknowledge it. Freeing mankind, I've created my prison. Nonetheless, I did not look for sentence so terrible, high on this precipice to droop and pine, having no neighbour but the desolate crags. And now, lament no more these ills I suffer, but come to earth and lend an attentive ear to the things that shall happen later. Listen, oh listen, and suffer as I suffer! Who knows, who knows, but on some other's injured head, will similar woes already be reserved, or a wandering doom soon descend?

CHORUS: Prometheus, we have heard your call: not on deaf ears do these awful words fall. Look! Lightly leaving our flying chariots at your words and holy air, the pathway of great birds, we long to tread this land of peak and scar, and understand myself by sure tidings all you have endured and must endure…

PROMETHEUS: Do not think that I am silent for pride or Prejudice: rather my heart is prey to gnawing thoughts, both for the past, and now seeing myself battered by vengeance. For who determine the precedence of these younger gods if not I? No more of that: I would only weary you with things you already know; but listen to the tale of human sufferings, and how at first, senseless as beasts, I gave men sense, gave them a mind. I do not speak in contempt of man; I only tell of the good gifts I conferred. In the beginning, seeing, they still saw amiss, and hearing, they heard not, but, like phantoms huddled in dreams, they were confounded by the perplexed story of their days; knowing neither wood-work, nor brick-built dwellings basking in the light, but dug for themselves holes, wherein like ants, that hardly may contend against a breath, they dwelled in burrows of their dark caves.

Neither by winter's cold had they a fixed sign, nor by the spring when she comes decked with flowers, nor yet by summer's heat with melting fruits had they any sure token: but utterly without knowledge they were enslaved, until I showed them the rising of the stars and when they set, though much obscure. Moreover, count the most excellent of all inventions – I devised them for humans, and gave them writing that records all, the useful mother of the Muse. I was the first that yoked unmanaged beasts, to serve as slaves with collar and with pack, and take upon themselves, to man's relief, the heaviest labour of his hands; and tamed to the rein and drove in wheeled cars the horse – an ornament of luxurious pride. And those sea-wanderers with the wings of cloth, the shipman's wagons – none but I contrived them. These varied inventions for mankind I perfected, I who have none – no not one stint – to rid me of this shame.

CHORUS: Your sufferings have been shameful, and your mind strays, at a loss: like a bad physician who has fallen sick, you are out of heart: nor can you prescribe for your own case the medicine to make you well.

PROMETHEUS: But hear more and admire more what arts, what aids I cleverly created. The chief one that, if any man fell sick, there was no help for him, no helpful lotion or potion; but for lack of drugs they dwindled away, until I taught them to compound liquids and sanative mixtures, by which they now are armed against disease. I formed the winding path of divination and was the first distinguisher of dreams, the true from false, and of ominous voices I interpreted obscure meaning, and the tokens seen when men take the road; and augury by flight of all the greater crook-clawed birds I defined with careful discrimination; these by their fair and favourable nature, those, flattered with fair name. And for each sort I described the habits. Their mutual feuds and friendships and the assemblies they hold. And of the plumpness of the inward parts what colour is acceptable to the Gods, the well-streaked liver and gall-bladder. Also by roasting limbs well wrapped in fat and the long backbond, I led men on the road of dark and riddling knowledge, and I purged the glancing eye of fire – dim before – and made its meaning plain. These are my works. Then, things beneath the earth, aids hid from man, bronze, iron, silver, gold, who dares to say he was before me in discovering? None, I know well, unless he loves to babble. And in a single word to sum up the whole – all manner of arts men were learned from Prometheus.

CHORUS: Shoot not beyond the mark in helping man while you yourself are comfortless: for I am of good hope that you shall one day escape from these bonds escaped and be mightier than Zeus.

PROMETHEUS: Fate, that which brings all things to an end, had not thus apportioned my lot: ten thousand pains must bow, ten thousand miseries afflict me before from these bonds I find freedom, for craft is much weaker than Necessity.

CHORUS: Who is the origin of Necessity?

PROMETHEUS: The three Fates, and the unforgetting Furies.

CHORUS: So then Zeus is of lesser might than these?

PROMETHEUS: Surely he shall not shun his apportioned lot.

CHORUS: What lot has Zeus but to reign the world without end?

PROMETHEUS: Tax me no further with importunate questions.

CHORUS: O, deep is the mystery that you shroud there!

PROMETHEUS: Of anything but this you freely may ask. But concerning this I order you to speak no word; no, veil it utterly: for, if strictly kept, the secret from these bonds shall set me free…

Io, a maiden transformed into a cow by Hera as punishment for being raped by Zeus, crazed by a long, miserable journey, arrives at the mountain. PROMETHEUS *prophesies her future wanderings and sufferings, but foretells of her descendants, including Heracles, who himself will free* PROMETHEUS *in thirteen generations. Io departs.*

CHORUS: I think him wise who first in his own mind fixed this doctrine and taught it to mankind: true marriage is the union that mates equal with equal; not where wealth emasculates, or mighty lineage is magnified, should he who earns his bread look for a bride. Therefore, grave mistresses of fate, I pray that I may never live to see the day when Zeus takes me for his bedmate; or draw near in love as a husband from on high. For I am full of fear when I behold Io, the virgin no human love may fold, and her disconsolate virginity, homeless and husbandless by Hera's hate. For me, when love is equal, fear is far away. May none of all the gods that are greater gaze at me with his irresistible regard; for in that war victory is hard, and from it plenty turns to emptiness. What should befall me then, I dare not guess, nor to where should I flee to shun the craft and subtlety of Cronos' son.

PROMETHEUS: I tell you that the self-willed pride of Zeus shall surely be abased, that even now he plots a marriage that shall hurl him forth far out of sight of his imperial throne and kingly dignity. Then, in that hour, shall be fulfilled, nor in one way fail, the curse by which his father Cronos cursed him, that time he fell from his majestic place, established so long ago. And such a stroke none of the Gods except me could turn aside. I know these things shall be and in what way. Therefore, let him feel secure in his seat, and put his trust in airy noise, and swing his bright, two-handed, blazing thunderbolt, for these shall not save him, nor avert such a great fall, and humbling of his glory. A wrestler of such might he makes ready for his own ruin; yes, a wonder, strong in unmatchable strength, and he shall find fire that shall set as nothing the burning bolt, and blast more dreadful that the thunder. The pestilence that scourges the deep seas and shakes solid earth, the three-pronged mace, Poseidon's spear, a mightier shall scatter; and when he stumbles, striking there his foot, fallen on evil days, the tyrant's pride shall measure all the miserable length that parts rule absolute from servitude...

HERMES *arrives on Zeus' orders to determine* PROMETHEUS' *prophesy of Zeus' descendants.* PROMETHEUS *insultingly refuses.*

HERMES: I have talked much, yet have not furthered my purpose, for you are in no way melted or moved by my prolonged requests: like a colt new to the harness, you jump back and plunge, snapping at the bit and fighting against the rein. And yet your confidence is in a straw; for stubbornness, if one is in the wrong, is in itself weaker than nothing at all. Look now, if you will not obey my words, what storm, what triple-crested wave of irresistible woe shall come upon you. First, this rocky chasm Zeus shall split with earthquake thunder and his burning bolt, and he shall hide your body, and you shall hang bolted upright, dangling in the rock's rude arms. Nor till you have completed your long term shall you come back into the light; and then the hound of Zeus, the tawny eagle, shall violently feast upon your flesh and rip it as if it were rags; and every day and all day long shall your unbidden guest sit at your table, feasting on your liver until he has gnawed it black. Look for no end to such an agony until there stands forth among the Gods one who shall take upon his shoulders tour sufferings and consent to enter hell far from the light of Sun, yes, the deep pit and mirk of Tartarus, for your. Be warned, this is not just talk framed to frighten, but woeful truth. For Zeus knows not to lie.

PROMETHEUS: The time is past for words. The earth quakes. Listen! Pent-up thunder rakes the depths, with bellowing sound of echoes rolling ever closer: lightning shakes out its locks of fire; the dust cones dance and spin; the skipping winds, as if possessed all the winds – north, south, east and west – blow at each other, the sea and sky are shaken together: there the swing and fury of the blow by which Zeus destroys me sweeps rapidly and visibly, to strike my heart with fear. See, see, Earth, awful Mother! Air, that bristles from the revolving sky on all the light they see you by, what bitter wrongs I bear!

The scene closes with earthquake and thunder, in the midst of which PROMETHEUS *and the* CHORUS OF DAUGHTERS OF OCEANUS *sink into the abyss.*

Adapted from G. M. Cookson, Aeschylus. Four plays (Oxford: Basil Blackwell, 1922).

READING 10:

AESCHYLUS' *AGAMEMNON*

Agamemnon is the first play in Aeschylus' *Oresteia* – the only tragic Athenian trilogy to have survived complete. It tells the story of the cursed house of Atreus, and how this curse endured to bring suffering on generation after generation. Agamemnon, the son of Atreus, is returning to Argos after the long and tragic conflict at Troy. Unbeknownst to him, his wife, Clytemnestra, furious at her husband's earlier decision to sacrifice their daughter, Iphigenia, for favourable winds for the voyage to Troy, has decided to murder him. She is aided somewhat by her new lover and Agamemnon's own cousin, Aegisthus. The latter acts out of vengeance, since Agamemnon's father, Atreus, had murdered and cooked Aegisthus' own brothers. Agamemnon and his prize from Troy, the prophetess Cassandra, are duly murdered on their return, and the play ends with the two jubilant, but not before the Chorus of Argive citizens call for Agamemnon's son, Orestes, to return home to exact vengeance in turn. The theme here is the inevitable and destructive nature of divine fate and human vengeance.

10a) Aeschylus, Agamemnon (1-257; 437-74; 1080-1673, passim)

SCENE: *Argos, at the royal palace of* **AGAMEMNON**. *The* **WATCHMAN** *appears at the palace's roof, and gazes into the night*

WATCHMAN: "Release me from this weary task of mine"
    Has been my plea to the gods throughout this long year's
    Watch, in which, lying upon the palace roof of the Atreidae
    Upon my bent arm, like a dog, I have learned to
    Know well the gathering of the night's stars,
    Those radiant potentates conspicuous in the heavens,
    Bringers of winter and summer to mankind
    The constellations, when they rise and set.

So now I am still watching for the signal-flame,
The gleaming fire that is to bring news from Troy and
Tidings of its capture. For thus commands my queen,
Woman in passionate heart yet man in strength of purpose.
And whenever I make here my bed,
Restless and dank with Dew and unvisited by dreams –
For instead of sleep fear stands ever by my side,
So that I cannot close my eyelids fast in sleep –
And whenever I care to sing or hum and thus
Apply an antidote of song to ward off drowsiness,
Then my tears burst forth, as I bewail the fortunes of this
House of ours, not ordered for the best as in days gone by.
But tonight may there come a happy release from my weary task!
May the fire with its glad tidings flash through the gloom!
A beacon-light is seen reddening the distant sky.
Oh welcome, you fire in the night, a light as if of day, y
You harbinger of many a choral dance in Argos in
Thanksgiving for this glad event!
Hallo! Hallo! To Agamemnon's queen I thus cry aloud the
Signal to rise from her bed, and as quickly as she can to
Lift up in her palace halls a shout of joy in welcome of this fire,
If the city of Ilium truly is taken, as this beacon unmistakably announces.
And I will make an overture with a dance upon my own account,
For my lord's lucky roll I shall count to my own score,
Now that this beacon has thrown me triple six.
Ah well, may the master of the house come home and may
I clasp his welcome hand in mine! For the rest I stay silent;
A great ox stands upon my tongue – yet the house itself,
Could it but speak, might tell a plain enough tale.
Since, for my part, by my own choice I have words for those who know,
And to those who do not know, I've lost my memory.

Watchman *exits. The* **Chorus of Old Men of Argos** *enter, each leaning on a staff. During their song,* **Clytemnestra** *appears in the background, kindling the altars.*

Chorus: This is now the tenth year since Priam's mighty adversary,
King Menelaus, and with him king Agamemnon,
The mighty pair of Atreus' sons, joined
In honor of throne and sceptre by Zeus, set forth
From this land with an army of a thousand ships
Manned by Argives, a warrior force to champion their cause.
Loud rang the battle-cry they uttered in their rage,

Just as eagles scream which, in lonely grief for their children,
Rowing with the oars of their wings, wheel high over their home,
Because they have lost the toil of guarding their nurslings' nest.
But some one of the powers supreme – Apollo perhaps or
Pan, or Zeus – hears the shrill wailing scream of the
Clamorous birds, these sojourners in his realm, and
Against the transgressors Sends vengeance at last, though late.
Just so Zeus, whose power is over all, Zeus,
Lord of host and guest, sends against Paris the sons of Atreus,
That for the sake of a woman with many husbands he may
Inflict many and wearying struggles – when the knee is
Pressed in the dust and the spear is splintered in the onset –
on Danaans and on Trojans alike.
The case now stands where it stands – it moves to fulfillment
At its destined end. Not by offerings burned in secret,
Not by secret libations, not by tears, shall man soften the
Stubborn wrath of unsanctified sacrifices.
But we, incapable of service by reason of our old age,
Discarded from that mustering for war of long ago,
Wait here at home, supporting on our canes a strength
Like a child's. For just as the vigor of youth, leaping up
Within the breast, is like that of old age, since the
War-god is not in his place; so extreme age, its leaves
Already withering, goes its way on triple feet, and,
No better than a child, wanders, a dream that is dreamed by day…
I have the power to proclaim the augury of triumph given on their way
To princely men – since my age still breathes Persuasion upon me
From the gods, the strength of song – how the twin-throned
Command of the Achaeans, the single-minded captains
Of Hellas' youth, with avenging spear and arm against the Trojan land,
Was sent off by the inspiring omen appearing to the kings of the ships –
Kingly birds, one black, one white in the tail, near the palace,
On the spear-hand, in a conspicuous place, devouring a hare
With offspring unborn caught in the last effort to escape.
Sing the song of woe, the song of woe, but may the good prevail!
Then the wise seer of the host, noticing how the two warlike
Sons of Atreus were two in temper, recognized the
Devourers of the hare as the leaders of the army, and thus
Interpreted the portent and spoke: "In time those who here
Issue forth shall seize Priam's city, and fate shall violently
Ravage before its towered walls all the public store of cattle.

Only may no jealous divinely-sent wrath cast its shadow
Upon the embattled host, the mighty bit forged for Troy's mouth,
And strike it before it reaches its goal! For, in her pity,
Holy Artemis is angry at the winged hounds of her father,
For they sacrifice a wretched fearful thing, together
With her young, before she has brought them forth.
An abomination to her is the eagles' feast."
Sing the song of woe, the song of woe, but may the good prevail!
"Although, O Lovely One, you are so gracious to the tender
Whelps of fierce lions, and take delight in the suckling
Young of every wild creature that roams the field,
Promise that the issue be brought to pass in accordance
With these signs, auspicious portents yet filled with ill.
And I implore Paean, the healer, that she may not raise
Adverse gales with long delay to stay the Danaan fleet
From putting forth, by urging another sacrifice,
One that knows no law, unsuited for feast, worker of family strife,
Dissolving wife's reverence for husband. For there abides wrath –
Terrible, not to be suppressed, a treacherous guardian of the home,
A wrath that never forgets and that exacts vengeance for a child."
Such utterances of doom, derived from auguries on the march,
Together with many blessings, did Calchas proclaim to the
Royal house; and in harmony with this,
Sing the song of woe, the song of woe, but may the good prevail...
Zeus, who sets mortals on the path to understanding,
Zeus, who has established as a fixed law that
Wisdom comes by suffering. But even as trouble,
Bringing memory of pain, drips over the mind in sleep,
So wisdom comes to men, whether they want it or not.
Harsh, it seems to me, is the grace of gods
Enthroned upon their awful seats.
So then the captain of the Achaean ships, the elder of the two
Holding no seer at fault, bending to the adverse blasts of fortune,
When the Achaean folk, on the shore over against Chalcis
In the region where Aulis' tides surge to and fro, were very
Distressed by opposing winds and failing stores.
The breezes that blew from the Strymon, bringing
Harmful leisure, hunger, and tribulation of spirit in a cruel port,
Idle wandering of men, and sparing neither ship nor cable,
Began, by doubling the season of their stay, to rub away and
Wither the flower of Argos; and when the seer,

Pointing to Artemis as cause, proclaimed to the chieftains
Another remedy, more oppressive even than the
Bitter storm, so that the sons of Atreus struck the ground
With their canes and did not stifle their tears –
Then the elder king spoke and said: "It is a hard fate to
Refuse obedience, and hard, if I must slay my child,
The glory of my home, and at the altar-side stain
A father's hand with streams of virgin's blood.
Which of these courses is not filled with evil?
How can I become a deserter to my fleet and fail my allies in arms?
For that they should with all too impassioned
Passion crave a sacrifice to lull the winds – even a virgin's blood –
Stands within their right. May all be for the best."
But when he had donned the yoke of Necessity,
With veering of mind, impious, unholy, unsanctified,
From that moment he changed his intention and
Began to conceive that deed of utmost audacity.
For wretched delusion, counselor of evil,
Primal source of woe, makes mortals bold.
So then he hardened his heart to sacrifice his daughter
So that he might continue a war waged to avenge a woman,
And as an offering for the voyage of a fleet!
For her supplications, her cries of "Father," and her virgin life,
The commanders in their eagerness for war cared nothing.
Her father, after a prayer, ordered his servants to lay hold of her
As, wrapped in her robes, she lay, fallen forward,
And with stout heart to raise her, as if she were a young goat,
High above the altar; and with a gag upon her lovely mouth
And by the strong power of a leather bit,
The shouted curse against her house was stifled.
Then, as she shed to earth her saffron robe, she struck
Each of her sacrificers with a glance from her eyes,
Beseeching pity, looking as if in a picture, wishing she could speak;
For she had often sung where men met at her father's hospitable table,
And with her virgin voice would lovingly honor her dear father's
Prayer for blessing at the third libation.
What happened next I did not see and do not tell.
The art of Calchas was not unfulfilled. Justice inclines her scales
So that wisdom comes at the price of suffering.
But the future, that you shall know when it occurs.
Until then, leave it be – it is just as someone weeping ahead of time.

Clear it will come, together with the light of dawn.
But as for what shall follow, may the issue be happy,
Even as she wishes, our sole guardian here, the
Bulwark of the Apian land, who stands nearest to our lord.

CLYTEMNESTRA *and her attendants enter the palace. She informs the* **CHORUS**, *skeptical of her information, of the Greeks' return. Having persuaded them, she exits, preparing to her husband's arrival.*

CHORUS: Ares barters the bodies of men for gold.
   He holds his balance in the contest of the spear,
   And back from Ilium to their loved ones he sends a
   Heavy dust passed through his burning,
   A dust cried over with plenteous tears,
   In place of men sending well made urns with ashes.
   So they lament, praising now this one: "How skilled in battle!"
   Now that one: "Fallen nobly in the carnage," –
   "For another's wife!" some mutter in secret, and
   Grief charged with resentment spreads stealthily
   Against the sons of Atreus, champions in the strife.
   But there far from home, around the city's walls,
   Those in their beauty's bloom have graves in Ilium –
   The enemy's soil has covered its conquerors.
   Dangerous is a people's voice charged with wrath –
   It acts as a curse of publicly ratified doom.
   In anxious fear I wait to hear something shrouded still in gloom.
   The gods are not blind to men with blood upon their hands.
   In the end the black Spirits of Vengeance bring to
   Obscurity that one who has prospered in unrighteousness
   And wear down his fortunes by reverse.
   Once a man is among the unseen, there is no more help for him.
   Glory in excess is fraught with peril;
   The lofty peak is struck by Zeus' thunderbolt. I choose prosperity
   Unsullied by envy. May I not be a sacker of cities, and may
   I not myself be despoiled and live to see my own life in another's power…

AGAMEMNON, *accompanied by his female captive,* **CASSANDRA**, *and the rest of the Achaeans eventually arrive, and are greeted by* **CLYTEMNESTRA**. *After* **AGAMEMNON'S** *arrogant and rather rude reunion with his wife, he goes into the palace.* **CLYTEMNESTRA** *speaks to the* **CHORUS** *(ironically) of her patient, devoted love to her husband, and eventually follows him inside.* **CASSANDRA**, *a former priestess of Apollo, enters a prophetic trance, and is questioned by the* **CHORUS**.

CASSANDRA: Apollo, Apollo! God of the Ways, my destroyer!
   For you have destroyed me—and utterly—this second time.

CHORUS: I think that she is about to prophesy about her own miseries.

The divine gift still abides even in the soul of one enslaved.

CASSANDRA: Apollo, Apollo! God of the Ways, my destroyer!
Ah, what way is this that you have brought me! To what a house!

CHORUS: To that of Atreus' sons. If you do not perceive this, I'll tell it to you.
And you shall not say that it is untrue.

CASSANDRA: No, no, rather to a god-hating house, a house that knows
Many a horrible butchery of kin, a slaughterhouse of
Men and a floor swimming with blood.

CHORUS: The stranger seems keen-scented as a hound.
She is on the trail where she will discover blood.

CASSANDRA: Here is the evidence in which I put my trust!
Behold those babies bewailing their own butchery
And their roasted flesh eaten by their father!

CHORUS: Your fame to read the future had reached our ears,
But we have no need of prophets here.

CASSANDRA: Alas, what can she be planning? What is this fresh woe
She contrives here within, what monstrous, monstrous horror,
Beyond love's enduring, beyond all remedy? And help stands far away!

CHORUS: These prophesies pass my comprehension,
But those I understood – the whole city rings with them.

CASSANDRA: Ah, damned woman, will you do this thing? Your husband,
The partner of your bed, when you have cheered him with the bath,
Will you – how shall I tell the end? Soon it will be done.
Now this hand, now that, she stretches out!

CHORUS: Not yet do I comprehend; for now, after riddles,
I am bewildered by dark oracles.

CASSANDRA: Ah! Ah! What apparition is this? Is it a net of death?
No, it is a snare that shares his bed, that shares the guilt of murder.
Let the fatal pack, insatiable against the race,
Raise a shout of jubilance over a victim accursed!

CHORUS: What Spirit of Vengeance is this that you bid to
Raise its voice over this house? Your words do not cheer me.
Back to my heart surge the drops of my pallid blood,
Even as when they drip from a mortal wound,
Ebbing away as life's beams sink low; and death comes speedily.

CASSANDRA: Alas, alas, the sorrow of my ill-starred doom! For it is my own affliction,
Crowning the cup, that I bemoan. Ah, to what end did you bring me here,

Unhappy as I am? For nothing except to die – and not alone. What else?

CHORUS: Frenzied in soul you are, by some god possessed,
And you wail in wild strains your own fate, like that brown bird
That never ceases making lament – ah me – and in the misery
Of her heart moans Itys, Itys, throughout
All her days abounding in sorrow, the nightingale.

CASSANDRA: Ah, fate of the clear-voiced nightingale! T
he gods clothed her in a winged form and gave to her a sweet life without tears.
But for me waits destruction by the two-edged sword.

CHORUS: From where come these vain pangs of prophecy that assail you?
And why do you mold to melody these terrors with
Dismal cries blended with piercing strains?
How do you know the bounds of the path of your ill-boding prophecy?

CASSANDRA: Ah, the marriage, the marriage of Paris, that destroyed his friends!
Ah me, Scamander, my native stream! Upon your banks in bygone days,
Unhappy maid, was I nurtured with fostering care,
But now by Cocytus and the banks of Acheron, I think, I soon must chant my prophecies.

CHORUS: What words are these you utter, words all too plain?
A newborn child hearing them could understand.
I am smitten with a deadly pain, while, by reason of your cruel fortune,
You cry aloud your pitiful moans that break my heart to hear.

CASSANDRA: O the sufferings, the sufferings of my city utterly destroyed!
Alas, the sacrifices my father offered,
The many pasturing cattle slain to save its towers!
Yet they provided no remedy to save the city from suffering even as it has;
And I, my soul on fire, must soon fall to the ground.

CHORUS: Your present speech chimes with your former strain.
Surely some malignant spirit, falling upon you with heavy swoop,
Moves you to chant your piteous woes fraught with death.
But the end I am helpless to discover.

CASSANDRA: And now, no more shall my prophecy peer forth from behind a
Veil like a new-wedded bride; but it will rush upon me clear as a
Fresh wind blowing against the sun's uprising so as to
Dash against its rays, like a wave, a woe far mightier than mine.
No more by riddles will I instruct you. And bear me witness, as,
Running close behind, I smell the track of crimes done long ago.
For from this roof never departs a choir chanting in unison,
But singing no harmonious tune; for it tells of no good.
And so, gorged on human blood, so as to be the more emboldened,

A revel-rout of kindred Furies haunts the house, hard to be drive away.
Lodged within its halls they chant their chant, the primal sin;
And, each in turn, they spurn with loathing a brother's bed,
For they bitterly spurn the one who defiled it.
Have I missed the mark, or, like a true archer, do I strike my quarry?
Or am I prophet of lies, a door-to-door babbler? Bear witness upon your
Oath that I know the deeds of sin, ancient in story, of this house.

CHORUS: How could an oath, a pledge although given in honor, effect any cure?
Yet I marvel at you that, though bred beyond the sea,
You speak truth of a foreign city, even as if you had been present there.

CASSANDRA: Ah, ah! Oh, oh, the agony! Once more the dreadful throes of
True prophecy whirl and distract me with their ill-boding onset.
Do you see them there – sitting before the house –
Young creatures like phantoms of dreams? Children, they seem,
Slaughtered by their own kindred, their hands
Full of the meat of their own flesh; they are clear to my sight,
Holding their vitals and their inward parts, which their father tasted.
For this cause I tell you that a weak lion, wallowing in his bed,
Plots vengeance, a watchman waiting for my master's coming home –
Yes, my master, for I must bear the yoke of slavery.
The commander of the fleet and the overthrower of Ilium knows
Little of what deeds shall be brought to evil accomplishment by the
Hateful hound, whose tongue licked his hand,
Who stretched forth her ears in gladness, like treacherous Ate.
Such boldness has she, a woman to slay a man.
What odious monster shall I fitly call her? An Amphisbaena?
Or a Scylla, tenanting the rocks, a pest to mariners,
A raging, devil's mother, breathing relentless war against her husband?
And how the all-daring woman raised a shout of triumph,
As when the battle turns, the while she feigned to joy at his safe return!
And yet, it is all one, whether or not I am believed. What does it matter?
What is to come, will come. And soon you, yourself present here,
Shall with great pity pronounce me all too true a prophetess…
Yet, we shall not die unavenged by the gods,
For there shall come in turn another, our avenger,
A descendent of the race, to slay his mother
And exact requital for his sire; an exile, a wanderer,
A stranger from this land, he shall return to put the
Coping-stone upon these unspeakable iniquities of his house.
For the gods have sworn a mighty oath that his slain father's
Outstretched corpse shall bring him home.

Why then thus raise my voice in pitiful lament?
Since first I saw the city of Ilium fare what it has fared
While her captors, by the gods' sentence, are coming to such an end,
I will go in and meet my fate. I will dare to die.
This door I greet as the gates of Death.
And I pray that, dealt a mortal stroke, without a struggle,
My life-blood ebbing away in easy death, I may close these eyes...

CASSANDRA *enters the palace, leaving the* CHORUS *to ponder her words. Soon they hear Agamemnon screaming inside the palace, but before they can assist him,* CLYTEMNESTRA *emerges, her hands bloody. She confronts them.*

CLYTEMNESTRA: Much have I said before to serve my need and
   I shall feel no shame to contradict it now.
   For how else could one, devising hate against a hated foe
   Who bears the semblance of a friend,
   Fence the snares of ruin too high to be overleaped?
   This is the contest of an ancient feud, pondered by me of old,
   And it has come, however long delayed.
   I stand where I dealt the blow; my purpose is achieved.
   Thus have I done the deed; I will not deny it!
   Round him, as if to catch a haul of fish, I cast an impassable net –
   Fatal wealth of robe – so that he should neither escape nor ward off doom.
   Twice I struck him, and with two groans his limbs relaxed.
   Once he had fallen, I dealt him yet a third stroke to
   Grace my prayer to the infernal Zeus, the savior of the dead.
   Fallen thus, he gasped away his life, and as he breathed forth quick spurts of blood,
   He struck me with dark drops of gory dew,
   While I rejoiced no less than the sown earth is gladdened in
   Heaven's refreshing rain at the birth of the flower buds.
   Since then the case stands thus, old men of Argos,
   Rejoice, if you would rejoice; as for me, I glory in the deed.
   And had it been a fitting act to pour libations on the corpse,
   Over him this would have been done justly, more than justly.
   With so many accursed lies has he filled the mixing-bowl in his own
   House, and now he has come home and himself drained it to the dregs.

CHORUS: We are shocked at your tongue, how bold-mouthed you are,
   That over your husband you can utter such a boastful speech.

CLYTEMNESTRA: You are testing me as if I were a witless woman. But my heart does not quail,
   And I say to you who know it well – and whether you wish to praise or to blame me,
   It is all one – here is Agamemnon, my husband, now a corpse,
   The work of this right hand, a just workman. So stands the case.

Chorus: Woman, what poisonous herb nourished by the earth have you tasted,
  What potion drawn from the flowing sea, that you have taken upon
  Yourself this maddened rage and the loud curses voiced by the public?
  You have cast him off; you have cut him off; and out from the land shall
  You be cast, a burden of hatred to your people…

Clytemnestra: Neither do I think he met an ignoble death.
  And did he not himself by treachery bring ruin on his house?
  Yet, as he has suffered – worthy penalty of worthy deed –
  For what he did to my sweet flower, shoot sprung from him,
  The sore-wept Iphigenia, let him make no great boasts in the halls of Hades,
  Since with death dealt him by the sword he has paid for what he first began.

Chorus: Bereft of any ready expedient of thought, I am
  Bewildered where to turn now that the house is tottering.
  I fear the beating storm of bloody rain that shakes the house;
  No longer does it descend in drops. Yet on other whetstones
  Destiny is sharpening justice for another evil deed…
  Chardge thus answeres charge in turn – hard is the struggle to decide.
  The spoiler is despoiled, the slayer pays penalty.
  Yet, while Zeus remains on his throne, it remains true that to him
  Who does it shall be done; for it is law.
  Who can cast from out the house the seed of the curse?
  The race is bound fast in calamity.…

Clytemnestra's *lover, and* **Agamemnon's** *nephew,* **Aegisthus,** *now enters the scene with guards. He recalls the justice regained for his family by the death of the son of Atreus. The* **Chorus** *accuses him of murder and weak, cowardly behavior. His enraged language against them is that of a tyrant, and he threatens to destroy them too if they resist. They remain unimpressed.*

Chorus: Aegisthus, excessive triumph amid distress I do not honor.
  You say that of your own intent you slew this man
  And did alone plot this pitiful murder. I tell you in the
  Hour of justice that you yourself, be sure of that,
  Will not escape the people's curses and death by stoning at their hand.

Aegisthus: You speak like that, you who sit at the lower oars
  When those upon the higher bench control the ship?
  Old as you are, you shall learn how bitter it is at your
  Age to be schooled when prudence is the lesson set before you.
  Bonds and the pangs of hunger are far the best
  Doctors of the spirit when it comes to instructing the old.
  Do you have eyes and lack understanding?
  Do not kick against the goads lest you strike to your own hurt.

Chorus: Woman that you are! Skulking at home and awaiting the
> Return of the men from war, all the while defiling a hero's bed,
> Did you contrive this death against a warrior chief?

Aegisthus: These words of yours likewise shall prove a source of tears.
> The tongue of Orpheus is quite the opposite of yours.
> He led all things by the rapture of his voice;
> But you, who have stirred our wrath by your silly yelping,
> Shall be led off yourself. You will appear tamer when put down by force!

Clytemnestra *stops* **Aegisthus** *from going too far, and convinces him to return inside the palace. The* **Chorus** *of Argives also exit the scene.*

Adapted from Herbert Weir Smyth, Aeschylus. Agamemnon (Cambridge, MA: Harvard University Press, 1926)

READING 11:

AESCHYLUS' *EUMENIDES*

Eumenides is the third part of Aeschylus' *Oresteia*. In the middle piece, *Libation-Bearers*, Orestes returns home to Argos from exile. With support from his sister, Electra, he manages to murder both Clytemnestra and Aegisthus, but is immediately set upon by the Furies: old, terrible goddesses who hunt and haunt anyone who murders their parents. *Eumenides*, then, must answer the questions posed by the two earlier plays: how can the cycle of bloodshed end? In *Eumenides*, Orestes is chased by the Furies to Delphi, where Apollo promises him his support. He proceeds to Athens, where Athena finally holds a trial, with a jury of Athenian citizens, to determine whether or not Orestes is guilty. In the end, Athena and the jury support Orestes, and to appease the Furies, Athena promises that they will be worshiped at Athens now as "kindly goddesses" (*eumenides*). Thus, the cycle of violence is brought to a close not by the destruction of all, but by the political institution of the Athenian polis. The play also offers new ideas on the importance of persuasion in contrast to force in dealings among humans, and the substitution of traditional bloodguilt with reason and law.

11a) Aeschylus, Eumenides (1-234; 397-680; 778-869, passim)

SCENE: *Outside Delphi, at the temple of* APOLLO. *The priestess of* APOLLO, *the* PYTHIA, *enters the scene.*

PYTHIA: First, in this prayer of mine, I give the place of highest honour among the gods to the first prophet, Earth; and after her to Themis, for she was the second to take this oracular seat of her mother, as legend tells. And in the third allotment, with Themis' consent and not by force, another Titan, child of Earth, Phoebe, took her seat here. She gave it as a birthday gift to Phoebus, who has his name from Phoebe. Leaving the lake and ridge of Delos, he landed on Pallas' ship-frequented shores, and came to this region and the dwelling places on Parnassus. The children of Hephaestus, road-builders taming the wildness of the untamed land, escorted him with mighty reverence. And at his arrival, the people and Delphus, helmsman and lord of this land, made a great celebration for him. Zeus inspired his heart with prophetic skill and established him as the fourth prophet on this throne; but Apollo is the spokesman of Zeus, his father....

PYTHIA *enters the temple, but quickly emerges in horror.*

PYTHIA: Horrors to tell, horrors for my eyes to see, have sent me back from the house of Apollo, so that I have no strength and I cannot walk upright. I am running on hands and knees, with no quickness in my limbs, for an old woman, overcome with fright, is nothing, or rather she is like a child.

I was on my way to the inner shrine, decked with wreaths, I saw on the center-stone a man defiled in the eyes of the gods, occupying the seat of suppliants. His hands were dripping blood, he held a sword just drawn and an olive-branch, from the top of the tree, decorously crowned with a large tuft of wool, a shining fleece; for as to this I can speak clearly.

Before this man an extraordinary band of women slept, seated on thrones. No! Not women, but rather Gorgons I call them, and yet I cannot compare them to forms of Gorgons either. Once before I saw some creatures in a painting, carrying off the feast of Phineus; but these are wingless in appearance, black, altogether disgusting; they snore with repulsive breaths, they drip from their eyes hateful drops; their attire is not fit to bring either before the statues of the gods or into the homes of men. I have never seen the tribe that produced this company, nor the land that boasts of rearing this brood with impunity and does not grieve for its labor afterwards.

Let what is to come now be the concern of the master of this house, powerful Apollo himself. He is a prophet of healing, a reader of portents, and for others a purifier of homes.

PYTHIA *departs.* ORESTES *and* APOLLO *emerge from the temple.*

APOLLO: No, I will not abandon you. Your guardian to the end, close by your side or far removed, I will not be gentle to your enemies. So now you see these mad women overcome, these loathsome maidens have fallen asleep, old women, ancient children, with whom no god or man or beast ever mingles. They were even born for evil, since they live in evil gloom and in Tartarus under the earth, creatures hateful to men and to the Olympian gods. Nevertheless, escape and do not be cowardly. For as you go always over the earth that wanderers tread, They will drive you on, even across the wide mainland, beyond the sea and the island cities. Do not grow weary too soon, brooding on this labor, but when you have come to Pallas' city, sit down and hold in your arms her ancient image. And there, with judges of your case and speeches of persuasive charm, we shall find means to release you completely from your labors. For I persuaded you to take your mother's life.

ORESTES: Lord Apollo, you know how to do no wrong, and, since you know this, learn not to be neglectful also. For your power to do good is certain.

APOLLO: Remember, do not let fear overpower your heart. You, Hermes, my blood brother, born of the same father, watch over him; true to your name, be his guide, shepherding this suppliant of mine – truly Zeus respects this right of outlaws – as he is sped on towards mortals with the fortune of a good escort.

ORESTES *departs and* APOLLO *enters his temple.* CLYTEMNESTRA'S GHOST *appears, calling out the Furies to avenge her, not to give up the chase after* ORESTES. *The* CHORUS OF FURIES *emerges.*

CHORUS: Awake! Wake her up, as I wake you! Still asleep? Get up, shake off sleep, let us see if any part of this beginning is in vain. Oh, oh! Alas! We have suffered, friends. Indeed I have suffered much and all in vain. We have suffered very painfully, oh, an unbearable evil! The beast has escaped from our nets and is gone. Overcome by sleep, I have lost my prey.

Oh! Child of Zeus, you have become a thief – you, a youth, have ridden down old divinities by showing respect to your suppliant, a godless man and cruel to a parent; although you are a god, you have stolen away a man that killed his mother. What is there here that anyone shall call just? Reproach, coming to me in a dream, struck me like a charioteer with goad held tight, under my heart, under my vitals. I can feel the cruel, the very cruel chill of the executioner's destroying scourge.

They do such things, the younger gods, who rule, wholly beyond justice, a throne dripping blood, about its foot, about its head. I can see the center-stone of the earth defiled with a terrible pollution of blood. Although he is a prophet, he has stained his sanctuary with pollution at its hearth, at his own urging, at his own bidding, against the law of the gods, he has honored mortal things and caused the ancient allotments to decay. And he brings distress to me too, but he shall not win his release, even if he escapes beneath the earth, he is never set free. A suppliant, he will acquire another avenger from his family.

APOLLO: Out, I order you! Go away from this house at once, leave my prophetic sanctuary, so that you may not be struck by a winged glistening snake shot forth from a golden bow-string, and painfully release black foam, vomiting the clots of blood you have drained from mortals. It is not right for you to approach this house; no, your place is where the punishments are beheading, gouging out of eyes, cutting of throats, and where young men's virility is ruined by destruction of seed – where there is mutilation and stoning, and where those who are impaled beneath their spine moan long and piteously. Do you hear what sort of feast is your delight? You are detested by the gods for it. The whole fashion of your form sets it forth. Creatures like you should live in the den of a blood-drinking lion, and not inflict pollution on all near you in this oracular shrine. Be gone, you goats without a herdsman! No god loves such a flock.

CHORUS: Lord Apollo, hear our reply in turn. You yourself are not partially guilty of this deed, you alone have done it all, and are wholly guilty.

APOLLO: What do you mean? Draw out the length of your speech this much.

CHORUS: Through your oracle, you directed the stranger to kill his mother.

APOLLO: Through my oracle, I directed him to exact vengeance for his father. What of it?

CHORUS: And then you agreed to take the fresh blood on yourself.

APOLLO: And I ordered him to turn for expiation to this house.

CHORUS: And do you then criticize us, the ones who escorted him here?

APOLLO: Yes, for you are not fit to approach this house.

CHORUS: But this function has been assigned to us –

APOLLO: What is this office of yours? Boast of your fine privilege!

CHORUS: We drive matricides from their homes.

APOLLO: But what about a wife who kills her husband?

CHORUS: That would not be murder of a relative by blood.

APOLLO: Then truly you dishonor and bring to nothing the pledges of Hera, the Fulfiller, and Zeus. Cypris too is cast aside, dishonored by this argument, and from her come the dearest things for mortals. For marriage ordained by fate for a man and a woman is greater than an oath and guarded by Justice. If, then, one should kill the other and you are so lenient as not to punish or visit them with anger, I claim that you unjustly banish Orestes from his home. For I see you taking the one cause very much to heart, but clearly acting more leniently about the other. But the goddess Pallas will oversee the pleadings in this case.

CHORUS: We will never, never leave that criminal!

APOLLO: Pursue him then and get more trouble for yourself.

CHORUS: Do not cut short our privileges by your words.

APOLLO: I would not take your privileges as a gift.

CHORUS: No, for in any case you are called great at the throne of Zeus. But as for us – since a mother's blood leads us, we will pursue our case against this man and we will hunt him down.

APOLLO: And I will aid my suppliant and rescue him! For the wrath of the one who seeks purification is terrible among mortals and gods, if I intentionally abandon him.

Scene is now in Athens. ORESTES *arrives, pursued by the* CHORUS *of Furies.* ATHENA, *the guardian of Athens, also arrives to judge the dispute.*

ATHENA: From afar I heard the call of a summons, from the Scamander, while I was taking possession of the land, which the leaders and chiefs of the Achaeans assigned to me, a great portion of the spoil their spears had won, to be wholly mine forever, a choice gift to Theseus' sons. From there I have come, urging on my tireless foot, without wings rustling the folds of my aegis, yoking this chariot to colts in their prime. As I see this strange company of visitors to my land, I am not afraid, but it is a wonder to my eyes. Who in the world are you? I address you all in common – this stranger sitting at my image, and you, who are like no race of creatures ever born, neither seen by gods among goddesses nor resembling mortal forms. But it is far from just to speak poorly of one's neighbor who is blameless, and Justice stands aloof.

CHORUS: Daughter of Zeus, you will hear it all in brief. We are the eternal children of Night. We are called Curses in our homes beneath the earth.

ATHENA: I now know your family and the names by which you are called.

CHORUS: You will soon learn our function.

ATHENA: I shall understand, if someone would tell the story clearly.

CHORUS: We drive murderers from their homes.

ATHENA: And where is the end of flight for the killer?

CHORUS: Where joy is absent and unknown.

ATHENA: And would you drive this man with your shrieks to such flight?

CHORUS: Yes, for he thought it right to be his mother's murderer.

ATHENA: Because of compulsion, or in fear of someone's wrath?

CHORUS: Where is there a spur so sharp as to compel the murder of a mother?

ATHENA: Two parties are present – only half the case is heard.

CHORUS: But he will not receive an oath nor does he want to give one.

Athena: You want to be called just rather than to act justly.

Chorus: How so? Teach us. For you are not weak in subtleties.

Athena: I say that oaths must not win victory for an injustice.

Chorus: Well then, question him, and make a straight judgment.

Athena: Then would you turn over the decision of the charge to me?

Chorus: How not? You are worthy and of worthy parentage.

Athena: What do you want to say to this, stranger, in turn? After you name your country and family and fortunes, then defend yourself against this charge; if indeed, relying on the justice of your case, you sit clinging to my image near my hearth, as a sacred suppliant, like Ixion. To all this give me a plain answer.

Orestes: Lady Athena, first of all I will take away a great anxiety from your last words. I am not a suppliant in need of purification, nor did I sit at your image with pollution on my hands. I will give you strong proof of this. It is the law for one who is defiled by shedding blood to be barred from speech until he is sprinkled with the blood of a newborn victim by a man who can purify from murder. Long before at other houses I have been thus purified both by victims and by flowing streams. And so I declare that this concern is out of the way. As to my family, you will soon learn. I am an Argive. My father – you rightly inquire about him – was Agamemnon, the commander of the naval forces. Along with him, you made Troy, the city of Ilium, to be no city at all. He did not die nobly, after he came home, but my black-hearted mother killed him after she covered him in a crafty snare that still remains to witness his murder in the bath. And when I came back home, having been an exile in the time before, I killed the woman who gave birth to me, I will not deny it, as the penalty in return for the murder of my dearly-loved father. Together with me Apollo is responsible for this deed, because he threatened me with pains, a goad for my heart, if I should fail to do this deed to those who were responsible. You judge whether I acted justly or not. Whatever happens to me at your hands, I will be content.

Athena: The matter is too great, if any mortal thinks to pass judgment on it. No, it is not lawful even for me to decide on cases of murder that is followed by the quick anger of the Furies, especially since you, by rites fully performed, have come a pure and harmless suppliant to my house. and so I respect you, since you do not bring harm to my city. yet these women have an office that does not permit them to be dismissed lightly, and if they fail to win their cause, the venom from their resentment will fall upon the ground, an intolerable, perpetual plague afterwards in the land.

So stands the case: either course – to let them stay, to drive them out – brings disaster and perplexity to me. But since this matter has fallen here, I will select judges of homicide bound by oath, and I will establish this tribunal for all time. Summon your witnesses and proofs, sworn evidence to support your case; and I will return when I have chosen the best of my citizens, for them to decide this matter truly, after they take an oath that they will pronounce no judgment contrary to justice.

Athena *departs, but eventually returns, accompanied by a group Athenian citizens to act as jurors.* **Apollo** *speaks on behalf of the defendant, the* **Chorus** *speaks as plaintiffs. They trade arguments…*

Chorus: Zeus, as you say, gave you this oracular command, to tell Orestes here to avenge his father's murder but to take no account at all of the honor due his mother?

APOLLO: Yes, for it is not the same thing – the murder of a noble man, honoured by a god-given scepter, and his murder indeed by a woman, not by shooting arrows from afar, as if by an Amazon, but as you will hear, Pallas, and those who are sitting to decide by vote in this matter. She received him from the expedition, where he had for the most part won success beyond expectation in the judgment of those favorable to him. Then, as he was stepping from the bath, on its very edge, she threw a cloak like a tent over it, tied her husband in an embroidered robe, and cut him down. This was his death, as I have told it to you. The death of a man wholly majestic, commander of the fleet. As for that woman, I have described her in such a way as to whet the indignation of the people who have been appointed to decide this case.

CHORUS: Zeus gives greater honor to a father's death, is that what you say? Yet he himself bound his aged father, Cronus. How does this not contradict what you say? I call on you as witness yourself for the judges to hear these things.

APOLLO: Oh, you utterly loathed monsters, detested by the gods! Zeus could undo fetters, and there is a remedy for that, and many means of release. But when the dust has drawn up the blood of a man, once he is dead, there is no return to life. For this, my father has made no magic spells, although he arranges all other things, turning them up and down. Nor does his exercise of force cost him a breath.

CHORUS: See how you advocate acquittal for this man! After he has poured out his mother's blood on the ground, shall he then live in his father's house in Argos? Which of the public altars shall he use? What purification rite of the brotherhood will receive him?

APOLLO: I will explain this, too, and see how correctly I will speak. The mother of what is called her "child" is not the parent, but the nurse of the newly-sown embryo. The one who penetrates is the parent, whereas she, as a stranger for a stranger, preserves the young offspring, if the god does not harm it. And I will show you proof of what I say: a father might exist without a mother. A witness is here at hand, the child of Olympian Zeus, who was not nursed in the darkness of a womb, and she is such a child as no goddess could give birth to. For my part, Pallas, as in all other matters, as I know how, I will make your city and people great, and I have sent this man as a suppliant to your sanctuary so that he may be faithful for all time, and so that you, goddess, might win him and those to come after him as a new ally and so that these pledges of faith might remain always, for the later generations of these people to cherish.

ATHENA: Am I to assume that enough has been said, and shall I now command these jurors to cast an honest vote according to their judgment?

APOLLO: For our part, every bolt is already shot. But I am waiting to hear how the trial will be decided.

ATHENA: Why not? As for you, To Apollo and Orestes. how shall I arrange matters so that I will not be blamed by you?

CHORUS: You have heard what you have heard, and as you cast your ballots, keep the oath sacred in your hearts, friends.

The jurors depart to deliberate, but then return to cast their vote. The result is a tie, but ATHENA *casts a tie-breaking vote in favour of* ORESTES. *Joyful,* ORESTES *promises that he and his ghost will protect Athenians for all time. He departs, and the* CHORUS *bewails the decision.*

CHORUS: Ah! Younger gods, you have ridden down the ancient laws and have taken them from my hands! And we are left dishonored, unhappy, and deeply angry! Upon this land, alas, we will release venom from our heart, venom in return for our grief, drops that the land cannot endure. From it, a blight that destroys leaves, destroys children – a just reward – speeding over the plain, will cast infection on the land to ruin mortals. We groan aloud. What shall we do? We are mocked by mortals. What we have suffered is unbearable. Ah, cruel indeed are the wrongs of the daughters of Night, mourning over dishonor!

ATHENA: Be persuaded by me not to bear it with heavy lament. For you have not been defeated; the trial resulted fairly in an equal vote, without disgrace to you. But clear testimony from Zeus was present, and he himself who spoke the oracle himself gave witness that Orestes should not suffer harm for his deed. Do not be angry, do not hurl your heavy rage on this land, or cause barrenness, letting loose drops whose savage spirit will devour the seed. For I promise you most sacredly that you will have a cavernous sanctuary in a righteous land, where you will sit on shining thrones at your hearths, worshipped with honor by my citizens here…

You are not dishonored. So, although you are goddesses, do not, in excessive rage, blight past all cure this land of mortals. I also rely on Zeus – what need is there to mention that? And I alone of the gods know the keys to the house where his thunderbolt is sealed – but there is no need for that. So yield to my persuasion and do not hurl the words of a reckless tongue against the land, so that all things bearing fruit will not prosper. Calm the black wave's bitter anger, since you will receive proud honors and will live with me. And when you have the first-fruits of this great land forever, offerings on behalf of children and of marriage rites, you will praise my counsel.

CHORUS: For us to suffer this, alas! For us, with ancient wisdom, to live beneath the earth, alas, without honor, unclean! We are breathing fury and utter rage! Oh, oh, the shame of it! What anguish steals into our breasts! Hear our anger, mother Night; for the deceptions of the gods, hard to resist, have deprived us of our ancient honors, bringing us to nothing.

ATHENA: I will endure your anger, for you are older, and in that respect you are surely wiser than me. Yet Zeus has given me, too, no dull understanding. But as for you, if you go to a foreign land, you will come to love this land – I tell you now. For time, flowing on, will bring greater honor to these citizens. And you, having a seat of honor at the house of Erechtheus, will obtain from hosts of men and women more than you could ever win from other mortals. So do not cast on my realm keen incentives to bloodshed, harmful to young hearts, maddening them with a fury not of wine. And do not, as if taking the heart out of fighting cocks, plant in my people the spirit of tribal war and boldness against each other. Let their war be with foreign enemies, and without stint for one in whom there will be a terrible passion for glory. But I say there will be no battling of birds within the home. It is possible for you to choose such things from me: bestowing good, receiving good, well honored in this land that is most beloved to the gods….

The CHORUS OF FURIES, *now called "Eumenides", finally accept the compensation, and Athenians celebrate and honour their new, kindly goddesses.*

Adapted from Herbert Weir Smyth, Aeschylus. Eumenides (Cambridge, MA: Harvard University Press, 1926)

READING 12:

SOPHOCLES' *OEDIPUS THE KING*

Sophocles (c. 496-406) was the second of the great Athenian playwrights. His first plays were later than those of Aeschylus, yet slightly earlier than those of his contemporary, Euripides. Among his many great works, his most famous are the three "Theban plays:" *Oedipus the King, Antigone*, and *Oedipus at Colonus*. These plays were not part of a trilogy, however, each having been written many years apart. They are compared with one another because they are based on myths associated with a royal family at Thebes. Oedipus was a prince of Thebes but was abandoned at birth by its King, Laius, because his son was fated to murder his father and marry his mother. Oedipus, however, was saved by a shepherd and raised at nearby Corinth. When he grew up and returned to Thebes, he unknowingly killed his father on the road home. He became king of Thebes soon after by solving the riddle of the Sphinx, who was terrorizing the city. He then married the widowed queen (and his mother), Jocasta.

Oedipus the King is not concerned with any of these famous events, but with a more fundamental problem: does Oedipus have free will in his actions? Or is fate inexorable? Oedipus is heroic, though not in a typical way. He is intelligent rather than strong, generous and selfless rather than aggressive and self-interested. He desires to rid his city of a plague of which he unknowingly is the cause, and he is determined to find the truth. Creon, the city's leading aristocrat, Teiresias, the blind seer of Thebes, and many others try to dissuade him, and the tragedy is that he ends up destroying himself in the pursuit of truth and justice. The suicide of Jocasta drives Oedipus to take out his own eyes, and he will become exiled from the city of which he was once king.

12a) Sophocles, Oedipus the King (1-145; 316-446; 707-1530, passim)

SCENE: *Thebes in front of the royal palace. A crowd of citizens carrying branches decorated with laurel garlands and wool and led by a* **PRIEST** *has gathered.* **OEDIPUS** *enters through the palace doors.*

OEDIPUS: My children, latest generation born from Cadmus, why are you sitting here with wreathed sticks in supplication to me, while the city fills with incense, chants, and cries of pain? Children, it would not be appropriate for me to learn of this from any other source, so I have come in person – I, Oedipus, whose fame all men acknowledge. But you there, old man, tell me – you seem to be the one who ought to speak for those assembled here. What feeling brings you to me – fear or desire? You can be confident that I will help. I shall assist you willingly in every way. I would be a hard-hearted man indeed, if I did not pity suppliants like these.

PRIEST: Oedipus, ruler of my native land, you see how people here of every age are crouching down around your altars, some fledglings barely strong enough to fly and others bent by age, with priests as well, for I'm priest of Zeus, and these ones here, the pick of all our youth. The other groups sit in the marketplace with suppliant sticks or else in front of Pallas' two shrines, or where Ismenus prophesies with fire. For our city, as you yourself can see, is badly shaken – she cannot raise her head above the depths of so much surging death. Disease infects fruit blossoms in our land, disease infects our herds of grazing cattle, makes women in labour lose their children. And deadly Smintheus, that fiery god, swoops down to blast the city, emptying the House of Cadmus, and fills black Hades with groans and howls. These children and myself now sit here by your home, not because we think you're equal to the gods. No. We judge you the first of men in what happens in this life and in our interactions with the gods. For you came here, to our Cadmeian city, and freed us from the tribute we were paying to that cruel singer – and yet you knew no more than we did and had not been taught. In their stories, the people testify how, with gods' help, you gave us back our lives. So now, Oedipus, our king, most powerful in all men's eyes, we're here as suppliants, all begging you to find some help for us, either by listening to a heavenly voice, or learning from some other human being. For, in my view, men of experience provide advice which gives the best results. So now, you best of men, raise up our state. Act to consolidate your fame, for now, thanks to your eagerness in earlier days, the city celebrates you as its saviour. Don't let our memory of your ruling here declare that we were first set right again, and later fell. No! Restore our city, so that it stands secure. In those times past you brought us joy – and with good omens, too. Be that same man today. If you're to rule as you are doing now, it's better to be king in a land of men than in a desert. An empty ship or city wall is nothing if no men share your life together there…

CREON *enters the scene.* OEDIPUS *calls to him as he approaches.*

OEDIPUS: My royal kinsman, child of Menoeceus, what message from the god do you bring us?

CREON: Good news. I tell you even troubles difficult to bear will all end happily if events lead to the right conclusion.

OEDIPUS: What is the oracle? So far your words inspire in me no confidence or fear.

CREON: If you wish to hear the news in public, I'm prepared to speak. Or we could step inside.

OEDIPUS: Speak out to everyone. The grief I feel for these citizens is even greater than any pain I feel for my own life.

CREON: Then let me report what I heard from the god. Lord Phoebus clearly orders us to drive away the polluting stain this land has harboured, which will not be healed if we keep nursing it.

OEDIPUS: What sort of cleansing? And this disaster, how did it happen?

CREON: By banishment, or atone for murder by shedding blood again. This blood brings on the storm which blasts our state.

OEDIPUS: And the one whose fate the god revealed, what sort of man is he?

CREON: Before you came, my lord, to steer our ship of state, Laius ruled this land.

OEDIPUS: I have heard that, but I never saw the man.

CREON: Laius was killed. And now the god is clear: those murderers, he tells us, must be punished, whoever they may be.

OEDIPUS: And where are they? In what country? Where am I to find a trace of this ancient crime? It will be hard to track.

CREON: Here in Thebes, so said the god. What is sought is found, but what is overlooked escapes.

OEDIPUS: When Laius fell in bloody death, where was he at home, or in his fields, or in another land?

CREON: He was abroad, on his way to Delphi. That's what he told us. He began the trip, but did not return.

OEDIPUS: Was there no messenger, since no companion who made the journey with him and witnessed what took place? A person who might provide some knowledge men could use?

CREON: They all died,e xcept for one who was afraid and ran away. There was only one thing he could inform us of with confidence about the things he saw.

OEDIPUS: What was that? We might get somewhere if we had one fact. We could find many things if we possessed some slender hope to get us going.

CREON: He told us it was robbers who attacked them – not just a single man, a gang of them – they came on with force and killed him.

OEDIPUS: How would a thief have dared to do this, unless he had financial help from Thebes?

CREON: That's what we guessed. But once Laius was dead, we were in trouble, so no one sought revenge.

OEDIPUS: When the ruling king had fallen in this way, what bad trouble blocked your path, preventing you from looking into it?

CREON: It was the Sphinx. She sang her enigmatic song and thus forced us to put aside something we found obscure to look into the urgent problem we now faced.

OEDIPUS: Then I will start afresh, and once again shed light on darkness. It is most fitting that Apollo demonstrates his care for the dead man, and worthy of you, too. And so, as is right, you will see how I work with you, seeking vengeance for this land, as well as for the god. This polluting stain I will remove, not for some distant friend, but for myself. For whoever killed this man may soon enough desire to turn his hand in the same way against me, too, and kill me. Thus, in avenging Laius, I serve myself. But now, my children, as quickly as you can stand up from these altar steps and take your suppliant branches. Someone must call the Theban people to assemble here. I'll do everything I can. With the god's help this will all come to light successfully, or else it will prove our common ruin.

CHORUS OF THEBAN CITIZENS *enters and bemoans their fate, and begs salvation.* OEDIPUS *promises them action and to find the truth. At* OEDPIUS' *request,* TEIRESIAS *is summoned with the hope that his prophetic powers can expose the problem.*

TEIRESIAS: Alas, alas! How dreadful it can be to have wisdom when it brings no benefit to the man possessing it. This I knew, but it had slipped my mind. Otherwise, I would not have journeyed here.

OEDIPUS: What's wrong? You've come, but seem so sad.

TEIRESIAS: Let me go home. You must bear your burden to the very end, and I will carry mine, if you'll agree with me.

OEDIPUS: What you are saying is not customary and shows little love toward the city state which nurtured you, if you deny us your prophetic voice.

TEIRESIAS: I see your words are also out of place. I do not speak for fear of doing the same.

OEDIPUS: If you know something, then, by heaven, do not turn away. We are all your suppliants, and we bend our knees to you.

TEIRESIAS: You are all ignorant. I will not reveal the troubling things inside me, which I can call your grief as well.

OEDIPUS: What are you saying? Do you know and will not say? Do you intend to betray me and destroy the city?

TEIRESIAS: I will cause neither me nor you distress. Why do you vainly question me like this? You will not learn a thing from me.

OEDIPUS: You most disgraceful of disgraceful men! You'd move something made of stone to rage! Will you not speak out? Will your stubbornness never have an end?

TEIRESIAS: You blame my temper, but do not see the one which lives within you. Instead, you are finding fault with me.

OEDIPUS: What man who listened to these words of yours would not be enraged? You insult the city!

TEIRESIAS: Yet events will still unfold, for all my silence.

OEDIPUS: Since they will come, you must inform me.

TEIRESIAS: I will say nothing more. Fume on about it, if you wish, as fiercely as you can.

OEDIPUS: I will. In my anger I will not conceal just what I make of this. You should know I get the feeling you conspired in the act, and played your part, as much as you could do, short of killing him with your own hands. If you could use your eyes, I would have said that you had done this work all by yourself.

TEIRESIAS: Is that so? Then I would ask you to stand by the very words that you yourself proclaimed and from now on not speak to me or these men. For the accursed polluter of this land is you.

OEDIPUS: You dare to utter shameful words like this? Do you think you can get away with it?

TEIRESIAS: I am getting away with it. The truth within me makes me strong.

OEDIPUS: Who taught you this? It could not have been your craft.

TEIRESIAS: You did. I did not want to speak, but you incited me.

OEDIPUS: What do you mean? Speak it again, so I can understand you more precisely.

TEIRESIAS: Did you not grasp my words before, or are you trying to test me with your question?

OEDIPUS: I did not fully understand your words. Tell me again.

TEIRESIAS: I say that you yourself are the very man you're looking for.

OEDIPUS: That's twice you've stated that disgraceful lie – something you'll regret.

TEIRESIAS: Shall I tell you more, so you can grow even more enraged?

OEDIPUS: As much as you desire. It will be useless.

TEIRESIAS: I say that with your dearest family, unknown to you, you are living in disgrace. You have no idea how bad things are.

OEDIPUS: Do you really think you can just speak out, say things like this, and still remain unpunished?

TEIRESIAS: Yes, I can, if the truth has any strength.

OEDIPUS: It does, but not for you. Truth is not in you, for your ears, your mind, your eyes are blind!

TEIRESIAS: You are a wretched fool to use harsh words, which all men soon enough will use to curse you.

OEDIPUS: You live in endless darkness of the night, so you can never injure me or any man who can glimpse daylight.

TEIRESIAS: It is not your fate to fall because of me. It's up to Apollo to make that happen. He will be enough.

OEDIPUS: Is this something Creon has devised, or is it your invention?

TEIRESIAS: Creon is no threat. You have made this trouble on your own....

OEDIPUS: Must I tolerate this insolence from him? Get out, and may the plague get rid of you! Off with you! Now! Turn your back and go! And don't come back here to my home again.

TEIRESIAS: I would not have come, but you summoned me.

OEDIPUS: I did not know you would speak so stupidly. If I had, you would have waited a long time before I called you here.

TEIRESIAS: I was born like this. You think I am a fool, but to your parents, the ones who made you, I was wise enough.

OEDIPUS: Wait! My parents? Who was my father?

TEIRESIAS: This day will reveal that and destroy you.

OEDIPUS: Everything you speak is all so cryptic, like a riddle.

TEIRESIAS: Well, in solving riddles, are you not the best there is?

OEDIPUS: Mock my excellence, but you will find out I am truly great.

TEIRESIAS: That quality of yours now ruins you.

OEDIPUS: I do not care, if I have saved the city.

TEIRESIAS: I will go now. Boy, lead me away.

OEDIPUS: Yes, let him guide you back. You're in the way. If you stay, you'll just provoke me. Once you're gone, you won't annoy me further.

TEIRESIAS *departs.* CREON *returns and disputes* OEDIPUS' *recent, public accusations of his treachery. After they toss accusations at one another,* JOCASTA *enters and helps to calm things.* CREON *departs.* OEDIPUS *tells* JOCASTA *of* TEIRESIAS' *assertion that he himself is the murderer.*

JOCASTA: All right, forget about those things you've said. Listen to me, and ease your mind with this. No human being has skill in prophecy. I'll show you why with this example. King Laius once received a prophecy. I won't say it came straight from Apollo, but it was from those who do assist the god. It said Laius was fated to be killed by a child conceived by him and me. Now, at least according to the story, one day Laius was killed by foreigners, by robbers, at a place where three roads meet. Besides, before our child was three days old, Laius fused his ankles tight together and ordered other men to throw him out on a mountain rock where no one ever goes. And so Apollo's plan that he'd become the one who killed his father didn't work, and Laius never suffered what he feared, that his own son would be his murderer, although that's what the oracle had claimed. So don't concern yourself with prophecies. Whatever gods intend to bring about they themselves make known quite easily.

OEDIPUS: Wife, as I listen to these words of yours, my soul is shaken, my mind confused . . .

JOCASTA: Why do you say that? What's worrying you?

OEDIPUS: I thought I heard you say that Laius was murdered at a place where three roads meet.

JOCASTA: That's what was said and people still believe.

OEDIPUS: Where is this place? Where did it happen?

JOCASTA: In a land called Phocis. Two roads lead there – one from Delphi and one from Daulia.

OEDIPUS: How long is it since these events took place?

JOCASTA: The story was reported in the city just before you took over royal power here in Thebes.

OEDIPUS: Oh Zeus, what have you done? What have you planned for me?

JOCASTA: What is it, Oedipus? Why is your spirit so troubled?

OEDIPUS: Not yet, no questions yet. Tell me, this "Laius" – how tall was he? How old a man?

JOCASTA: He was big – his hair was turning white. In shape he was not all that unlike you.

OEDIPUS: The worse for me! I may have just set myself under a dreadful curse without my knowledge!

JOCASTA: What do you mean? As I look at you, my king, I start to tremble.

OEDIPUS: I am afraid, full of terrible fears the prophet sees. But you can reveal this better if you now will tell me one thing more.

JOCASTA: I'm shaking, but if you ask me, I will answer you.

OEDIPUS: Did Laius have a small escort with him or a troop of soldiers, like a royal king?

JOCASTA: Five men, including a herald, went with him. A carriage carried Laius.

OEDIPUS: Alas! Alas! It's all too clear! Lady, who told you this?

JOCASTA: A servant – the only one who got away. He came back here.

OEDIPUS: Is there any chance he's in our household now?

JOCASTA: No. Once he returned and understood that you had now assumed the power of slaughtered Laius, he clasped my hands, begged me to send him off to where our animals graze out in the fields, so he could be as far away as possible from the sight of town. And so I sent him. He was a slave but he'd earned my gratitude. He deserved an even greater favour.

OEDIPUS: I'd like him to return back here to us, and quickly, too…

The SERVANT is sent for, while OEDIPUS retires inside the palace. JOCASTA address the CHORUS briefly on how prophesies cannot be trusted…

JOCASTA: You leading men of Thebes, I think it is appropriate for me to visit our god's sacred shrine, bearing in my hands this garland and an offering of incense. For Oedipus has let excessive pain seize his heart and does not understand what's happening now by thinking of the past, like a man with sense. Instead he listens to whoever speaks to him of dreadful things. I can do nothing more for him with my advice, and so, Lycean Apollo, I come to you, who stand here beside us, a suppliant, with offerings and prayers for you to find some way of cleansing what corrupts us. For now we are afraid, just like those who on a ship see their helmsman terrified…

*A **Messenger** from Corinth arrives, declaring that **Oedipus**' "father" and the King of Corinth, Polybus, has died. The citizens of Corinth are now requesting **Oedipus** become their king as well. **Oedipus** and **Jocasta** are summoned and given the news.*

Messenger: If I must first report my news quite plainly, then I should let you know that Polybus has passed away. He's gone.

Oedipus: By treachery, or was it the result of some disease?

Messenger: With old bodies a slight weight on the scales brings final peace.

Oedipus: Apparently his death was from an illness?

Messenger: Yes, and from old age.

Oedipus: Alas! Indeed, lady, why should any man pay due reverence to Apollo's shrine, where his prophet lives, or to those birds, which scream out overhead? For they foretold that I was going to murder my own father. But now he's dead and lies beneath the earth, and I am here. I never touched my spear. Perhaps he died from a desire to see me – so in that sense I brought about his death. But as for those prophetic oracles, they're worthless. Polybus has taken them to Hades, where he lies.

Jocasta: Was I not the one who predicted this some time ago?

Oedipus: You did, but then I was misguided by my fears.

Jocasta: You must not keep on filling up your heart with all these things.

Oedipus: But my mother's bed – I am afraid of that. And surely I should be?

Jocasta: Why should a man whose life seems ruled by chance live in fear – a man who never looks ahead, who has no certain vision of his future? It's best to live haphazardly, as best one can. Do not worry you will wed your mother. It's true that in their dreams a lot of men have slept with their own mothers, but someone who ignores all this bears life more easily.

Oedipus: Everything you say would be commendable, if my mother were not still alive. But since she is, I must remain afraid, although what you are saying is right.

Jocasta: But still, your father's death is a great comfort to us.

Oedipus: Yes, it is good, I know. But I do fear that lady – she is still alive.

Messenger: This one you fear, what kind of woman is she?

Oedipus: Old man, her name is Merope, wife to Polybus.

Messenger: And what in her makes you so fearful?

Oedipus: Stranger, a dreadful prophecy sent from the god.

Messenger: Is it well known? Or something private, which another person has no right to know?

Oedipus: No, no. It's public knowledge. Apollo once said it was my fate that I would marry my own mother and shed my father's blood with my own hands. That's why, many years ago, I left my home in Corinth. Things turned out well, but nonetheless it gives the sweetest joy to look into the eyes of one's own parents.

Messenger: And because you were afraid of her you stayed away from Corinth?

Oedipus: And because I did not want to be my father's killer.

Messenger: My lord, since I came to make you happy, why don't I relieve you of this fear?

OEDIPUS: You would receive from me a worthy thanks.

MESSENGER: That's really why I came: so your return might prove a benefit to me back home.

OEDIPUS: But I will never go back to my parents.

MESSENGER: My son, it is so clear you have no idea what you are doing...

OEDIPUS: What do you mean, old man? In the name of all the gods, tell me.

MESSENGER: ...if that's the reason you're a fugitive and won't go home....because you and Polybus were not related...

The MESSENGER explains to OEDIPUS that he was not the biological son of Merope and Polybus, but had been found. The MESSENGER himself had been given the abandoned boy, his feet tied and pierced, in forests near Thebes by a local shepherd, whom the MESSENGER remembers to have been a servant of King Laius. OEDIPUS requests the whereabouts of this SERVANT.

OEDIPUS: My wife, do you know the man we sent for just minutes ago, the one we summoned here? Is he the one this messenger refers to?

JOCASTA: Why ask me what he means? Forget all that. There's no point in trying to sort out what he said.

OEDIPUS: With all these indications of the truth here in my grasp, I cannot end this now. I must reveal the details of my birth.

JOCASTA: In the name of the gods, no! If you have some concern for your own life, then stop! Do not keep investigating this. I will suffer – that will be enough!

OEDIPUS: Be brave. Even if I should turn out to be born from a shameful mother, whose family for three generations have been slaves, you will still have your noble lineage.

JOCASTA: Listen to me, I beg you. Do not do this!

OEDIPUS: I will not be convinced I should not learn the whole truth of what these facts amount to.

JOCASTA: But I care about your own wellbeing. What I tell you is for your benefit.

OEDIPUS: What you're telling me for my own good just brings me more distress.

JOCASTA: Oh, you unhappy man! May you never find out who you really are!

OEDIPUS: (to Chorus): Go, one of you, and bring that shepherd here. Leave the lady to enjoy her noble family.

JOCASTA: Alas, you poor miserable man! There's nothing more that I can say to you. And now I'll never speak again!

JOCASTA runs into the palace. The old SERVANT arrives and is asked by OEDIPUS and the messenger from Corinth to speak. The SERVANT begs not to say more, but OEDIPUS threatens him.

SERVANT: By all the gods, don't torture an old man!

OEDIPUS: One of you there, tie up this fellow's hands.

SERVANT: Why are you doing this? It's too much for me! What is it you want to know?

OEDIPUS: That child this messenger mentioned: did you give it to him?

SERVANT: I did. How I wish I'd died that day!

OEDIPUS: Well, you're going to die if you don't speak the truth.

SERVANT: And if I do, there's an even greater chance that I'll be killed.

OEDIPUS: It seems to me the man is trying to stall.

SERVANT: No, no, I'm not. I've already told you, I did give him the child.

OEDIPUS: Where did you get it? Did it come from your home or somewhere else?

SERVANT: It was not mine – I got it from…someone.

OEDIPUS: Which of our citizens? Whose home was it?

SERVANT: In the name of the gods, my lord, don't ask! Please, no more questions!

OEDIPUS: If I have to ask again, then you will die.

SERVANT: The child was born in Laius' house.

OEDIPUS: From a slave or from some relative of his?

SERVANT: Alas, what I'm about to say now…it's horrible!

OEDIPUS: And I'm about to hear it. But nonetheless I have to know this.

SERVANT: If you must know, they said the child was his. But your wife inside the palace is the one who could best tell you what was going on.

OEDIPUS: You mean she gave the child to you?

SERVANT: Yes, my lord.

OEDIPUS: Why did she do that?

SERVANT: So I would kill it.

OEDIPUS: That wretched woman was the mother? Ah, so it all came true. It's so clear now. O light, let me look at you one final time, a man who stands revealed as cursed by birth, cursed by my own family, and cursed by murder where I should not kill!

OEDIPUS *runs into the palace. After a choral ode, a* SECOND MESSENGER *emerges to describe* JOCASTA'S *suicide and* OEDIPUS' *torment.*

SECOND MESSENGER: She killed herself. You did not see it, so you'll be spared the worst of what went on. But from what I recall of what I saw you'll learn how that poor woman suffered. She left here frantic and rushed inside, fingers on both hands clenched in her hair. She ran through the hall straight to her marriage bed. She went in, slamming both doors shut behind her and crying out to Laius, who's been a corpse a long time now. She was remembering that child of theirs born many years ago – the one who killed his father, who left her to conceive cursed children with that son. She lay moaning by the bed, where she, poor woman, had given birth twice over: a husband from a husband, children from a child. How she died after that I don't fully know. With a scream Oedipus came bursting in…with a dreadful howl, as if someone had pushed him, he leapt at the double doors, bent the bolts by force out of their sockets, and burst into the room. Then we saw her. She was hanging there, swaying, with twisted cords roped round her neck. When Oedipus saw her, with a dreadful groan he took her body out of the noose in which she hung, and then, when the poor woman was lying on the ground – what happened next was a horrific sight!

From her clothes he ripped the golden brooches she wore as ornaments, raised them high, and drove them deep into his eyeballs, crying as he did so: "You will no longer see all those atrocious things I suffered, the dreadful things I did! No. You have seen those you never should have looked upon, and those I wished to know you did not see. So now and for all future time be dark!" With these words he raised his hand and struck, not once, but many times, right in the sockets. With every blow blood spurted from his eyes down on his beard, and not in single drops, but showers of dark blood spattered like hail. So what these two have done has overwhelmed not one alone – this disaster swallows up a man and wife together. That old happiness they had before in their rich ancestry was truly joy, but now lament and ruin, death and shame, and all calamities which men can name are theirs to keep.

OEDIPUS *emerges, blinded. The* CHORUS *address him.*

Chorus Leader: You have carried out such dreadful things! How could you dare to blind yourself this way? What god drove you to it?

Oedipus: It was Apollo, friends, it was Apollo. He brought on these troubles, the awful things I suffer. But the hand which stabbed out my eyes was mine alone. In my wretched life, why should I have eyes when nothing I could see would bring me joy?

Chorus Leader: What you have said is true enough.

Oedipus: What is there for me to see, my friends? What can I love? Whose greeting can I hear and feel delight? Hurry now, my friends, lead me away from Thebes: take me somewhere, a man completely lost, utterly accursed, the mortal man the gods despise the most.

Creon *arrives, informed of the situation, and informs* **Oedipus** *that Delphi must be contacted to learn what to do.* **Oedipus**, *intent on his own exile, has his daughters,* **Ismene** *and* **Antigone**, *brought out and informed as well. He requests that they accompany him into exile, since they have no happy future here.*

Creon: You have grieved enough. Now go into the house.

Oedipus: I must obey, although that's not what I desire.

Creon: In due time all things will work out for the best.

Oedipus: I will go. But you know there are conditions.

Creon: Tell me. Once I hear them, I'll know what they are.

Oedipus: Send me away to live outside of Thebes.

Creon: Only the god can give you what you ask.

Oedipus: But I've become abhorrent to the gods!

Creon: Then you should quickly get what you desire.

Oedipus: So you agree?

Creon: I don't like to speak thoughtlessly and say what I don't mean.

Oedipus: Come then, lead me off.

Creon: All right, but let go of the children.

Oedipus: No, no! Do not take them away from me!

Creon: Don't try to be in charge of everything. Your life has lost the power you once had.

Creon, Oedipus, Antigone, Ismene, *and* **Attendants** *all enter the palace.*

Chorus: You residents of Thebes, our native land, look on this man, this Oedipus, the one who understood that celebrated riddle. He was the most powerful of men. All citizens who witnessed this man's wealth were envious. Now what a surging tide of terrible disaster sweeps around him. So while we wait to see that final day, we cannot call a mortal being happy before he's passed beyond life free from pain.

Adapted from Sir Richard Jebb, Sophocles. The Oedipus Tyrannus of Sophocles (Cambridge: Cambridge University Press, 1887)

READING 12:

SOPHOCLES' *OEDIPUS AT COLONUS*

Oedipus is now old, yet not broken. He is now escorted by his devoted daugters Ismene and Antigone. He has arrived at Athens, eager for protection and acceptance, both of which he finds from the king, Theseus. In his blindness, he has acquire prophetic abilities, and informs the Athenians of the benefits that will come to them if he may die there. Others have learned of this, however, and several men attempt to take him away, including Creon, now king of Thebes, and Polyneices, Oedipus' son, who wants his father's support for his coming war to wrest Thebes away from Creon and Oedipus' other son, Eteocles.

Oedipus at Colonus (406 BCE) is Sophocles' last play, and it carries the hallmarks of such a late effort: an old man who considers the mistakes of his life; a quest for resolution of past wrongs; a concern for passing to the next life, and what passing entails. Oedipus' famous contention here, that "nothing escapes all-ruinous time," is a reminder of his acceptance of the power of divine fate. The heart of the play, however, is Oedipus' love for Antigone and Ismene, and is contrasted with his hatred for his sons. When Oedipus eventually passes into the spiritual world in spectacular fashion, we are left both with a sense of hope for Oedipus' final rest, but also foreboding, for Antigone's own coming tragedy, told in Sophocles' earlier play, *Antigone*.

12a) Sophocles, Oedipus at Colonus (1-668; 898-1118, 1348-1779, passim)

SCENE: *The blind* **OEDIPUS** *enters led by his daughter,* **ANTIGONE** *at Colonus, a district on the outskirts of Athens*

OEDIPUS: Child of a blind old man, Antigone, to what region have we come, or to what city? Who will entertain the wandering Oedipus today with scanty gifts? I crave little, and obtain still less than that, and with that I am content. For patience is the lesson of suffering, and of the long years upon me, and lastly of a noble mind. My child, if you see any resting-place, either on profane ground or by groves of the gods, stop me and set me down, so that we may inquire where we are. We have come to learn as foreigners from the townsmen, and to bring to completion whatever we hear.

ANTIGONE: Father, toil-worn Oedipus, the towers that ring the city, to judge by sight, are far off, and this place is sacred, to judge from its appearance: laurel, olive, and vine grow thickly, and a feathered crowd of nightingales makes music within. So sit here on this unshaped stone; you have travelled a long way for an old man.

OEDIPUS: Seat me, then, and watch over the blind.

ANTIGONE: If time can teach me, I need not learn that.

OEDIPUS: Can you tell me, now, where we have arrived?

ANTIGONE: Athens I know, but not this place.

OEDIPUS: Yes, so much every traveller told us.

ANTIGONE: Well, shall I go and learn what the spot is called?

OEDIPUS: Yes, child, if indeed it is inhabited.

ANTIGONE: It surely is inhabited. But I think there is no need – I see a man nearby.

They find out from a stranger passing by that he is at Colonus, a region of Athens. **OEDIPUS** *learns that he has trespassed into a sacred grove dedicated to worshipping the Eumenides, kindly chthonic spirits at Athens. When Oedipus learns this, he says he will not move from here. He asks that King* **THESEUS** *come to him, to hear something for his benefit. Meanwhile, a* **CHORUS OF PEOPLE OF COLONUS** *come to see the curious beggar.*

OEDIPUS: Goddesses of terrible form, since your seat is the first in this land at which I have bent my knee, show yourselves not ungracious to Apollo or to myself, who, when he proclaimed that doom of many woes, spoke to me of this rest after long years: on reaching my goal in a land where I should find a seat of the terrible goddesses and a shelter for foreigners, there I should close my weary life, with benefit, through my having fixed my home there, for those who received me, but ruin for those who sent me forth, who drove me away. And he went on to warn me that signs of these things would come, in earthquake, or in thunder, or in the lightning of Zeus. Now I perceive that in this journey some trusty omen from you has surely led me home to this grove. For never otherwise could I have met with you, first of all, in my wanderings – I, in my sobriety, with you who touch no wine, or taken this august seat not shaped by men. Then, goddesses, according to the word of Apollo, give me at last some way to accomplish and close my journey – unless, perhaps, I seem too lowly, enslaved as I am evermore to the sorest woes on the earth. Listen, sweet daughters of ancient Darkness! Listen, you that are called the city of great Pallas, Athens, given most honor of all cities! Pity this poor ghost of the man Oedipus! For in truth it is the former living body no more.

ANTIGONE: Hush! Here come some aged men to spy out your resting-place.

OEDIPUS: I will be silent. But hide me in the grove, apart from the road, till I learn how these men will speak. For in learning is the safeguard of our course.

CHORUS: Zeus defend us! Who may this old man be?

OEDIPUS: Not really a friend of fate that you would call him fortunate, guardians of this land! It is plain; otherwise I would not be creeping, as you see, by the eyes of others, and buoying my strength upon weakness.

CHORUS: Alas! Were you sightless even from birth? Evil have been your days, and many, it appears. But at least if I can help it, you shall not add this curse to your lot. You go too far, too far! That your rash steps may intrude on the field of this voiceless, grassy glade, where the waters of the mixing bowl blend their stream with the flow of honied offerings, beware, unhappiest of strangers, Leave! Withdraw! Let a wide space part us. Do you hear, toil-worn wanderer? If you have anything to say in converse with us, leave this forbidden ground, and speak where it is lawful for all. But, until then, keep back.

OEDIPUS: Daughter, what counsel shall we choose?

ANTIGONE: My father, we must behave just as the townspeople do, listening and giving way where it is necessary.

OEDIPUS: Then give me your hand.

ANTIGONE: I lay it in yours.

OEDIPUS: Strangers, let me not suffer wrong when I have trusted in you, and have passed from my refuge!

The CHORUS *questions him as to his identity and past, and his current state. He finally reveals his identity to them. The* CHORUS *is shocked, and wants him to leave.*

OEDIPUS: What help comes, then, for repute or fair fame, if it ends in idle breath? Seeing that Athens, as men say, is god-fearing beyond all, and alone has the power to shelter the outraged stranger, and alone the power to help him? And where are these things for me, when, after making me rise up from this rocky seat, you then drive me from the land, afraid of my name alone? Not, surely, afraid of my person or my acts, since my acts, at least, have been in suffering rather than doing. If I must mention the tale of my mother and my father, because of which you fear me. That I know full well. And yet how was I innately evil? I, who was merely requiting a wrong, so that, had I been acting with knowledge, even then I could not be accounted evil. But, as it was, all unknowing, I went where I went, while they who wronged me knowingly sought my ruin. Therefore, strangers, I beg you by the gods: just as you made me leave my seat, so protect me, and do not, while you render honor to the gods, consider those gods to be fools. But rather consider that they look on the god-fearing man and on the godless, and that never yet has an impious man found escape. With the help of those gods, do not obscure the prosperity of Athens by paying service to unholy deeds. As you have received the suppliant under your pledge, rescue me and guard me to the end. Do not dishonor me when you look on this face unlovely to behold, for I have come to you as one sacred and pious, bearing comfort for this people. But when the master has come, whoever is your leader, then you will hear and know all; meanwhile show yourselves in no way evil.

CHORUS: The thoughts you urge, old man, must move us. They have been set forth in grave words. But we are content that the rulers of our country should judge in this case.

OEDIPUS: And where, strangers, is the lord of this realm?

CHORUS: He is at the city of his fathers in our land. The messenger who sent us here has gone to fetch him.

OEDIPUS: Do you think that he will have any regard or care for the blind man, so as to come here himself?

CHORUS: Yes, surely, as soon as he learns of your name.

OEDIPUS: Who is there to bring him that word?

CHORUS: The way is far, and many words from travellers often wander about. When he hears them, he will soon be with us, never fear. For your name, old man, has been loudly trumpeted through all lands, so that even if he is taking his ease, and slow to move, when he hears of you he will swiftly arrive.

OEDIPUS: Well, may he come with good fortune both for his own city and for me! What noble man is not his own friend?

ANTIGONE: O Zeus! What shall I say? What shall I think, my father?

OEDIPUS: What is it, Antigone, my child?

ANTIGONE: I see a woman coming towards us, mounted on a colt of Etna. She wears a Thessalian bonnet to screen her face from the sun. What shall I say? Is it she, or is it not? Does my judgment err? Yes…no…I cannot tell…ah, me! It is no other, yes! She greets me with bright glances as she draws near, and makes a signal. Here is Ismene, clearly, and no other before me.

OEDIPUS: What is that you say, my child?

ANTIGONE: That I see your daughter, my sister. By her voice right away you can know her.

ISMENE: Father and sister, names most sweet to me! How hard it was to find you! And how hard now to look upon you for my tears!

ISMENE, OEDIPUS' *other daughter arrives and informs him of the coming battle between his sons, Eteocles and* POLYNEICES. *Initially both content to leave the throne to* CREON, *Eteocles has now driven* POLYNEICES *from Thebes, but the latter has raised an army from Argos and prepares to march on Argos.* ISMENE *also warns* OEDIPUS *that* CREON *may try to drag him back to Thebes because of a Delphic oracle that prophesies that his burial place will bring military victory to its community.* OEDIPUS *himself prophesies destruction for Thebes and his ungrateful sons.*

OEDIPUS: Then may the gods not end their fated conflict, and may it fall to me to decide this war on which they are now setting their hands, raising spear against spear! For then neither would he who now holds the scepter and the throne survive, nor would the exile ever return, seeing that when I, their father, was being thrust without honor from my country, they did not stop or defend me. No, they saw me sent forth homeless, and heard the crier proclaim my sentence of exile. Perhaps you will say that that was my own wish then, and that the city fittingly granted me that gift. Not so! For on that first day, when my heart seethed, and my sweetest wish was for death (indeed, death by stoning), no one was found to help me in that desire. But after a time, when all my anguish was now softened, and when I began to feel that my heart had been excessive in punishing those past errors, then it was that the city set about to drive me by force from the land, after all that time. And my sons, when they had the strength to bring help – as sons should – they would not do it. For lack of one little word from them, I was left to wander, an outcast and a beggar forever. Instead, it is from these, young women as they are, insofar as nature enables them, that I obtain my daily food, and a shelter in the land, and the aid of family. Their brothers have bartered their father for the throne, the scepter of power, and the rule of the realm. No, never will they win Oedipus for an ally, nor will good ever come to them from this reign at Thebes; that I know, when I hear this maiden's oracles and reflect on the old prophecies stored in my own mind, which Phoebus has fulfilled for me at last. Therefore let them send Creon, or whoever else is mighty in Thebes, to seek me. For if you, strangers, with the help of the great goddesses who reign among your district, are willing to defend me, you will obtain a great savior for this city, and troubles for my enemies.

ISMENE *departs, but King* THESEUS *arrives on the scene. He knows of* OEDIPUS *and is curious why he has come to Athens.* OEDIPUS *explains the good fortune that his burial will bring to Athens, but warns that Thebans may try to abduct him.* THESEUS *accepts his supplication, and promises his support.*

THESEUS: Through hearing from many in the past about the bloody marring of your sight, I recognized it was you, son of Laius. And now on coming here, through sight I am more fully certain. For your clothing and that heart-rending face alike assure me that it is you. And in all compassion I ask you, ill-fated Oedipus, with what petition to the city and to me have you taken your place here, you and the poor maiden at your side. Declare it. Dire indeed must be the fortune that you tell, for me to stand aloof from it; since I know that I myself also was reared in exile, just as you, and that in foreign lands I wrestled with perils to my life, like no other man. Never, then, would I turn aside from a stranger, such as you are now, or refuse to help in his deliverance. For I know well that I am a man, and that my portion of tomorrow is no greater than yours.

Oedipus: Theseus, in a few words your nobleness has come to such a point that I need to make only a brief reply. You have said who I am, from what father I am sprung, and from what land I have come, and so nothing else remains for me but to speak my wish, and the tale is told.

Theseus: Then inform me of this very thing, so that I may learn it.

Oedipus: I come to offer you my care-worn body as a gift – not one fine to look on, but the gains from it are better than beauty

Theseus: And what gain do you claim to have brought?

Oedipus: Later you may learn it…but not yet.

Theseus: At what time, then, will the benefit become clear?

Oedipus: When I am dead, and you have given me burial.

Theseus: You crave life's last service; but for all between you have no memory, or no care.

Oedipus: Indeed, for by that service I gather in all the rest.

Theseus: Well then, this favor you crave from me is brief indeed.

Oedipus: Yet take care: the struggle here is no light one. No, indeed.

Theseus: Do you mean in respect to your sons, or to me?

Oedipus: They will compel you to convey me there to Thebes.

Theseus: But if you are willing, then exile is not suitable.

Oedipus: No, when I was willing, they refused.

Theseus: Foolish man, anger amidst woes is not suitable.

Oedipus: When you have heard my story, criticize me; until then, withhold.

Theseus: Speak. I must not pronounce without knowledge.

Oedipus: I have suffered, Theseus, terrible woes upon woes.

Theseus: Will you speak of the ancient trouble of your people?

Oedipus: No, indeed. all Greeks speak of that.

Theseus: How, then, do you suffer beyond what is mortal?

Oedipus: The circumstance is this: from my country I have been driven by my own sons, and I may not return, since I am guilty of a father's blood.

Theseus: Why would they have you brought back, if you must dwell apart?

Oedipus: The word of the god will compel them.

Theseus: What suffering do they fear from the oracles?

Oedipus: That they must be struck down in this land.

THESEUS: And how should bitterness come between them and me?

OEDIPUS: Dearest son of Aegeus, to the gods alone old age and death never come, but everything else sinks into chaos from time which overpowers all. Earth's strength decays, and so too the strength of the body, trust dies, distrust is born, and the same spirit is never steadfast among friends, or between city and city. For some now, for others tomorrow, sweet feelings turn to bitter, and then once more to being dear. And if now the sun shines brightly between Thebes and you, yet time in his course gives birth to days and nights untold, in which from a small cause they will scatter with the spear today's pledges of concord. Then one day my slumbering and buried corpse, cold in death, will drink their warm blood, if Zeus is still Zeus, and Phoebus, the son of Zeus, speaks clearly. But, since I would not break silence concerning words that must not spoken, allow me to stop where I began. Only keep your own pledge, and never will you say that in vain you welcomed Oedipus to dwell in this land – if indeed the gods do not deceive me.

CHORUS: Lord, from the first this man has shown a will to bring these words, or similar ones, to completion for our land.

THESEUS: Who, then, would reject the goodwill of such a man? To whom, first, the hearth of a comrade is always available on our side, by equal right. Then too he has come as a suppliant to our gods, paying no small recompense to this land and to me. In reverence for these claims, I will never spurn his favor, and I will establish a dwelling for him as a citizen in the land. And if it is the pleasure of the stranger to remain here, I will command you to protect him; or, if it pleases him, to come with me. This choice or that, Oedipus, you may take; your desire will be mine.

OEDIPUS: O Zeus, may you be good to men such as these!

THESEUS: What is your wish, then? Will you come to my house?

OEDIPUS: Yes, I would, if it were right. But this is the place…

THESEUS: What will you do here? Speak, for I will not hinder you.

OEDIPUS: …Where I will conquer those who cast me out.

THESEUS: The promised gift of your presence would be great.

OEDIPUS: It shall be, if you keep your pledge with me.

THESEUS: Have courage concerning me; never will I betray you.

OEDIPUS: I will not bind you with an oath as if an evil man.

THESEUS: Well, you would win nothing more than by my word.

OEDIPUS: What will you do, then?

THESEUS: What is it that you fear?

OEDIPUS: Men will come…

THESEUS: But these men here will see to them.

OEDIPUS: Beware that if you leave me…

THESEUS: Do not instruct me in my duties.

OEDIPUS: Fear constrains me…

THESEUS: My heart feels no fear.

OEDIPUS: You do not know the threats…

THESEUS: I know that none will lead you from here against my will. Often threats have blustered in men's hearts with words loud and vain. But when the mind comes to itself once more, the threats have vanished. For those men, too, perhaps – yes, even if in boldness they have spoken dreadful things of bringing you back, the voyage here will prove long and hard to sail. Now I encourage you, apart from any decision of mine, to take heart, if indeed Phoebus Apollo has been your escort here. Even if I am not present, still my name, I know, will shield you from harm.

THESEUS *departs to make arrangements. While gone,* CREON *arrives, desiring to take* OEDIPUS *back to Thebes and having already abducted* ISMENE. *He tries to trick* OEDIPUS *to come home, feigning friendliness and forgiveness.* OEDIPUS *sees through him, and again prophesies destruction for* CREON *and Thebes.* CREON *then has his guards rip* ANTIGONE *away from* OEDIPUS, *but he is blocked by the citizens of Colonus and* THESEUS *himself. He then confronts* CREON.

THESEUS: Hurry, one of you attendants, to the altars there, and order the people to leave the sacrifice and race on foot and by horse full speed to the region where the two highways meet, so that the maidens may not pass and I not become a mockery to this stranger as one worsted by force. Quick, I say! As for this man, if my anger went as far as he deserves, I would not let him go uninjured from my hand. But now, just such law as he himself has brought will be the rule for his correction. You, Creon, will never leave this land until you bring those maidens and produce them in my sight. For your action is a disgrace to me, and to your own ancestors, and to your country. You have come to a city that practices justice and sanctions nothing without law, yet you have spurned her lawful authorities and made this violent assault. You are taking captives at will and subjugating them by force, as if you believed that my city was void of men, or manned by slaves, and that I counted for nothing. Yet it was not Thebes that trained you to be evil. Thebes is not accustomed to rearing unjust men, nor would she praise you, if she learned that you are despoiling me, and despoiling the gods, when by force you drive off their unfortunate suppliants. If my foot were upon your land, never would I drag off or lead away someone without permission from the ruler of the land, whoever he might be – no, even if my claim were the most just of all. I would know how a stranger ought to live among citizens. But you are disgracing a city that does not deserve it: your own, and your years, despite their fullness, bring you an old age barren of sense. Now, I have said before, and I say it once again: let the maidens be brought here speedily, unless you wish to be an unwilling immigrant to this country by force. These are the words from my lips, and my mind is in accord.

CHORUS: Do you see your plight, stranger? You are judged to be just by where you are from, but your deeds are found to be evil.

CREON: It is not because I thought this city void of men, son of Aegeus, or of counsel, as you say, that I have done this deed, but because I judged that its people could never be so zealous for my relatives as to support them against my will. And I knew that this people would not receive a parricide and a polluted man, a man whose unholy marriage – a marriage with children – had been found out. Such wisdom, I knew, was immemorial on the Areopagus, which does not allow such wanderers to dwell within this city. Trusting in that, I sought to take this prize. And I would not have done so, had he not been calling down bitter curses on me and on my race. As I was wronged in this way, I judged that I had a right to this requital. For anger knows no old age, until death comes. The dead alone feel no galling pain. In response to this, you will do what pleases you, for, although my case is just, the lack of aid makes me weak. Yet in the face of your actions, despite my age, I will endeavor to pay you back.

OEDIPUS: Such shameless arrogance, where do you think this outrage falls: on my old age, or on your own? Bloodshed, incest, misery – all this your tongue has launched against me, and all this I have borne in my wretchedness by no choice of mine. For this was dear to the gods, who were angry, perhaps, with my race from of old. Taking me alone, you could not find a blame for any crime, in retribution for which I was driven to commit these sins against myself and against my kin. Tell me now: if, by the voice of an oracle, some divine doom was coming on my father, that he should die by a son's hand, how could you justly reproach me with this, when I was then unborn, when no father had yet begotten me, no mother's womb conceived me? But if, having been born to misery, as I was born, I came to blows with my father and slew him, ignorant of what I was doing and to whom, how could you reasonably blame the unwitting deed? And my mother – poor wretch – do you feel no shame in forcing me to speak of her marriage, when she was your sister, and when it was such as I will now tell? For I will not be silent, when you have gone so far in impious speech.

Yes, she was my mother – alas, for my miseries! I did not know it, nor did she, and to her shame she bore children to the son whom she had borne. But one thing, at least, I know: that you willingly revile her and me, but I did not willingly marry her, and I do not willingly speak now. No, I will not be called evil on account of this marriage, nor in the slaying of my father, which you charge me with again and again in bitter insult. Answer just one thing of those I ask. If, here and now, someone should come up and try to murder you, would you ask if the murderer was your father, or would you revenge yourself on him straightaway? I think that if your life is dear to you, you would requite the criminal, and not look around for a justification. Such then were the evils into which I came, led by the gods. And in this, I think, my father's soul, could it come back to life, would not contradict me. But you are not just. You are one who considers it a fine thing to utter every sort of word, both those which are sanctioned and those which are forbidden – such are your taunts against me in the presence of these men. And to you it seems a fine thing to flatter the renowned Theseus, and Athens, saying how well it is governed. Yet while giving such generous praise, you forget that if any land knows how to worship the gods with honors, this land excels in that. It is from her that you had planned to steal me, a suppliant and an old man, and tried to seize me, having already carried off my daughters. Therefore I now call on the goddesses here, I supplicate them, I beseech them with prayers, to bring me help and to fight on my behalf, that you may learn well what kind of men this by which this city is guarded.

THESEUS *is unconvinced by* CREON. *He arrests him and orders that he surrender* ISMENE *and* ANTIGONE *back to* OEDIPUS. *Both are returned to their father's embrace.*

ANTIGONE: Father, father, I wish some god would grant that your eyes might see this excellent man, who has brought us here to you!

OEDIPUS: My child, are you really here?

ANTIGONE: Yes, for these strong arms have saved us – Theseus and his dearest followers.

OEDIPUS: Come here, my children, to your father! Grant me your embrace – restored beyond all hope!

ANTIGONE: We shall grant your wish, for we crave the favor we bestow.

OEDIPUS: Where, then, where are you?

ANTIGONE: Here we are, approaching you together.

OEDIPUS: My dearest children!

ANTIGONE: Everything is dear to its parent.

Oedipus: Supports of a man...

Antigone: Ill-fated as he is ill-fated.

Oedipus: I hold my dearest. Now, if I should die, I would not be wholly wretched, since you have come to me. Press close to me on either side, children, cling to your father, and rest from your wandering, so desolate, so grievous! And tell me what has happened as briefly as you can, since brief speech suffices for young maidens.

Antigone: Here is our savior, Theseus: you should hear the story from him, father, since the deed was his. So short will by part be.

Polyneices, *aware of the oracle foretelling the fortune brought by his father's burial, has come to ask for his support, and to try to justify why he had ignored his father during his wanderings.* **Oedipus** *scorns and curses him, prophesying how he and his brother will both kill each other in their destructive greed for the throne of Thebes.*

Oedipus: Guardians of this land, if it were not Theseus who had sent him here to me, thinking it just that he should hear my response, then never would he have heard my voice of prophecy. But now he will be graced with it, before he goes, and hear from me such words as never will gladden his life. Worst of men, when you had the scepter and the throne, which now your brother has in Thebes, you drove me, your own father, into exile, and by making me an exile you caused me to wear this clothing at whose sight you weep, now that you have come to the same state of misery as me. The time for tears is past. I must bear this burden as long as I live, and keep you before my mind as a murderer. For it is you that have made me subject to this anguish, it is you that have thrust me out, and because of you I wander, begging my daily bread from strangers. And had these daughters not been born to me to be my comfort, in truth I would be dead, for lack of help from you. But now these girls preserve me, they are my nurses, they are men, not women, in sharing my toil. But you are from another and are no sons of mine.

Therefore the divinity looks upon you – not yet as he soon will look, if indeed those armies of yours are moving against Thebes. There is no way in which you can ever overthrow that city. Before that you will fall, polluted by bloodshed, and so too your brother. Such curses as my heart before now sent up against you both, I now invoke to fight for me, in order that you may think it fit to revere your parents and not to dishonor your father utterly, because he who begot such sons is blind. For my daughters here did not act in this way. This supplication of yours, and this throne of yours, will lie in the power of my curses, if indeed Justice, revealed long ago, sits beside Zeus, to share his throne through sanction of primordial laws. But to damnation with you, abhorred by me and disowned! Suffer these curses which I call down on you, most evil of evil men: may you never defeat your native land, and may you never return to the valley of Argos. I pray that you die by a related hand, and slay him by whom you have been driven out. This is my prayer. And I call on the hateful darkness of Tartarus that your father shares, to take you into another home; and I call on the divinities of this place, and I call on the god of war, who has set dreadful hatred in you both. Go with these words in your head! Go and announce to all the Cadmeans, and to your own faithful allies that Oedipus has distributed such portions to his sons.

Fearful and dejected, **Polyneices** *departs.* **Antigone** *begs him to stop the war with their brother, but* **Polyneices**, *understanding the truth in his father's prophesy, sees the inevitable. The scene is set for* **Antigone's** *eventual heroism and sacrifice.*

Antigone: Do you see where the prophecies of this man are leading, who declares mutual death for you two?

POLYNEICES: Yes, for he wishes it. But I must not yield.

ANTIGONE: Ah, wretched me! But who will dare follow you, when he hears what prophecies this man has uttered?

POLYNEICES: I will not report ill-tidings. A good leader should tell the better news, and not the worse.

ANTIGONE: Is this then your final decision, my brother?

POLYNEICES: Yes, and do not detain me. This path now will be my destiny, ill-fated and evil, because of my father here and his Furies. But as for you two, may Zeus grant you good things, if you bring these things to completion for me when I am dead, since in life you will see me no more. Now release me, and farewell; for nevermore will you behold me living.

POLYNEICES *departs. Thunder and lightning then begin to crash.* OEDIPUS *calls for* THESEUS *and his daughters, knowing that the storm is a sign of his coming death and transformation.*

OEDIPUS: Children, children! If there is any man still here, send him forth to bring back Theseus, excellent in all respects.

ANTIGONE: And what, father, is the purpose of your call?

OEDIPUS: This winged thunder of Zeus will soon lead me to Hades. So send someone with speed.

OEDIPUS: Children, the appointed end of life has reached this man; he can turn from it no more.

ANTIGONE: How do you know? By what means do you understand this?

OEDIPUS: I know it well. But let some one go, I beg you, as quickly as he can, and bring back the lord of this land.

THESEUS *arrives, and then departs with* OEDIPUS *and his daughters. Eventually, a* MESSENGER *comes to inform the chorus what has transpired.*

MESSENGER: Citizens, my news might be summed up most briefly thus: Oedipus is dead. But the story of the event cannot be told in brief words, as the deeds done there were not brief.

CHORUS: Is he gone, the unfortunate man?

MESSENGER: You may be sure that he has left this life.

CHORUS: How? By a fate divine and painless, the wretched man?

MESSENGER: On that you touch upon what is indeed worthy of wonder. How he departed from here, you yourself must know since you were here: with no one of his friends as guide, but rather with himself leading the way for us all…They went to the hill which was in view, the hill of Demeter who guards the tender plants, and in a short time brought what their father had commanded. Then they washed him and dressed him, as is the custom. But when all his desire was fulfilled, and nothing that he required was still unfinished, then Zeus of the Underworld sent forth his thunder, and his daughters shuddered as they heard. They fell weeping at their father's knees, and did not cease from beating their breast, and from wailing loud. When he heard their sudden bitter cry, he put his arms around them and said: "My children, on this day your father no longer exists. Now I have perished utterly, and no longer will you bear the burden of tending me, which was no easy one, I well know, my children. Yet just one word turns all those toils to nothing: you have been treated as friends by no one more than by this man; and now you will have me with you no longer, through all your days to come."

In this way, clinging close to one another, the father and his daughters stood and wept. But when they came to the end of their crying, and the sound of wailing went forth no more, there was a silence. Suddenly a voice called aloud to him, so that everyone felt hair rising from the sudden terror. The god called him again and again: "Oedipus, Oedipus, why do you delay our going? Too long you have been lingering." And when he perceived that he was called by the god, he asked that lord Theseus should come to him, and when he did, he said: "Friend, give me the sworn pledge of your right hand for my children. And you, my daughters, for him. Promise never to betray them by your own free will, but always to accomplish whatever you think for their benefit." And Theseus, as a man of noble spirit, without lamentation swore to keep that promise to the stranger. When he had done this, straightway Oedipus felt for his children with blind hands, and said: "Children, you must bear nobly in your hearts and depart from this place. Do not consider it just to look upon what is not right, or to hear such speech as you may not hear. Go in haste, and let only Theseus be entitled to remain to learn of those things which will be done." So he spoke, and everyone of us listened with streaming tears and mourning we followed the maidens away. But when we had departed, very soon we looked back and saw that Oedipus was nowhere any more and our lord was alone, holding his hand in front of his face to screen his eyes, as if he had seen some terrifying sight, one that no one could endure to behold. And then after a short time, we saw him adore together the earth and Olympus of the gods in the same prayer. But by what fate Oedipus perished, no man can tell, except Theseus alone. It was no fiery thunderbolt of the god that removed him, nor any rising of whirlwind from the sea. It was either an escort from the gods, or else the dark world of the dead kindly split open to receive him. The man passed away without lamentation or sickness or suffering, and beyond all mortal men he was wondrous. And if in anyone's eyes I seem to speak senselessly, I would not try to win his belief when he counts me senseless.

Chorus: Where are his daughters and the escort of their friends?

Messenger: Not far away – the sounds of mourning show plainly that they are approaching.

Oedipus' daughters and the chorus are distraught. Theseus returns and says that Oedipus' resting place will forever remain a secret. The scene is now set for Antigone to return to Thebes and reach her own tragic end.

Theseus: Children, he told me that no one should draw near that place, or approach with prayer the sacred tomb in which he sleeps. He said that, so long as I saw to this, I would always keep the country free from pain. The divinity heard me say these things, as did the all-seeing oath of Zeus.

Antigone: If this is his intention, we must be content with it. Send us to ancient Thebes, in case we may somehow stop the bloodshed that threatens our brothers.

Theseus: I will do both this and whatever other favorable service I can, for you and for the recently-departed under the earth, according to the gratitude I owe. I am bound to spare no pains.

Chorus: Stop, raise such grieving no further. These things are established…firm and fixed.

Adapted from Sir Richard Jebb, Sophocles. Oedipus at Colonus of Sophocles (Cambridge: Cambridge University Press, 1889)

READING 14:
EURIPIDES' *HIPPOLYTUS*

Euripides (c. 480-406 BCE) is considered the last of Athens' three great tragedians, though he was roughly a contemporary of Sophocles. His plays are marked by a strong thematic break from the previous two tragedians. Rather than concern primarily with fate or the nature of the gods, Euripides approached his material with an eye firmly on the human level. His plays are concerned with human suffering, desires, and prejudices, although always still in the context of a world in which the divine were responsible for all great matters. Only 18 of his 88 plays survive. *Hippolytus* is arguably is best.

The myth on which the play is based is rather bland. Theseus' wife, Phaedra, falls in love with Hippolytus. When he spurns her, she kills herself in shame, but leaves a note, implicating Hippolytus in rape. Theseus, in a rage, exiles his son, who is killed before Theseus can learn of the truth. Euripides, ever interested in new interpretations, brings the affairs of gods and family together. Implicating Aphrodite in Phaedra's lust and Artemis in Hippolytus' chastity. The polar interests of these two goddesses are manifested through the destruction of the son and step-mother, with Hippolytus being punished by Aphrodite for ignoring her rites. More interesting, however, is the dynamic of family in the play. Hippolytus is a bastard, an outsider, respected but never really loved by his father. The debate and conflict between the characters may be based on immediate events, but the underlying tensions and backstory are always just beneath the surface, which only adds to both the realism and tragedy.

14a) Euripides, Hippolytus (1-120; 203-668; 902-1101; 1283-1466, passim)

SCENE: *Troezen, a great city in the Northeast Peloponnesus.* **APHRODITE** *enters from the stage from above.*

APHRODITE: Wide over man my realm extends, and proud the name that I, the goddess Cypris, bear, both in heaven's courts and among all those who dwell within the limits of the sea and the bounds of Atlas, and who can behold the sun-god's light. Those that respect my power I advance to honour, but bring to ruin all who vaunt themselves at me. For even among the race of gods this feeling finds a home: they gain pleasure at receiving honour from men. And the truth of this I soon will show, for that son of Theseus, born of the Amazon, Hippolytus, whom holy Pittheus taught, alone of all the dwellers in this land of Trœzen, calls me lowest of the deities. Love he scorns, and, as for marriage, will take none of it. But instead he honours Artemis, daughter of Zeus, sister of Phoebus, counting her the chief of goddesses, and ever through the woods, accompanying his virgin goddess, he clears the earth of wild beasts with his swift hounds, enjoying the comradeship of one too high for mortals. It is not this I grudge him, no! Why should I? But for his sins against me, I will this very day take vengeance on Hippolytus, for long ago I prepared the ground for my action, so it needs only a little more work. For as he came one day from the home of Pittheus to witness the solemn mystic rites and be initiated them in Pandion's land, Phædra, his father's noble wife, caught sight of him, and by my designs she found her heart was seized with wild desire for him. And before she came to this Troezenian realm, a dedicated a temple to Cypris near the rock of Pallas where it overlooks this country, all for the love of the youth in another land, and to win his love in days to come she called after his name the temple she had founded for the goddess. Now, when Theseus left the land of Cecrops, fleeing the pollution of the blood of Pallas' sons, and with his wife sailed to this shore, content to suffer exile for a year, at this time the wretched wife began to pine away in silence, moaning beneath love's cruel scourge, and none of her servants knows what ails her. But this passion of hers must not fail. No, I will reveal the matter to Theseus, and all shall be laid bare. Then will the father slay his child, my bitter foe, by curses, for the lord Poseidon granted this gift to Theseus: three wishes of the god to ask, nor ever ask in vain. So Phaedra is to die – an honoured death, true – but still to die, for I will not let her suffering outweigh my desire for my enemies to pay the penalty that will satisfy my heart. But look! I see the son of Theseus coming here: Hippolytus, fresh from the labours of the hunt. I will depart. At his back follows a long train of servants, in joyous cries of revelry, singing hymns of praise to Artemis, his goddess; for little does he realize that Death has opened his gates for him, and that this is his last look upon the light.

APHRODITE *exits.* **HIPPOLYTUS** *enters in front, carrying a garland, with a chorus of servants.*

HIPPOLYTUS: All hail the most beautiful Artemis, lovelier far than all the daughters of Olympus! For you, O goddess, I bring this woven garland, culled from a virgin meadow, where nor shepherd dares to herd his flock nor ever scythe has cut, but over the virginal meadow the bee wings its way in Spring, and with the dew drawn from rivers purity tends the garden. Such a place knows no cunning, yet in its nature self-control, made perfect, has a home. Such among the pure may pluck the flowers here, but not the wicked. Accept, I pray, dear goddess, this garland from my holy hand to crown your golden locks; for I, and none other of mortals, have this high privilege, to be with you, to speak with you, hearing your voice, though not seeing your face. May my life end my life as it began!

SERVANT: My lord – since we must call our masters as we do the gods – will you listen to a friendly word from me?

HIPPOLYTUS: Why, of course! Otherwise I would seem a fool.

SERVANT: Do you know the law preserved by mortals?

HIPPOLYTUS: I don't, but what are you talking about?

SERVANT: To hate the proud, which is no friend to anyone.

HIPPOLYTUS: And rightly too. For who is proud who does not hurt?

SERVANT: But there's a charm in courteous affability?

HIPPOLYTUS: The greatest surely. Yes, and profit, too, at little cost.

SERVANT: Do you think the same law holds in heaven as well?

HIPPOLYTUS: Yes, since we men draw all our laws from heaven.

SERVANT (POINTING TO THE STATUE OF APHRODITE): Why, then, do you neglect to greet this revered goddess?

HIPPOLYTUS: Whom are you talking about? Watch out that your tongue causes no mischief.

SERVANT: Aphrodite I mean, whose image is stationed over your gate.

HIPPOLYTUS: I greet this one from afar, since I am pure.

SERVANT: Yet is she a revered goddess, far renowned on earth.

HIPPOLYTUS: I do not like any god who is worshipped at night.

SERVANT: My son, it is only just to honor the gods.

HIPPOLYTUS: Among gods as well as men we have our favourites.

SERVANT: I wish you luck, and wisdom too, so far as you need it.

HIPPOLYTUS: Go in, my faithful followers, and make ready food within the house; a well-filled table is pleasurable after the hunt is over. Rub down my horses, so that when I have had my fill I can yoke them to the chariot and give them proper exercise. As for your "Queen of Love," I bid her goodbye!

Exit HIPPOLYTUS and other servants into the palace.

SERVANT: In the meantime, I with a more sober mind – for I must not copy my young master – offer my prayer to your image, lady Aphrodite, in such words as fits a slave to use. But you should pardon all who, in youth's impetuousness, speak idle words to you. Do not hear them, for gods must be wiser than the sons of men!

The SERVANT exits into the palace. The scene shifts to the bedchamber of PHAEDRA, who lies in agony, burning with the sickness given to her by APHRODITE. She is tended by a NURSE and the CHORUS OF WOMEN OF TROEZEN.

NURSE: Be of good heart, dear child; do not toss so wildly to and fro. Lie still, be brave, so you will find your sickness easier to bear. Suffering for mortals is nature's iron law.

PHAEDRA: Ah! If only I could draw a draught of pure water from some dew-fed spring, and lay down to rest in the grassy meadow beneath the poplar's shade!

NURSE: My child, what wild speech is this? Do not say such things in public – such wild, whirling words produced by some frenzy!

PHAEDRA: Away to the mountain take me! To the wood, to the pine-trees I will go, where hounds pursue the prey, hard on the scent of dappled fawns. Ye gods! What joy to shout at the hounds, to grasp the barbed javelin, to poise Thessalian hunting-spears close to my golden hair, then let them fly.

NURSE: Why, why, my child, these anxious cares? What have you to do with the hunt? Why so eager for the flowing spring, when near by these towers stands a hill well watered, from which you may freely draw water?

Phaedra: Ah me! What have I done? Where have I strayed, my senses leaving me? Mad, mad! Stricken by some god's curse! Woe is me! Cover my head again, nurse. Shame fills me for the words I have spoken. Hide me then. From my eyes the tear-drops fall, and for shame I turn them away. It is painful coming to one's senses again, and madness, evil though it be, has this advantage, that one has no knowledge of reason's overthrow.

Nurse: There, I'm covering you, but when will death hide my body in the grave? Many a lesson old age is teaching me. Yes, mortal men should pledge themselves to moderate friendships only, not to such as reach the very heart's core! Love's ties should be light upon us, in order to let them slip or draw them tight. For one poor heart to grieve for two, as I do for my mistress, is a burden too sore to bear. Men say that too engrossing pursuits in life often cause more disappointment than pleasure, and too often are enemies to health. For this reason, I do not praise excess so much as "nothing in excess," and with me wise men will agree. Come on, why so silent? You should not remain this way, my child, but scold me if I speak wrongly, or, if I give good advice, yield to me. One word, one look this way! Ah me! Friends, we waste our time to no purpose, for we are as far away as ever. She would not relent to my arguments then, nor is she yielding now. Well, fine, grow more stubborn than the sea, yet be assured of this, that if you die, you are a traitor to your children, for they will never inherit their father's halls. No, it will be by that queenly the Amazon who bore a son to lord it over your children – a bastard born but not bred a bastard, whom you know well, Hippolytus…

Phaedra: Oh!

Nurse: Does this strike you quickly?

Phaedra: You are killing me, Nurse! I beg by the gods that you mention nothing of him again!

Nurse: Ah ha! You now seem to be in your right mind, but you still refuse to aid your children and save your own life.

Phaedra: I love my children. It is another fate that curses me.

Nurse: Lady, are your hands clean of bloodshed?

Phaedra: My hands are clean. It is my soul that's polluted…Oh, my poor mother, what a passion you had!

Nurse: Her love for the bull? What is this you mean?

Phaedra: My poor sister, a bride to Dionysus.

Nurse: What's are you doing this, child? Why speak of your family in this way?

Phaedra: And I myself, the third to suffer! How I am undone!

Nurse: What, my child? Are you in love?

Phaedra: The son of an Amazon, whatever his name is…

Nurse: You mean Hippolytus?

Phaedra: Your words, not mine.

Nurse: O heavens! What is this, my child? You've ruined me. Outrageous! Friends, I will not live and bear it. Hateful is my life, hateful to my eyes the light. This body I give up, I will cast it off, and rid myself of existence by my death. Farewell, my life is over! Yes, for the pure have wicked passions, against their will maybe, but still they have them. Cypris, it seems, is not a goddess after all, but something greater by far, for she has been the ruin of my lady and of me and our whole family…

Phaedra: I will tell you all of my judgment's path. When love wounded me, I though how I best might bear the wound. So from that day I began to hide in silence what I suffered. For

I put no faith in counselors, who know well to lecture others for presumption, yet themselves have countless troubles of their own. Next I devised noble endurance for these horrible thoughts, striving by moderation for success. And at last when I could not succeed in mastering love, I thought it best to die, and none can criticize my purpose. For just as I would wish my virtue to be open, I wish few to witness my shame. I understood my sickly passion now. To yield to it would be infamous. And more, I learned to know so well that I was but a woman, a thing the world detests. Curses, hideous curses on that wife, who first shamed her marriage-vow for lovers other than her man! It was from noble families that this curse began to spread among our sex. For when the nobility show disgrace, poor folk of course will think that it is right. Those too I hate who profess purity, though in secret are reckless sinners. How can these, queen Cypris, ocean's child, ever look their husbands in the face? Do they never feel guilty thrill that their accomplice, nighttime, or the chambers of their house, will find a voice and speak? This it is that calls on me to die, kind friends, that so I may never be found to have disgraced my lord, or the children I have born; no! May they grow up and dwell in glorious Athens, free to speak and act, heirs to such fair fame as a mother can give to them. For to know that father or mother have sinned turns the stoutest heart to slavishness. This alone, men say, can stand the slings and arrows of life's battle: a just and virtuous soul. For time unmasks the villain sooner or later, holding up to them a mirror as to some blooming girl. Among such may I be never seen!

Nurse: Will you, then, because of love, destroy yourself? It is little gain, I think, for those who love or yet may love their fellows, if death must be their end. For although Aphrodite's assault in her might is more than humans can bear, yet she also gently visits yielding hearts, and only when she finds a proud unnatural spirit, does she take it and mock it past belief. Her path is in the sky, and amid the ocean's surge she rides; from her all nature springs, and she sows the seeds of love, inspires the warm desire to which we sons of earth all owe our being. They who have experience with books of ancient scribes, or themselves engage in studious pursuits, know how Zeus was enamored with Semele, how the bright-eyed goddess of the Dawn once stole Cephalus to dwell in heaven for the love she bore him; yet these in heaven live on, and do not shun the gods' approach, content, I think, to yield to their misfortune. Why such solemn intentions? No need of clever phrases, but of the man himself, telling him frankly how it is with you. Had your life not come to such a crisis, or if you weren't endowed with such self-control, never would I gratify your passions and urge you to this course, but now it is a fierce struggle to save your life, and therefore less to blame.

Phaedra: Monstrous! Quiet, woman, and never say such vile things again!

Nurse: Vile, yes, but better for you than your "code of honour." Better the evil deed to save your life, than the pride of your name for which you will kill yourself!

Phaedra: I beg you, go no further! For your words are plausible but terrible, for although love has not yet undermined my soul, still, if in specious words you disguise your foul idea, I shall be tricked into the snare from which I am now trying to escape.

Nurse: Peace, my child! I will do all things well. Queenly Cypris, Ocean's child, be my partner in the task! And for the rest of my purpose, it will be enough for me to tell it to our friends within the house.

*The **Nurse** exits the room. **Phaedra** and the **Chorus** of women hear outraged shouting beyond the chamber. **Phaedra** realizes that the **Nurse** has* *told* HIPPOLYTUS *about the sickness, and withdraws. The* NURSE *and* HIPPOLYTUS *enter, shouting at one another.*

NURSE: My son, do not dishonour your oath!

HIPPOLYTUS: My tongue swore it, not my heart.

NURSE: Son, what will you do? Destroy your friends and family?

HIPPOLYTUS: Friends indeed! No criminals are my friends!

NURSE: Pardon me! To err is human, my son!

HIPPOLYTUS: Great Zeus, why did you, to man's sorrow, put woman, an evil curse, to dwell where the sun shines? If you intended that the human race should multiply, it was not from women they should have drawn their stock, but in your temples they should have paid gold or iron or heavy bronze and bought a family, each man proportioned to his offering, and so dwell in independence, free from women. But now, as soon as ever we bring this curse into our home, we bring our own fortune to the ground. It is clear from this how great a curse a woman is; the very father that begot and nurtured her, in order to rid him of this mischief, gives her a dowry and packs her off, while the husband, who takes the noxious weed into his home, fondly decks her sorry form in fine jewels and tricks her out in robes, squandering his fortune by degrees, unhappy wretch! For he is in this dilemma: say his marriage has brought him good connections, he is glad then to keep the wife he loathes; but, if he gets a good wife but useless relations, he tries to stifle the bad luck with the good.

But it is easiest for him who has settled in his house to have an idiot as a wife, incapable of simplicity. I hate a clever woman; may she who aims at knowing more than women need, never set foot in my house! For in these clever women Cypris implants a larger store of villainy, while the artless woman is by her shallow wit from debarred from cleverness. No servant should ever have had access to a wife, but men should live with beasts, which bite, not talk, in which case they could not speak to any one nor be answered back by them. But, as it is, the wicked plot wickedness in their chambers, and their servants carry it abroad. Even thus, you vile wretch, you try to make me partner in an outrage on my father's honour! For this reason, I must wash that stain away in running streams, dashing the water into my ears. How could I commit so foul a crime when by the very mention of it I feel myself polluted? Be well assured, woman, it is only my religious purity saves you. For had not I unawares been caught by an oath, before heaven! I would not have refrained from telling all to my father. But now I will leave the house, so long as Theseus is abroad, and will maintain strict silence. But, when my father comes, I will return and see how you and your mistress face him, and so shall I learn by experience the extent of your audacity. May Hell seize you both! I can never satisfy my hate for women, no! Not even though some say this is always my theme, in truth they always are evil. So either let some one prove them pure, or let me still trample on them forever.

After this rant, HIPPOLYTUS *storms off.* PHAEDRA *emerges, having heard everything. She sends the* NURSE *away, and has the* CHORUS *of women swear not to reveal what they have heard. She declares again her intention to kill herself, but promises that she will bring harm to* HIPPOLYTUS *for his arrogance and teach him to be moderate before she dies.* THESEUS *returns home and finds that his wife has hung herself.* THESEUS *is devastated, but finds a "suicide note" beside the corpse, declaring that* PHAEDRA *had been raped by* HIPPOLYTUS, *and that it was for this dishonor that she killed herself.* THESEUS *calls for his son to confront him.*

HIPPOLYTUS: I heard your voice, father, and hasted to come here; yet I do not know the cause of your present sorrow, but would like to learn it from you. What! What is this? Your wife is a corpse? This is strange; it was just now that I left her, a moment since she looked upon the light. How came she to this end? What was the manner of her death? This I need to learn from you, Father. Why silent? Silence is no use in this, no, for the heart that desires to know all must show its curiosity even in sorrow's hour. Be sure it is not right, father, to hide misfortunes from those who love, indeed, more than love thee!

Theseus: O the mind of mortal man! To what lengths will it go? What limit to its audacity? For if it goes on growing as man's life advances, and each successor outdoes the man before him in wickedness, the gods will have to add another sphere to the world, which shall take in the fools and villains. Behold this man; he, my own son, has outraged my honour, his guilt most clearly proven by my dead wife. Now, since you have dared to commit this terrible crime, come, look your father in the face. Are you the man who consorts with gods, as one above the vulgar herd? Are you really the "pure" and sinless saint? Your boasts will never persuade me to be guilty of attributing ignorance to gods. Go then, boast about yourself, and make a show of your petty desire for your diet of vegetables; take Orpheus for your lord and go reveling, with all honour for the vapourings of many a written scroll, seeing you now are caught. Let everyone beware, I say, of such hypocrites! Those who hunt their prey with fine words, and all the while are scheming villainy. She is dead – do you think that this will save you? Why this convicts you more than anything, abandoned wretch! What oaths, what pleas can outweigh this letter, so that you should escape your doom? You will assert that she hated you, that between the bastard and the true-born child nature has herself put war; it seems then by your show she made a sorry bargain with her life, if to gratify her hate of you she lost what most she prized. It is said, no doubt, that frailty finds no place in man but is innate in woman – my experience is, however, that young men are no more secure than women, when the Queen of Love excites a youthful breast, although their sex comes in to help them all the more. Yet why do I bandy words with you, when before me lies the corpse, to be the clearest witness? Leave at once, an exile from this land, and never set foot again in god-built Athens nor in the confines of my dominion. For if I am tamely to submit to this treatment from such as you, no more will Sinis, robber of the Isthmus, bear me witness how I slew him, but say my boasts are idle, nor will those Scironian rocks, that fringe the sea, call me the miscreants' scourge.

Hippolytus: Father, your wrath and the tension of your mind are terrible; yet this charge, hollow though its arguments appear, becomes a disaster, if one lays it bare. I have little skill in speaking to a crowd, but have a readier wit for comrades of mine own age and small companies…Upon this sun-lit earth there is no man, although you deny it, purer than me. To reverence God I count the highest skill, and to adopt as friends not those who attempt injustice, but such as would blush to propose to their companions any evil orders to disgraceful services; to mock at friends is not my way, father, but I am still the same behind their backs as to their face. The very crime you think I have committed, is just the one I am untainted with, for to this day have I remained pure from women. Nor do I know anything about it, except what I hear or see in pictures, for I have no wish to look even on these, so pure my virgin soul…Now by Zeus, the god of oaths, and by the earth, upon which we stand, I swear to you I never laid a hand upon your wife nor would have wished to, or have harboured such a thought. Slay me, gods! Rob me of name and honour, from home and city cast me out, a wandering exile over the earth! Nor sea nor

...eive my bones when I am dead, if I am wicked man! I cannot say if she through fear destroyed herself, for more than this am I forbid to say. Her discretion took the place of chastity, while I, though chaste, was not discreet in using this virtue

Theseus: A wizard or magician must the child be, to think he can deceive me, his father, then by playing it cool, master my resolve.

Hippolytus: Father, your part in this fills me with amazement. If you were my son and I your father, by heaven! I would have had you killed, not let you off with banishment, if you violated my honour.

Theseus: A just remark! Yet you shall not die by the sentence your own lips pronounced. For death that comes in a moment is an easy end for wretchedness. No, you shall be exiled from your fatherland, and wandering to a foreign shore, drag out a life of misery – for such are the wages of your crime.

Hippolytus: Great gods! Why do I not unlock my lips, seeing that I am ruined by you, the object of my reverence? No, I will not; I still could not persuade those whom I ought to, and in vain would break the oath I swore.

Theseus: Oh! Your "purity" will be the death of me! Leave your father's land at once! Servants, drag him away! You heard my proclamation long ago condemning him to exile.

Hippolytus: The sentence then, it seems, is passed. Ah, misery! How well I know the truth in this, but know no way to tell it! O daughter of Leto, dearest to me of all deities, partner, comrade in the chase, far from glorious Athens must I fly. Farewell, city and land of Erechtheus; farewell, Troezen, most joyous home in which to pass the spring of life; it is my last sight of thee, farewell! Come, my comrades in this land, young like me, greet me kindly and escort me out, for never will you behold a purer soul, for all my father's doubts.

Hippolytus departs with his companions. After an ode by the Chorus, a Messenger returns and informs Theseus that his son is near death. Theseus is eager to hear how justice has avenged him by killing his seemingly wicked son. The Messenger describes how Hippolytus was riding his chariot when a monstrous bull rose from the sea. His horses panicked and flipped the chariot, mangling his body. Theseus asks that he be brought back, so that he can still refute anything he says before he dies. The goddess Artemis then arrives, and informs Theseus of his folly.

Artemis: Listen, I command you, noble son of Aegeus: look! It is I, Leto's child, that speak: I, Artemis. Why, Theseus, to your own sorrow do you rejoice at this news, seeing that you hast slain your son most impiously, listening to a charge not clearly proved, but falsely sworn to by your wife? Though clearly have you brough a curse on yourself. Why do you not for shame hide beneath the dark places of the earth, or change your human life and soar on wings to escape this tribulation? Among men of honour you have now no share in life. Listen, Theseus: I will inform you of your wretched case. Yet it will not help you at all, if I do, but only vex your heart. Still, with this intent I came, to show your son's pure heart, so that he may die with honour, as well as the frenzy, and, in a sense, the nobleness of your wife; for she was cruelly stung with a passion for your son by that goddess whom all of us who take joy in virgin purity, detest. And though your wife tried to conquer love by resoluteness, yet by no fault of hers, she fell, thanks to her nurse's action, who revealed her sickness to your son, while under oath. But he would accept none of her plans, as indeed was right, nor yet, when your reviled him, would he break the oath he swore, out of his own piety. She meanwhile, fearful of being found out, wrote a lying letter, destroying by guile your son, and persuading you.

THESEUS: No!

ARTEMIS: Does my story wound your, Theseus? Be still awhile; hear what follows, so you will have more cause to groan. Do you remember those three prayers your father granted you, so certain in their consequence? It is one of these you misused, unnatural wretch, against your own son, instead of aiming it at an enemy. Your sea-god father, it is true, for all his kind intent, has granted that gift he was compelled, by reason of his promise, to grant. But you alike in his eyes and in mine have shown your evil heart, in that you ignored the need of all proof or prophetic voice, you made no inquiry, nor taken time for consideration, but with undue haste cursed your son even to the death.

THESEUS: Lady, may I live no longer!

ARTEMIS: An awful deed is this, but still even for this you may yet obtain pardon; for it was Aphrodite that would have it so, satisfying the fury of her soul. For this is law among us gods; none of us will thwart the other's will, but always we stand aloof. For be well assured, had I not feared Zeus, never would I have incurred the bitter shame of handing over to death a man of all his kind to me most dear. As for your sin, first your ignorance acquits you from villainy, next your wife, who is dead, was lavish in her arguments to influence your mind. On you in chief this storm of woe has burst, yet is it some grief to me as well; for when the righteous die, there is no joy in heaven, albeit we try to destroy the wicked, house and home.

HIPPOLYTUS *is brought in, barely alive.*

HIPPOLYTUS: Ah! I smell the fragrance from my goddess! Even in my agony I feel you near and find relief; she is here in this very place, my goddess Artemis!

ARTEMIS: She is, poor one – the dearest of gods to you.

HIPPOLYTUS: Do you see me, goddess, suffering in my wretched state?

ARTEMIS: Yes, but it is not right that I shed any tears for you.

HIPPOLYTUS: You no longer have your huntsman or your servant!

ARTEMIS: None now, but even in death, I cherish you.

HIPPOLYTUS: No one to groom your horses or tend to your sanctuary!

ARTEMIS: No, it was Aphrodite – treacherous – who devised this.

HIPPOLYTUS: Ah me! Now know I the goddess who destroyed me!

ARTEMIS: She faulted you for your homage, and was galled by your purity.

HIPPOLYTUS: Ah, I see that her one hand destroyed us three.

ARTEMIS: Your father, you, and your father's wife third.

HIPPOLYTUS: Then I groan for my father's misfortune as my own.

ARTEMIS: He too was deceived by the goddess.

HIPPOLYTUS: Such a misfortune for you, my unhappy father!

THESEUS: I am finished, my son. Life has no joys for me.

HIPPOLYTUS: For your mistake I mourn you more than myself.

THESEUS: If only I could have died, my son, instead of you!

HIPPOLYTUS: Oh, those fatal gifts that your father, Poseidon, brought!

Theseus: If only my lips had never uttered that curse!

Hippolytus: You still would have killed me in your anger.

Theseus: Yes, for the gods corrupted my ability to think.

Hippolytus: Oh! If only that the race of men could curse the gods!

Artemis: Enough! For though you pass to gloom beneath the earth, the wrath of Aphrodite shall not, at her will, fall on you without penalty, simply because you had a noble, pure soul. For I with my own hand will with unerring arrows avenge myself on another who is her favourite, dearest to her of all the sons of men. And to you, poor sufferer, for your anguish now will I grant high honours in the city of Troezen; for you shall virgins before their marriage cut off their hair, your harvest through the long roll of time of countless bitter tears. Yes, and forever shall the virgin choir sing about your sad story, nor shall Phaedra's love for you fall into oblivion and pass away unnoticed. But you, son of old Aegeus, take your son in your arms, draw him close, for unwittingly you slew him, and men may well commit an error when gods put it in their way. And I advise you, Hippolytus: do not hate your father, for in this death you are only meeting your destined fate. And now farewell! It is not right for me to gaze upon the dead, or pollute my sight with death, and even now I see for you that moment is close.

Artemis *departs.*

Hippolytus: Farewell, blessed virgin goddess! Leave me now! How easily you turn from our long friendship! I am reconciled with my father at your desire, yes, for always before I would obey your bidding. Ah me! Darkness is settling even now upon my eyes. Take me, father, in your arms, lift me up!

Theseus: No, no, my son! What are you doing to your father?

Hippolytus: I am finished. I see the gates of the Dead.

Theseus: And will you leave me with my murder on my hands?

Hippolytus: Oh no. I set you free from this bloodguilt.

Theseus: What are you saying? You set me free of bloodguilt?

Hippolytus: The archer-goddess Artemis is my witness!

Theseus: My dearest son, how noble you are to your father, even now.

Hippolytus: Farewell my father, and be joyful.

Theseus: Oh, what a noble, pure soul you have!

Hippolytus: Pray to have sons such as me born in wed-lock.

Theseus: Do not leave me, son, but endure!

Hippolytus: My endurance is spent, father. Quickly cover my face with my clothes!

Hippolytus *falls silent.* **Theseus** *covers his face.*

Theseus: Glorious Athens, Pallas' territory, what a splendid man you have lost! No, no! How often shall I remember your evil work, Aphrodite!

Adapted from E. P. Coleridge, Euripides. The Plays of Euripides (London: G. Bell & Sons, Ltd., 1910).

READING 15:

EURIPIDES' *BACCHAE*

Bacchae tells the myth of Dionysus' return to Thebes, the home of his mortal mother, Semele, who had died giving birth to him. The city has disrespected her and, by extension, refuses to honour his own sacred rites of the grape and ecstasy. Dionysus drives the women of Thebes into alcoholic frenzy, making them his attendant Maenads (bacchae). Pentheus, the young and impetuous king, hears of this, and demands that they and this trouble-maker be arrested. He is warned by the old king, Cadmus, and the seer, Teiresias, against challenging one who is clearly a god, but stubbornly ignores them. His attempts to stop the Bacchic rites, however, inevitably end in failure, and Dionysus punishes Pentheus for his lack of respect for the god by driving the frenzied bacchae to him apart. Pentheus' own mother, Agave, only realizes too late what she and the other women have done, and Dionysus emerges once again to foretell the fate of the family, and announce that he has indeed arrived in Greece.

Bacchae is Euripides' most famous play. Not only does it boast one the most incredible scenes in drama, when Pentheus' own mother bears his head to the palace, but it is also one of the few tragedies that honours the god of drama and tragedy: Dionysus. It is more than a simple story of the punishment for someone who failed to acknowledge a god – Pentheus' own attempts to hide his desires for reveling and his youthful curiosity about sexuality are his primary undoing. The play thus addresses the central importance of Dionysiac worship in Greek life, in particular the natural and necessary need from humans to revel in the rites of Dionysus: music, dance, drink and ecstasy.

15a) Euripides, Bacchae (1-369; 451-510; 664-829; 1051-1392, passim)

Scene: *In the hills outside of Thebes. Dionysus is alone and addresses the audience.*

Dionysus: I, the son of Zeus, have come to this land of the Thebes. I, Dionysus, whom once Semele, Kadmos' daughter, bore, delivered by a lightning-bearing flame. And having adopted a mortal form instead of a god's, I am here at the fountains of Dirke and the water of Ismenus. And I see the tomb of my thunder-stricken mother here near the palace, and the remnants of her house, smouldering with the still living flame of Zeus' fire, the everlasting insult of Hera against my mother. I praise Kadmos, who has made this place hallowed, the shrine of his daughter, and I have covered it all around with the cluster-bearing leaf of the vine. I have left the wealthy lands of the Lydians and Phrygians, the sun-parched plains of the Persians, and the Bactrian walls, and have passed over the wintry land of the Medes, and blessed Arabia, and all of Asia, which lies along the coast of the salt sea with its beautifully-towered cities full of Greeks and barbarians mingled together. And I have come to this Greek city first, having already set those other lands to dance and established my mysteries there, so that I might be a deity manifest among men. In this land of Greece, I have first excited Thebes to my cry, fitting a fawn-skin to my body and taking a thyrsos in my hand, a weapon of ivy. For my mother's sisters, the ones who least should, claimed that I, Dionysus, was not the child of Zeus, but that Semele had conceived a child from a mortal father and then ascribed the sin of her bed to Zeus, a trick of Kadmos', for which they boasted that Zeus killed her, because she had told a false tale about her marriage.

Therefore I have struck them from the house in frenzy, and they dwell in the mountains, out of their wits; and I have compelled them to wear the outfit of my mysteries. And all the female offspring of Thebes, as many as are women, I have driven maddened from the house, and they, mingled with the daughters of Kadmos, sit on roofless rocks beneath green pines. For this city must learn, even if it is unwilling, that it is not initiated into my Bacchic rites, and that I plead the case of my mother, Semele, in appearing manifest to mortals as a divinity whom she bore to Zeus. Now Kadmos has given his honor and power to Pentheus, his daughter's son, who fights against the gods as far as I am concerned and drives me away from sacrifices, and in his prayers makes no mention of me, for which I will show him and all the Thebans that I was born a god. And when I have set matters here right, I will move on to another land, revealing myself. But if ever the city of Thebes should in anger seek to drive the Bacchae down from the mountains with arms, I, the general of the Maenads, will join battle with them. On which account I have changed my form to a mortal one and altered my shape into the nature of a young man. But, you women who have left Tmolus, the bulwark of Lydia, my sacred band, whom I have brought from among the barbarians as assistants and companions to me, take your drums, native instruments of the city of the Phrygians, the invention of mother Rhea and myself, and going about this palace of Pentheus beat them, so that Kadmos' city may see. I myself will go to the folds of Cithaeron, where the Bacchae are, to share in their dances.

Enter **Chorus of Bacchae** *with musical instruments.*

Chorus: From the land of Asia, having left sacred Tmolus, we are swift to perform for Bromius our sweet labor, and toil easily borne, celebrating the god Bacchus! Who is in the way? Who is in the way? Who? Let him get out of the way indoors, and let everyone keep his mouth pure, speaking propitious things. For we will celebrate Dionysus with hymns according to eternal custom. Blessed is he who, being fortunate and knowing the rites of the gods, keeps his life pure and has his soul initiated into the Bacchic revels, dancing in inspired frenzy over the mountains with holy purifications, and who, revering the mysteries of great mother Cybele, brandishing the thyrsos, garlanded with ivy, serves Dionysus. Go, Bacchae, go, Bacchae, escorting the god Bromius, child of a god, from the Phrygian mountains to the broad streets of Hellas – Bromius, whom once, in the compulsion of birth pains, the thunder of Zeus flying upon her, his mother cast from her womb, leaving life by the stroke of a thunderbolt. Immediately Zeus, Kronos' son, received him in a chamber fit for birth, and having covered him in his thigh shut him up with golden clasps, hidden from Hera.

And he brought forth, when the Fates had perfected him, the bull-horned god, and he crowned him with crowns of snakes, for which reason Maenads cloak their wild prey over their locks. O Thebes, nurse of Semele, crown yourself with ivy, flourish, flourish with the verdant yew bearing sweet fruit, and crown yourself in honor of Bacchus with branches of oak or pine. Adorn your garments of spotted fawn-skin with fleeces of white sheep, and sport in holy games with insolent thyrsoi. At once all the earth will dance – whoever leads the sacred band is Bromius – to the mountain, to the mountain, where the crowd of women waits, goaded away from their weaving by Dionysus. O secret chamber of the Curetes and you holy Cretan caves, parents to Zeus, where the Corybantes with triple helmet invented for me in their caves this circle, covered with stretched hide; and in their excited revelry they mingled it with the sweet-voiced breath of Phrygian pipes and handed it over to mother Rhea, resounding with the sweet songs of the Bacchae. Nearby, raving Satyrs were fulfilling the rites of the mother goddess, and they joined it to the dances of the biennial festivals, in which Dionysus rejoices…

Scene shifts to just outside of Thebes, where **Teiresias**, *an old seer of Thebes, and* **Kadmos**, *the first king and patriarch of Thebes, are enjoying their revels, having already been influenced by* **Dionysus'** *presence.*

Teiresias: Who is at the gates? Call from the house Kadmos, son of Agenor, who, after leaving the city of Sidon built this towering city of the Thebans. Let someone go and announce that Teiresias is looking for him. He knows why I have come and what agreement I, an old man, have made with him, older still: to twine the thyrsoi, to wear fawn-skins, and to crown our heads with ivy branches.

Kadmos: Dearest friend, for inside the house I heard and recognized your wise voice, the voice of a wise man; I have come prepared with this equipment of the god. For we must praise him, the child of my daughter, as much as is in our power. Where must I dance, where set my feet and shake my grey head? Show me the way, Teiresias, one old man leading another – for you are wise. And so I shall never tire night or day striking the ground with the thyrsos. Gladly I have forgotten that I am old.

Teiresias: Then you and I have the same feelings, for I too feel young and will try to dance…

Kadmos: Are we the only ones in the city who will dance in Bacchus' honor?

Teiresias: Yes, for we alone think rightly, the rest wrongly…

Kadmos: …Having been born mortal I do not scorn the gods.

Teiresias: We mortals have no cleverness in the eyes of the gods. Our ancestral traditions, and those which we have held throughout our lives, no argument will overturn, not even if some craftiness should be discovered by the depths of our wits. Will anyone say that I do not respect old age, being about to dance with my head covered in ivy? No, for the god has made no distinction as to whether it is right for men young or old to dance, but wishes to have common honors from all and to be praised, setting no one apart.

PENTHEUS, **KADMOS**' *grandson and the current king of Thebes, enters the scene with servants holding several of the* **CHORUS OF BACCHAE** *under guard.*

PENTHEUS: I happened to be at a distance from this land, when I heard of strange evils throughout this city, that the women have left our homes in contrived Bacchic rites, and rush about in the shadowy mountains, honoring with dances this new deity Dionysus, whoever he is. I hear that wine-bowls stand full in the midst of their assemblies, and that they each creep off different ways into secrecy to serve the lusts of men, on the pretext that they are Maenads worshipping – but they consider Aphrodite before Bacchus! As many of them as I have caught, servants keep in the public strongholds with their hands bound, and as many as are absent I will hunt from the mountains, and having bound them in iron fetters, I will soon stop them from this ill-working drunkenness. And they say that some stranger has come, a sorcerer, some quack from the Lydian east, fragrant in hair with golden curls, having in his eyes the wine-dark graces of Aphrodite. He is with the young girls day and night, seducing them with joyful mysteries. If I catch him within this house, I will stop him from making a noise with the thyrsos and shaking his hair, by cutting his head off.

That one claims that Dionysus is a god, claims that he was once stitched into the thigh of Zeus – Dionysus, who was burnt up with his mother by the flame of lightning, because she had falsely claimed a marriage with Zeus. Is this not worthy of a terrible death by hanging, for a stranger to insult me with these insults, whoever he is? But here is another wonder – I see Teiresias the soothsayer in dappled fawn-skins and my mother's father – how absurd – raging about with a thyrsos. I shrink, Father, from seeing your old age devoid of sense. Won't you cast away the ivy? Grandfather, will you not free your hand of the thyrsos? You persuaded him to this, Teiresias? Do you wish, by introducing another new god to men, to examine birds and receive rewards for sacrifices? If your gray old age did not defend you, you would sit in chains in the midst of the Bacchae, for introducing wicked rites. For where women have the delight of wine at a feast, I say that none of their rites is healthy any longer.

CHORUS LEADER: Oh, what blasphemy! Stranger, do you not reverence the gods and Kadmos who sowed the earth-born crop? Do you, child of Echion, bring shame to your race?

TEIRESIAS: Whenever a wise man has an opportunity to try a speech, it is not a great task to speak well. You have a rapid tongue as though you were sensible, but there is no sense in your words. [270] A man powerful in his boldness, one capable of speaking well, becomes a bad citizen in his lack of sense. This new god, whom you ridicule, I am unable to express how great he will be throughout Greece. For two things, young man, are first among men: the goddess Demeter – she is the Earth, but call her whatever name you wish – she nourishes mortals with dry food. But he who came afterwards, the offspring of Semele, discovered a match to it, the liquid drink of the grape, and introduced it to mortals. It releases wretched mortals from grief, whenever they are filled with the stream of the vine, and gives them sleep, a means of forgetting their daily troubles, nor is there another cure for hardships. He who is a god is poured out in offerings to the gods, so that by his means men may have good things…

But this god is a prophet – for Bacchic revelry and madness have in them much prophetic skill. For whenever the god enters a body in full force, he allows the frantic to foretell the future. He also possesses a share of Ares' nature.

For terror sometimes flutters an army under arms and in its ranks before it even touches a spear, and this too is a frenzy from Dionysus. You will see him also on the rocks of Delphi, bounding with torches through the highland of two peaks, leaping and shaking the Bacchic branch, mighty throughout Greece. But believe me, Pentheus, do not boast that sovereignty has power among men, nor, even if you think so, and your mind is diseased, believe that you are being at all wise. Receive the god into your land, pour libations to him, celebrate the Bacchic rites, and garland your head.

KADMOS: My child, Teiresias has advised you well. Dwell with us, not apart from the laws. For now you flit about and have thoughts without thinking. Even if, as you say, he is not a god, call him one anyway, and tell a glorious falsehood, so that Semele might seem to have borne a god, and honor might come to all our race. You've hears of the wretched fate of Actaeon, who was torn apart in the meadows by the blood-thirsty hounds he had raised, having boasted that he was superior in the hunt to Artemis. May you not suffer this. Come, let me crown your head with ivy. Honor the god along with us!

PENTHEUS: Don't lay a hand on me! Go off and hold your revels, but don't wipe your foolishness off on me. I will seek the punishment of this teacher of your idiocy. Let someone go quickly to the place where he watches the flights of birds, and upset and overturn it with levers, turning everything upside down! Release his garlands to the winds and storms! In this way I will especially wound him. And some of you hunt throughout the city for this effeminate stranger, who introduces a new disease to women and pollutes our beds. If you catch him, bring him here bound, so that he might suffer as punishment a death by stoning, having seen a bitter Bacchic revelry in Thebes.

TEIRESIAS: O wretched man, how little you know what you are saying! You are mad now, and even before you were out of your wits. Let us go, Kadmos, and pray to the god, on behalf of your grandson, though he is savage, and on behalf of the city, to do no ill. But follow me with the ivy-clad staff, and try to support my body, and I will try to support yours. It would be shameful for two old men to fall down. But let that pass, for we must serve Bacchus, the son of Zeus. Beware, so that Pentheus brings no trouble to your house, Kadmos! I do not speak in prophecy, but judging from the state of things, for a foolish man speaks foolishness.

CHORUS: Misfortune is the result of unbridled mouths and lawless folly, but the life of quiet and wisdom remains unshaken and holds houses together. Though they dwell far off in the heavens the gods see the deeds of mortals. But cleverness is not wisdom, nor is thinking on things unfit for mortals. Life is short, and on this account the one who pursues great things does not achieve that which is present. In my opinion, these are the ways of mad and ill-advised men.

TEIRESIAS *and* KADMOS *depart. A* SERVANT *arrives with* DIONYSUS *as his prisoner. He informs* PENTHEUS *that although this "young man" came without resisting, the* CHORUS OF BACCHAE *whom Pentheus had arrested earlier have miraculously escaped.* PENTHEUS *examines his prisoner.*

PENTHEUS: Release his hands, for caught in the nets he is not so swift as to escape me. Hmm, your body is not ill-formed, stranger, for women's purposes, for which reason you have come to Thebes. For your hair is long, not through wrestling, scattered over your cheeks, full of desire, and you have a white skin from careful preparation, hunting after Aphrodite by your beauty not exposed to strokes of the sun, but beneath the shade. First then tell me who your family is.

DIONYSUS: I can tell you this easily, without boasting. I suppose you are familiar with flowery Tmolus.

PENTHEUS: I know of it. It surrounds the city of Sardis.

DIONYSUS: I am from there, and Lydia is my fatherland.

PENTHEUS: Why do you bring these rites to Greece?

DIONYSUS: Dionysus, the child of Zeus, sent me.

PENTHEUS: Is there a Zeus who breeds new gods there?

DIONYSUS: No, but the one who married Semele here.

PENTHEUS: Did he compel you at night, or in your sight?

DIONYSUS: Seeing me just as I saw him, he gave me sacred rites.

PENTHEUS: What appearance do your rites have?

DIONYSUS: They cannot be told to mortals uninitiated in Bacchic revelry.

PENTHEUS: And do they have any profit to those who sacrifice?

DIONYSUS: It is not lawful for you to hear, but they are worth knowing.

PENTHEUS: You have made this up skillfully, so that I desire to hear.

DIONYSUS: The rites are hostile to whoever practices impiety.

PENTHEUS: Did you come here first, bringing the god?

DIONYSUS: All the barbarians celebrate these rites.

PENTHEUS: Yes, for they are far more foolish than Greeks.

DIONYSUS: In this at any rate they are wiser, though their laws are different.

PENTHEUS: Do you perform the rites by night or by day?

DIONYSUS: Mostly by night: darkness conveys awe.

PENTHEUS: This is dangerous towards women, and shameful.

DIONYSUS: Even during the day someone may devise what is shameful.

PENTHEUS: You must pay the penalty for your evil plans.

DIONYSUS: And you for your ignorance and impiety toward the god…

PENTHEUS (TO ATTENDANTS): Seize him! He insults me and Thebes!

DIONYSUS *is led away to a prison, but only after warning* PENTHEUS *that the gods will punish him for his acts of impiety. Soon afterwards, however,* DIONYSUS *breaks out of prison, and destroys* PENTHEUS' *palace in a great fire and earthquake.* PENTHEUS *finds* DIONYSUS *free, and just as he begins questioning him as to how he managed to escape, a* MESSENGER *arrives from the nearby woods.*

MESSENGER: Having seen the holy Bacchae, who, struck with madness have darted from this land with their fair feet, I have come to tell you and the city, lord, that they are doing terrible things, beyond belief… I saw three companies of dancing women, one of which Autonoe led, the second your mother Agave, and the third Ino. All were asleep, their bodies relaxed, some resting their backs against pine foliage, others laying their heads at random on the oak leaves, modestly, not as you say drunk with the goblet and the sound of the flute, hunting out Aphrodite through the woods in solitude. Your mother raised a cry, standing up in the midst of the Bacchae, to wake their bodies from sleep, when she heard the lowing of the horned cattle.

And they, casting off refreshing sleep from their eyes, sprang upright, a marvel of orderliness to behold, old, young, and still unmarried virgins. First they let their hair loose over their shoulders, and secured their fawn-skins, as many of them as had released the fastenings of their knots, girding the dappled hides with serpents licking their jaws. And some, holding in their arms a gazelle or wild wolf-pup, gave them white milk, as many as had abandoned their new-born infants and had their breasts still swollen. They put on garlands of ivy, and oak, and flowering yew.

One took her thyrsos and struck it against a rock, from which a dewy stream of water sprang forth. Another let her thyrsos strike the ground, and there the god sent forth a fountain of wine. All who desired the white drink scratched the earth with the tips of their fingers and obtained streams of milk; and a sweet flow of honey dripped from their ivy thyrsoi; so that, had you been present and seen this, you would have approached with prayers the god whom you now blame. We herdsmen and shepherds gathered in order to discuss with one another concerning what strange and amazing things they were doing. Someone, a wanderer about the city and practiced in speaking, said to us all: "You who inhabit the holy plains of the mountains, do you wish to draw Pentheus' mother Agave out from the Bacchic revelry and do the king a favor?" We thought he spoke well, and lay down in ambush, hiding ourselves in the foliage of bushes. They, at the appointed hour, began to wave the thyrsos in their revelries, alling on Bacchus, the son of Zeus, Bromius, with united voice. The whole mountain revelled along with them and the beasts, and nothing was unmoved by their running. Agave happened to be leaping near me, and I sprang out, trying to snatch her, abandoning the ambush where I had hidden myself. But she cried out: "O my fleet hounds, we are hunted by these men, but follow me! Follow armed with your thyrsoi in your hands!"

We fled and escaped from being torn apart by the Bacchae, but they, with unarmed hands, sprang on the heifers browsing the grass. And you might see one ripping apart a fatted lowing calf, while others tore apart cows. You might see ribs or cloven hooves tossed here and there, caught in the trees they dripped, dabbled in gore. Bulls who before were fierce, and showed their fury with their horns, stumbled to the ground, dragged down by countless young hands…Some people in rage took up arms, being plundered by the Bacchae, and the sight of this was terrible to behold, lord. For their pointed spears drew no blood, but the women, hurling the thyrsoi from their hands, kept wounding them and turned them to flight – women did this to men, not without the help of some god. And they returned where they had come from, to the very fountains that the god had sent forth for them, and washed off the blood, and snakes cleaned the drops from the women's cheeks with their tongues. Receive this god then, whoever he is, into this city, master. For he is great in other respects, and they say this too of him, as I hear, that he gives to mortals the vine that puts an end to grief. Without wine there is no longer Aphrodite or any other pleasant thing for men.

Pentheus: Already like fire does this insolence of the Bacchae blaze up, a great reproach for the Greeks. But we must not hesitate. Go to the Electran gates, order all the shield-bearers and riders of swift-footed horses to assemble, as well as all who brandish the light shield and pluck bowstrings with their hands, so that we can make an assault against the Bacchae. For it is indeed too much if we suffer what we are suffering at the hands of women. Bring me my armor. (To Dionysus) And you! Stop talking!

Dionysus: Ah! Do you wish to see them sitting together in the mountains?

(At this point, Dionysus begins to put Pentheus under his spell).

PENTHEUS: Certainly. I'd give an enormous amount of gold for that.

DIONYSUS: Why do you desire this so badly?

PENTHEUS: I would be sorry to see them in their drunkenness.

DIONYSUS: Would you see gladly what is grievous to you?

PENTHEUS: To be sure, sitting quietly under the pines.

DIONYSUS: But they will track you down, even if you go in secret.

PENTHEUS: You are right: I will go openly.

DIONYSUS: Shall I guide you? Will you attempt the journey?

PENTHEUS: Lead me as quickly as possible. I grudge you the time.

DIONYSUS: Put linen clothes on your body then.

PENTHEUS: What is this? Shall I then, instead of a man, be reckoned among the women?

DIONYSUS: So that they do not kill you if you are seen there as a man.

PENTHEUS: Again you speak correctly: how wise you have been all along!

DIONYSUS: Dionysus taught me these things fully.

PENTHEUS: How can your advice to me be well carried out?

DIONYSUS: I will go inside and dress you.

PENTHEUS: In what clothing? Female? But shame holds me back.

DIONYSUS: Are you no longer eager to view the Maenads?

PENTHEUS *sheepishly agrees and goes into a room to change into women's clothing and acquire the necessary accessories, including the Bacchic thyrsus. The scene is reminiscent of the preparation of a bull for sacrifice.* PENTHEUS *and* DIONYSUS *depart for the woods so that* PENTHEUS *may see the Bacchae. After a choral ode, a* MESSENGER *returns, informing the* CHORUS *that* PENTHEUS *has been killed, ripped apart by the Bacchae, who caught him snooping from behind a bush.*

MESSENGER: There was a little valley surrounded by precipices, irrigated with streams, shaded by pine trees, where the Maenads were sitting, their hands busy with delightful labors. Some of them were crowning again the worn thyrsos, making it leafy with ivy, while some, like colts freed from the painted yoke, were singing a Bacchic song to one another. And the unhappy Pentheus said, not seeing the crowd of women: "Stranger, from where we are standing I cannot see these false Maenads. But on the hill, ascending a lofty pine, I might view properly the shameful acts of the Maenads." And then I saw the stranger perform a marvelous deed. For seizing hold of the lofty top-most branch of the pine tree, he pulled it down, pulled it to the dark earth. It was bent just as a bow or a curved wheel, when it is marked out by a compass, describes a circular course: in this way the stranger drew the mountain bough with his hands and bent it to the earth, doing no mortal's deed. He sat Pentheus down on the pine branch, and let it go upright through his hands steadily, taking care not to shake him off. The pine stood firmly upright into the sky, with my master seated on its back. He was seen by the Maenads more than he saw them, for sitting on high he was all but apparent, and the stranger was no longer anywhere to be seen, when a voice, that of Dionysus I guess, cried out from the air: "Young women, I bring the one who has made you and me and my rites a laughing-stock. Now punish him!" And as he said this a light of holy fire was placed between heaven and earth.

The air became quiet and the woody glen kept its leaves silent, nor would you have heard the sounds of animals. But they, not having heard the sound clearly, stood upright and looked all around. He repeated his order, and when the daughters of Kadmos recognized the clear command of Bacchus, they rushed forward, swift as a dove, running with eager speed of feet, Pentheus' mother Agave, and her sisters, and all the Bacchae. They leapt through the torrent-streaming valley and mountain cliffs, frantic with the inspiration of the god. When they saw my master sitting atop the pine, first they climbed a rock towering opposite the tree and began to hurl boulders at him. Some aimed with pine branches and other women hurled their thyrsoi through the air at Pentheus, a sad target indeed. But they did not reach him, for the wretched man, caught with no way out, sat at a height too great for their eagerness. Finally like lightning they smashed oak branches and began to tear up the roots of the tree with ironless levers. When they did not succeed in their toils, Agave shouted: "Come, standing round in a circle, each seize a branch, Maenads, so that we may catch the beast who has climbed up, and so that he does not make public the secret dances of the god." They applied countless hands to the pine and dragged it up from the earth. Pentheus fell crashing to the ground from his high seat, wailing greatly: for he knew he was in terrible trouble.

His mother, as priestess, began the slaughter, and fell upon him. He threw the headband from his head so that the wretched Agave might recognize and not kill him. Touching her cheek, he said: "It is I, mother, your son, Pentheus, whom you bore in the house of Echion. Pity me, mother, and do not kill me, your child, for my sins." But she, foaming at the mouth and twisting her eyes all about, not thinking as she ought to have, was possessed by Bacchus, and he did not persuade her. Seizing his left arm at the elbow and propping her foot against the unfortunate man's side, she tore out his shoulder, not by her own strength, but the god gave facility to her hands. Ino began to work on the other side, tearing his flesh, while Autonoe and the whole crowd of the Bacchae pressed on. All were making noise together, he screaming as much as he had life left in him, while they shouted in victory. One of them bore his arm, another a foot, boot and all. His ribs were stripped bare from their tearings. The whole band, hands bloodied, were playing a game of catch with Pentheus' flesh.

The **Messenger** *departs. Soon after,* **Kadmos** *enters solemnly, with* **Kadmos** *bearing the remains of his grandson. The* **Chorus of Bacchae,** *meanwhile, return triumphantly, believing, in their frenzy, that they had killed vicious animals in a hunt.* **Agave** *leads them in triumph and holds Pentheeus' head in her hands, utterly oblivious to what she has done.* **Kadmos** *attempts to bring her out of her frenzy to realize what she holds in her hand.*

Kadmos: O grief beyond measuring, one that I cannot stand to see – that you have performed murder with miserable hands. Having cast down a fine sacrificial victim to the gods, you invite Thebes and me to a banquet. Alas, first for your troubles, then for my own. How justly, yet too severely, lord Bromius the god has destroyed us, though he is a member of our own family.

Agave: How morose and sullen in its appearance is man's old age! I hope that my son is a good hunter, taking after his mother's ways, when he goes after wild beasts together with the young men of Thebes. But all he can do is fight with the gods. You must admonish him, father. Who will call him here to my sight, so that he may see how lucky I am?

Kadmos: Alas, alas! When you realize what you have done you will suffer a terrible pain. But if you remain forever in the state you are in now, though hardly fortunate, you will not imagine that you are unfortunate.

AGAVE: But what of these matters is not right, or what is painful?

KADMOS: First cast your eye up to this sky.

AGAVE: All right…why do you tell me to look at it?

KADMOS: Is it still the same, or does it appear to have changed?

AGAVE: It is brighter than before and more translucent.

KADMOS: Is your soul still quivering?

AGAVE: I don't understand your words. I have become somehow sobered, changing from my former state of mind.

KADMOS: Can you hear and respond clearly?

AGAVE: Yes, for I forget what we said before, father.

KADMOS: To whose house did you come in marriage?

AGAVE: You gave me, as they say, to Echion, the sown man.

KADMOS: What son did you bear to your husband in the house?

AGAVE: Pentheus, from my union with his father.

KADMOS: Whose head do you hold in your hands?

AGAVE: A lion's, as they who hunted him down said.

KADMOS: Examine it correctly then…it takes but little effort to see.

AGAVE: Gods! What do I see? What is this that I carry in my hands?

KADMOS: Look at it and learn more clearly.

AGAVE: I see the greatest grief, wretched that I am.

KADMOS: Does it seem to you to be like a lion?

AGAVE: No! I am holding the head of Pentheus!

KADMOS: Yes, much lamented before you recognized him.

AGAVE: Who killed him? How did he come into my hands?

KADMOS: Miserable truth, how inconveniently you arrive!

AGAVE: Tell me! My heart leaps at what is to come.

KADMOS: You and your sisters killed him.

AGAVE: Where did he die? Was it here at home, or in what place?

KADMOS: Where formerly dogs divided Actaeon among themselves.

AGAVE: And why did this ill-fated man go to Cithaeron?

KADMOS: He went to mock the god and your revelry.

AGAVE: But in what way did we go there?

KADMOS: You were mad, and the whole city was frantic with Bacchus.

AGAVE: Dionysus destroyed us – now I understand.

KADMOS: Being insulted with insolence, for you did not consider him a god.

AGAVE: What part did Pentheus have in my folly?

KADMOS: He, like you, did not revere the god, who therefore joined all in one ruin, both you and this, your son here, and thus destroyed the house and me, who am bereft of my male children and see this offspring of your womb, wretched woman, most miserably and shamefully slain. He was the hope of our line – you, child, who supported the house, son of my daughter, an object of fear to the city; seeing you, no one wished to insult the old man, for you would have given a worthy punishment. But now I, great Kadmos, who sowed and reaped [1315] a most glorious crop, the Theban people, will be banished from the house without honor…

Chorus Leader: I grieve for you, Kadmos. Your daughter's child has a punishment deserved indeed, but grievous to you.

Agave: Father, for you see how much my situation has changed…

Dionysus, *until this point silent, now enters the conversation. He reveals himself and why he has punished the city. He prophesies a future of exile for* **Kadmos** *and his family line.*

Adapted from T. A. Buckley, Euripides. The Tragedies of Euripides (London. Henry G. Bohn. 1850).